Heavenly Readings

PEFC

PEFC/16-33-111

CATG-PEFC-052

www.pefc.org

NEW PERSPECTIVES ON LANGUAGE AND EDUCATION
Series Editor: Professor Viv Edwards, *University of Reading, Reading, Great Britain*
Series Advisor: Professor Allan Luke, *Queensland University of Technology, Brisbane, Australia*

Two decades of research and development in language and literacy education have yielded a broad, multidisciplinary focus. Yet education systems face constant economic and technological change, with attendant issues of identity and power, community and culture. This series will feature critical and interpretive, disciplinary and multidisciplinary perspectives on teaching and learning, language and literacy in new times.

Recent Books in the Series
Distance Education and Languages: Evolution and Change
  Börje Holmberg, Monica Shelley and Cynthia White (eds)
Ebonics: The Urban Education Debate (2nd edn)
  J.D. Ramirez, T.G. Wiley, G. de Klerk, E. Lee and W.E. Wright (eds)
Decolonisation, Globalisation: Language-in-Education Policy and Practice
  Angel M. Y. Lin and Peter W. Martin (eds)
Travel Notes from the New Literacy Studies: Instances of Practice
  Kate Pahl and Jennifer Rowsell (eds)
Social Context and Fluency in L2 Learners: The Case of Wales
  Lynda Pritchard Newcombe
Social Actions for Classroom Language Learning
  John Hellermann
Teaching English as an International Language: Identity, Resistance and Negotiation
  Phan Le Ha
Language Teacher Identities: Co-constructing Discourse and Community
  Matthew Clarke

Other Books of Interest
Developing Minority Language Resources
  Guadalupe Valdés, Joshua A. Fishman, Rebecca Chávez and William Pérez
Deep Culture: The Hidden Challenges of Global Living
  Joseph Shaules
From Foreign Language Education to Education for Intercultural Citizenship
  Michael Byram
Imagining Multilingual Schools: Language in Education and Glocalization
  Ofelia García, Tove Skutnabb-Kangas and María Torres-Guzmán (eds)
Language Learning and Teacher Education: A Sociocultural Approach
  Margaret R. Hawkins (ed.)
Medium or Message? Language and Faith in Ethnic Churches
  Anya Woods
Online Intercultural Exchange: An Introduction for Foreign Language Teachers
  Robert O'Dowd (ed.)
Understanding Deaf Culture: In Search of Deafhood
  Paddy Ladd

For more details of these or any other of our publications, please contact:
Multilingual Matters, St Nicholas House, 31-34 High Street
Bristol, BS1 2AW, England
http://www.multilingual-matters.com

NEW PERSPECTIVES ON LANGUAGE AND EDUCATION
Series Editor: Viv Edwards

Heavenly Readings
Liturgical Literacy
in a Multilingual Context

Andrey Rosowsky

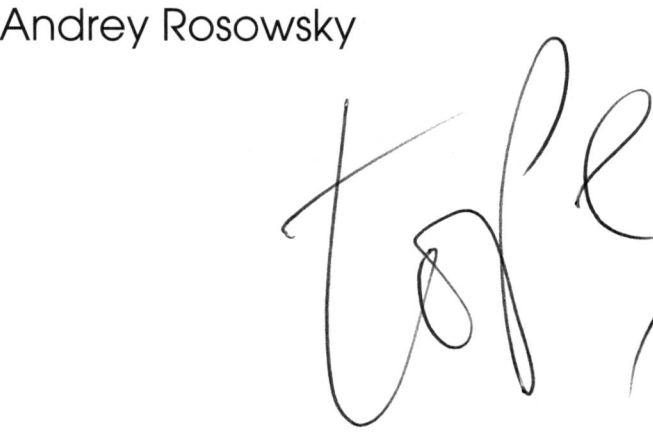

MULTILINGUAL MATTERS
Bristol • Buffalo • Toronto

Library of Congress Cataloging in Publication Data
Rosowsky, Andrey
Heavenly Readings: Liturgical Literacy in a Multilingual Context
Andrey Rosowsky. 1st ed.
Includes bibliographical references and index.
1. Islamic religious education. 2. Islam–Rituals. 3. Language and languages–Study
and teaching. 4. Literacy. I. Title.
BP44.R67 2008
297.7'70941–dc22   2008012754

British Library Cataloguing in Publication Data
A catalogue entry for this book is available from the British Library.

ISBN-13: 978-1-84769-093-7 (hbk)
ISBN-13: 978-1-84769-092-0 (pbk)

Multilingual Matters
UK: St Nicholas House, 31-34 High Street, Bristol, BS21 7HH.
USA: UTP, 2250 Military Road, Tonawanda, NY 14150, USA.
Canada: UTP, 5201 Dufferin Street, North York, Ontario M3H 5T8, Canada.

The policy of Multilingual Matters/Channel View Publications is to use papers that
are natural, renewable and recyclable products, made from wood grown in
sustainable forests. In the manufacturing process of our books, and to further support
our policy, preference is given to printers that have FSC and PEFC Chain of Custody
certification. The FSC and/or PEFC logos will appear on those books where full
certification has been granted to the printer concerned.

Typeset by Wordworks Ltd.
Printed and bound in Great Britain by MPG Books Ltd.

Contents

Part 3: The Settings for Liturgical Literacy

Acknowledgements

Obviously, this book could not have been written without the cooperation and good will of the community that is its subject. I owe a significant debt of gratitude to pupils, past and present, of 'Fieldworth' secondary school, to their parents, to their siblings, to their grandparents and to all who attend, or who have attended, 'Church Walk' and 'University Road' mosques. I am also aware of the privilege that was granted me in gaining the trust and friendship of many other members of the community of 'Midbrough', including mosque trustees and other elders, the respective imams of the two mosques and other teachers of liturgical literacy.

Secondly, I must acknowledge a debt to my former head teacher, Melvin Whale, and to his deputy, Howard Thomas, who encouraged me all those years ago to pursue an incipient interest in literacy and who, subsequently, supported my re-entry into the world of research and writing. It was there that I was mentored by Elaine Millard of the University of Sheffield who never stinted of her advice and time whilst I carried out the research that has led to this book. The latter would not have been written without their timely interventions. I would also like to thank all my colleagues past and present. In particular, thanks should go to Mick Connell, a towering pillar of good sense and wise counsel in what seems, at times, to be an age of unhelpful 'policy' and banal 'strategy'.

I would also like to acknowledge my best friend, Abdullah, for all the discussions we have had down the years. His counsel is always valued and informs much of my thought on this and on other subjects.

Many thanks are also due, more recently, to everyone at Multilingual Matters: Viv Edwards for accepting my manuscript in the first place, Marjukka Grover for her cheery emails and my latest collaborators, Anne and Alex Gray at Wordworks, whom I fear I may have exasperated with my figures and maps.

Finally, and most importantly, this book would never have happened without the support and encouragement of my beloved wife, Amal, who provided me with the invaluable gift of time and space to allow me to shirk, at times, the usual family responsibilities and to concentrate on completing this work.

wa min allahi at-tawfiq ['ultimately, success is from Allah']

Illustrations

Plates

Tables

Figures

Foreword

I am indeed honoured to be invited to write this foreword having had the prior privilege of working with Andrey Rosowsky in my capacity as co-editor of the volume *Explorations in the Sociology of Language and Religion* (John Benjamins, 2006) to which he contributed the chapter titled 'The role of liturgical literacy in UK Muslim communities'. I am pleased to observe that the promise of that chapter is now fleshed out as a full length mono-graph. It is not only confirmation that minority ethnoreligious communities present us with a rich context for sociolinguistic scholarship, but also that they represent legitimate sites for exploring the interface between religion and the sociology of language.

Rosowsky's research population both constitutes a significant demog-raphy culturally and politically in the United Kingdom, as well as one within which language (in) education issues had until recently received rather scant if not superficial treatment. In this regard, the research reported in this book is evidently cutting-edge and will no doubt serve as a trail blazer for further research. It contributes in large measure to extending the frontier of the emerging discipline of the Sociology of Language and Religion as well as to establishing and fine-tuning its methodologies.

Designing the study on which the book is based as an ethnographic investigation has enabled Rosowsky to write deftly about his subject community from the perspective of a co-opted outsider, a position from which he has obviously garnered unique, incisive and well-informed insider perspectives. As a white middle-class intellectual and a practising Muslim living in the community about which he writes, he skilfully avoids the pitfalls we very often expect of those who research the Other. The critical mind with which he attends the issues he covers, together with the benefit of his perspectives, ensures that the arguments he advances are flawless and certainly not those of an apologist.

The richness of this work is evident in the smooth mind journeys Rosowsky undertakes as he criss-crosses communities in the UK and several locations in Western and Eastern Punjab, which constitute his frames of reference for engaging with language and literacy issues. These translocal and transnational connections are interlaced with movement through historical periods as he attempts vigorously to trace the trajectories

responsible for the contemporary literacy practices of his research population. His claims, intricate as these are, are lucidly argued and with seeming
ease but without necessarily compromising the rigour one expects from
work of first grade scholarship such as this.

Rosowsky employs a number of strategies, the consequence of which is
the potentially broad appeal of the monograph. The discussion chapters
3–7 open with a vignette which set the tone as well as serve as a backdrop
for the arguments they advance. These are complemented by pictorial data
which complexify but nevertheless authenticate the analysis by triangula-
tion. Through all these we enter the community whose ethnography the
monograph presents. Our entry is further facilitated by the construction of
a unique materiality through the close attention to detail that we find in
accounts such as:

> Tenter Street, close to the railway, in 1950, could boast of two Italian resi-
> dents, Antonio Maccio, at number 65, and Franco Annibaldi, at number
> 69, but its other residents all had local names. By 1970, Mohammad
> Azam was at number 39, Ali Sher at 43 and Arif Mohammad at 45. We
> also notice here the custom of buying houses adjacent to one another
> which characterised the early purchase of houses by the Mirpuri
> community in the 1960s.

The manner in which Rosowsky successfully links the skills acquired
from ordinary everyday social and religious practices of community life to
the acquisition of skills necessary for school literacy practice via an adaptive
process is ingenious. There is an obvious departure from the normative
centre-staging of English in works of this kind which presents a different
but creatively fresh focus and aesthetics. By the time we come to Chapter
12, which is dedicated to English, the minority and community languages
and culture have received sufficient attention and treatment of detail to the
extent that they can hold their own as reference points for a discussion of
mainstream school literacy activities in English.

The consequence of Rosowsky's sophisticated discussion, I shall
conclude, is a book that is at once entertaining, informative and highly
educative. I say this without an iota of doubt and I am convinced you will
find this to be self-evident truth.

Tope Omoniyi
Roehampton, April 2008

Part 1

The Study of Liturgical Literacy

Chapter 1

Introduction to Liturgical Literacy, or Heavenly Readings

This book aims to account for some of the social, cultural, linguistic and religious processes that give rise to what I shall call 'liturgical literacy'. Wagner *et al.* (1986) use the term 'religious literacy' to describe one of the objectives of having attended a Qur'anic school in urban or rural Morocco. Fishman (1989) uses 'religious classical' as a general category of language used for religious purposes only. I prefer 'liturgical' as it restricts the literacy involved to that used exclusively for ritual and devotional practices, which is the topic of this book, and, in itself, is a word intimately linked with notions of words, texts and scripts.

The domain of liturgical literacy is wide and complex. It has a long and often controversial history. Its place in the 21st century is also varied and contested. It has often had a bad press, particularly in its Islamic form, and compared unfavourably with other forms of literacy. Nearly 100 years ago, MacDonald, for example, emphasised the 'rote' nature of the learning involved:

> It trains the memory and the power of reasoning – always in formal methods – and then gives to neither any adequate material on which to work. The memory is burdened with verbatim knowledge of the Qur'an and some outlines of Theology and law, and the reason is exhausted in elaborate argumentations therefrom deduced. (MacDonald, 1911: 228–289)

Another writer, much later in the century, echoed these sentiments with:

> Qur'anic school imposes on the child a purely mechanical, monotonous form of study in which nothing is likely to rouse his interest. (Zerdoumi, 1970: 96)

And, at the beginning of the 21st century we even have Muslim writers weighing in with similar comments:

> Inevitably, their experiences of rote learning without any understanding left them bored and alienated not only from the madrassah but from religion itself. (Lewis, 2001)

3

And when an attack on such literacy is not intended, writers often reveal their unconscious disapproval with value-laden words and expressions making invidious comparisons between learning how to read the Qur'an and Western learning as in Bledsoe and Robey:

> Arabic is traditionally studied from the Qur'an under a karamoko (Arabic teacher, Islamic scholar) who demands *stringent discipline, laborious work, and long-term* commitments from his students. (Bledsoe & Robey, 1993: 116; my emphasis)

English (or any other non-liturgical literacy) is obviously taught and learnt effortlessly in an environment of perfect motivation needing only a short time for its mastery ...

This point of view can be interpreted, in many respects, as an example of that dismissive or condescending attitude to the East, and to Islam in particular, discussed by writers such as Said (1997) and Asad (2003). Although this book does not directly deal with Western attitudes to things oriental, it is relevant inasmuch as the marginalisation of literacies, which *is* one of the themes of this book, is a manifestation of a tendency in dominant cultures to emphasise, and thus exacerbate, cultural differences which, in turn, leads to 'othering', an elected ignorance and deliberate sidelining of alternative cultural practices. A lack of detailed knowledge about other cultures, forgivable if confessed, but criminal if suppressed, inevitably leads to unfounded generalisations and platitudes that inform nobody. In the bigger picture, which may involve communities, nations, or nation-blocs, this ignorance leads to stand-off, distrust and suspicion, with all that these positions may entail. And, indeed, since the events of September 11th 2001 and July 7th 2005, there is even more onus upon those who discuss and write about matters pertaining to aspects of Islamic culture or to Muslim communities to do so in an informed and intelligent manner. When discussing the Other in terms of *literacy practices* one is mindful of the responsibility to avoid short-cut assumptions and ascribing motives and to present as accurate and honest a description of the literacy practice as is possible whilst admitting any limitations on such a description as might arise.

> Respect for the concrete detail of human experience, understanding that arises from viewing the Other compassionately, knowledge gained and diffused through moral and intellectual honesty: surely these are better, if not easier, goals at present than confrontation and reductive hostility. (Said, 1981: lxx)

However, it is not only Qur'anic liturgical literacy which is thus disparaged. Reder and Wikelund (1993) report that the Old Church Slavonic liturgy of the Russian Orthodox Church still present in Alaska is being slowly but surely replaced by the dominant English literacy introduced by Baptists.

> The technology of the Baptists' literacy was English-based and used the Roman alphabet, whereas the Orthodox literacy used Cyrillic script in Slavonic and Alutiiq. Few if any Orthodox parishioners understood the Slavonic services they attended; participation was by rote, and comprehension of the oral languages was limited. (Reder & Wikelund, 1993: 184)

Note here the substitution of not only language but also script (there are no linguistic reasons why Alutiiq could not be maintained with a Slavonic script). This colonising aspect of the seemingly neutral technology of a script is expanded upon below (Chapter 5: Teachers) where the script associated with a dominant language comes to be used for other languages. One might argue that a single script, when dealing with several languages, would be economic and more practical, allowing for the transfer of skills learnt acquiring the script in one language to facilitate learning literacy in another. It is rare that such a decision (one that is likely to be made officially once official resources come into play) is made solely on linguistic grounds. Rather, the dominant script will be adopted by default for political reasons. Azerbaijan is currently experiencing its fourth major alphabet change in a century. Originally using an Arabic-Persian script reflecting its geographical position and political ties to the Ottoman Empire, the language briefly flirted with Roman script immediately following the Communist takeover, was obliged to conform with the rest of the Soviet Union and adopt a form of Cyrillic, and is now once again attempting to re-introduce a Roman script in the light of the break-up of the Soviet Union (Grimes, 1992). A script is rarely neutral. The use of other scripts is a vital issue for the community involved in this book (see Chapter 11: Mirpuri-Punjabi).

The ethnocentrism of the quotes cited earlier is sometimes matched by the 'chronocentrism' of other writers describing literacy practices from the past. Graff (1979) argues that the claims for universal literacy in Sweden before the end of the 18th century are weakened when we bear in mind that the literacy in question was guided by religious considerations.

> ... good reading ability did not relate strongly to the ability to understand. Popular skills tested well in assessments of oral reading and in memorisation. They were, however, much less useful when it came to comprehension ... (Graff, 1979: 310)

With religion becoming less and less of an influence on the lives of many people living in the world today, particularly the Western world, it may seem bizarre to focus upon a literacy practice which, to some minds, appears irrelevant, outmoded and clearly unsatisfactory. As Frank Smith reminds us, exclusive attention to the phonic dimension of the reading act leads to what he terms 'barking at print'. Reading without meaning? Where is the point in that? (Smith, 1994: 7). Yet, at the time of writing, in the UK, at least, there is a government-approved initiative to introduce a reading scheme into primary schools that relies more heavily on the process of systematic phonics teaching than ever before in recent history, and is akin in many ways to the methods employed in traditional settings for the acquisition of liturgical literacy (DfES, 2007; DCSF, 2007).

What is important to note is that, whatever current orthodoxies may be regarding the meaning of 'reading', millions of the world's citizens participate in this literacy practice and do not, in the slightest, perceive their practice to be meaningless, but rather understand it as a meaningful and fulfilling part of their daily lives, informing their notions of both personal identity and community.

Liturgical Literacy: Defining Remarks

Liturgical literacy is understood as that use of reading, more rarely of writing, which is essential to ritual and other devotional practices connected with an established religion, usually a 'religion of the book', such as Judaism, Christianity or Islam. The language of the liturgy is often different from that spoken by the congregation, such as Classical Arabic in non-Arab Muslim countries and communities, Old Church Slavonic in the Russian Orthodox Church, or the retention of Latin in some aspects of Roman Catholicism.[1] Even when the language of the liturgy can be considered, in some senses, the same as the spoken tongue of the congregation, there are often major differences in register, style and vocabulary that can problematise meaning for participants. This is the case in the Arabic-speaking world, where the Classical Arabic of the Qur'an is not the same as the spoken Arabic of the congregation, or even the same as the Standard Arabic of more formal settings. Ferguson and others (1957; Fishman, 1967) have described this general sociolinguistic phenomenon as an example of diglossia where there is a functional distinction between varieties of the same language. When a liturgical language is involved, as it is, for example, in Muslim communities, the diglossia is of a particular kind. It is more often the case that the liturgical language, or more specifically liturgical literacy, is not a variant of the spoken language of the congregation. However, the linguistic 'compartmentalisation' that Fishman argues for (1991, 2001), and which needs to take place for a language variety to survive in a minority language setting, appears to be enhanced when the variety is a liturgical one. I hope that this book will show how this compartmentalisation, where the domain for the use of liturgical literacy is clearly demarcated and defended, takes place. That there is a difference, in this example, is due to the considerable passage of time that has elapsed from the period of the first scripted Qur'an (650AD) to the present moment and to the extensive geographical spread of the Arabic language. Although the written form of the Qur'an crystallises a moment in the history of Arabic, and indeed has acted as a conservative force on the Arabic language throughout its history, the spoken language moves inexorably on through time and place. An English reader with little appreciation of the diglossic situation that exists with many languages in the world would do well to think of the differences between the language of Shakespeare, a version of English crystallised at a particular moment in history, and the spoken language of today, 400 years later. For most first-language English speakers, much of what Shakespeare has written is incomprehensible on first hearing without the aid of the text.

Islamic Liturgical Literacy or Qur'anic Literacy

The liturgy often is derived from the central scripture of the religion involved. For the liturgical literacy described in this book, the liturgy is derived from the Qur'an. The Qur'an, according to Muslim belief, was a book revealed to the Arabian Prophet Muhammad in the 7th century AD. It was revealed in Arabic and committed to memory by the early 'companions' of Muhammad, many of whom memorised the entire book. Soon after the death of Muhammad, when many of the memorisers of the Qur'an had died and there was a fear that the Qur'an might be lost, the Prophet's successor as leader, or *khalifah*, Abu Bakr, ordered the Qur'an to be transcribed in full. The first transcribed version of the Qur'an made in the 7th century AD is almost identical to any copy of the book found in any mosque today.

Islam is, par excellence, a religion centred on literacy. The first word of the Qur'anic revelation was the imperative *'iqra'* ('read!').[1] This was, in Islamic tradition, a miraculous event in many ways. The Prophet Muhammad was said to have never been taught to read. Despite the primacy of the overwhelmingly oral culture of 7th century Arabia and the Prophet's own lack of literacy, from the very first days of Islamic history reading was always of the utmost importance and was considered a pathway to virtue. An early instruction of the Prophet was to free prisoners-of-war who were able to teach someone to read. Alongside memorisation of the Qur'an, a common practice was to memorise sayings of the Prophet. These too were eventually written down after the compilers of collections of these sayings[3] devoted their lives to their authentication and arrangement. In the Islamic religion, therefore, there are two principal scriptural sources. However, it is the Qur'an that is used most extensively in the liturgy in the mosques and in private devotions. Chapters and verses of the book are used regularly in congregational and individual prayers. Indeed, it is impossible for a Muslim to pray without reading the first chapter of the Qur'an, *The Opening*,[4] usually followed by other verses.

> *The Opening*
> In the name of God, Most Merciful, Most Compassionate
> Praise be to God, Lord of all worlds,
> The Merciful, the Compassionate,
> The King of the Day of Judgement.
> It is You we worship and it is from You we seek help.
> Show us the straight path,
> The path of those you have favoured
> Not the path of those with whom you are angry,
>   or of those who are astray
> Amen   (author's translation)

The Qur'an is read individually as part of one's individual devotions. It can also be read in a group as part of group devotions. It is often read aloud for people to listen to. It is often read in its entirety during the month of Ramadan, either individually or by the congregation as a whole during the nightly extra prayers of *tarawih*.[5] It is read aloud to accompany birth and to accompany death. It is read in times of distress and in times of joy. It is referred to in nearly every sermon and religious talk or lecture with verses quoted and explained. In the Arabic-speaking world, its language has entered common parlance. As the human form is not generally depicted in art form in the Islamic world, the words of the Qur'an have become of great significance in the art form of calligraphy. Most mosques will have decorations featuring Qur'anic verses and words. Copies of the Qur'an will also be very much in evidence on window shelves or in bookcases. The Qur'an will also feature in the home, with decorative calligraphy on walls and copies of the Qur'an on shelves often decorated. The car will also usually contain a Qur'an. Wallets may have small credit-card size verses. Jewellery will often feature verses, in particular the 'Throne' verse for protection (see Chapter 9: Homes).

The community who are the subject of this book do not speak or usually understand Arabic, the language of the Qur'an. For them, the language of the Qur'an has a sound they can replicate, a form they can recognise, but a meaning that often eludes them. For an understanding of their religion, they have to be taught in their mother tongue by, in theory, someone with access to the meaning, or they have to read in a language they understand. When they pray, they use their liturgical language which is Arabic. They will also be able, at varying levels of proficiency, to read the Qur'an. This will be decoding, and may be aloud or silent. They will probably also know, in common with all Muslims, a few common interjections and sayings in Arabic which they will use sometimes in conversation such as *'alhamdulillah'* ('thanks be to God'), *'subhan Allah'* ('glory to God') and *'astaghfirullah'* ('may God forgive us').

In order for this community to be able to participate in this liturgical language, considerable investment in terms of time and money has to be expended. Instruction for children is begun on a part-time basis from the age of six and continues until a reasonable level of proficiency in decoding is achieved. At the end of this period a young person is left able to read, or decode, the Qur'an and able to conduct his or her prayers correctly.

The meaning of the individual words that are read or recited in the prayer are usually not known, apart from a general sense that the words are sacred and are related to God and the religion of Islam. In theory, the imam of the mosque, who is often the Qur'anic instructor as well, has a competent enough command of Arabic to understand what he reads. In practice, in the UK context, this is not necessarily so. Many imams, though studying for many years a range of Islamic sciences, can end up with an imprecise knowledge of Classical Arabic that renders their interpretations insecure, were they to attempt them. Thankfully, it may be argued, this they do not generally do. There is a lengthy and respectable tradition of commentaries in Urdu, the preferred literary language of the community in this book, which provides them with all the interpretations and explanations they will ever need. Sadly, for many of the members of the community involved, particularly the young, these Urdu commentaries and explanations are, too, beyond their understanding, as literacy in the mother tongue is often lacking. Such members of the congregation often find themselves marginalised in their communities and some have argued recently that this experience has been one of the factors leading to radicalisation among some Muslim youth in the UK. As we will see later, circumstances like these have led some to call for much greater use of English in the mosque, and the UK government at present (and similar initiatives are taking place in other European countries) is leading moves to introduce legislation and advice to facilitate this development (DCLG, 2006).

However, forms of liturgical literacy, where the language of the literacy is removed both geographically and temporally from the language of the participants, are not that uncommon, and can be found in many other settings from around the world. For example, the Jewish community in the United Kingdom, although not native speakers of Hebrew, learn to read and recite Biblical Hebrew in order to allow them to fulfil their religious responsibilities. Until recently, Latin was an integral part of the liturgy in both the English and French Catholic Churches. The Coptic Church in Egypt has a liturgy in Copt, a language not spoken for over 1500 years.

Liturgical literacy, where it is practised, does not exist in a vacuum, there to be learnt and used regardless of the social context in which it finds itself. In the community described in this book, alongside the role of the liturgical literacy, there are other languages and literacies, each with its varying social role and function. The fate of the liturgical literacy is intimately linked with the trajectories of those other literacies, and the interplay among them is crucial in any understanding of the literacy practices of this community. Thus it is important to note the respective importance given to liturgical literacy in comparison to literacy in English or literacy in Urdu, or knowledge of poetry in Punjabi. Gregory and Williams (2000) have used a model of contrasting literacies in order to illustrate this interplay and have suggested that teachers in mainstream schools who ignore community-based literacy practices deprive themselves of important knowledge about the children they teach:

> It is a model based on the belief that contrasting rather than similar home and school strategies and practices provide a child with a larger treasure trove from which to draw for school learning. The key task for teachers is to tap into this knowledge and to teach children to become conscious of existing knowledge and skills, to enable children to compare and contrast different languages and literacy practices. It is a model that is particularly relevant for children whose families do not share the literacy practices of the teachers and the school and whose reading skills, therefore, risk remaining invisible. (Gregory & Williams, 2000: 10–11)

A substantial part of the present book is devoted to some of those 'invisible' reading skills mentioned above.

The amount of investment in liturgical literacy evinced by this community suggests that it has a very high priority. This is not to say that the community does not value other literacies. In fact, it is fundamentally unfair to claim that this community, or any other similar minority community, can make a genuine choice regarding preferred cultural and social practices when its marginalised position militates against realistic choices. Would not every community, given the appropriate amount of resources and support, wish to maintain and nourish its cultural heritage, as well as confidently adapting to new situations – preserving literacies as well as developing new ones? However, Fishman (1989) reminds us that, universally, the status of liturgical literacy, which he categorises socio-linguistically as a *religious classical*, once in competition with other languages (vernaculars) and literacies for community support, is privileged:

> Ethnocultural minorities with religious classicals are engaged in a two-front struggle. Not only must they seek to maintain control of their inter-group and intragroup boundaries insofar as their vernaculars are concerned ... but they must also seek to do the same insofar as their religious classicals are concerned ... *[W]hen differentials develop, it is recurringly the religious classical that is retained longer than the vernacular.* The religious domain has more authoritative (and, therefore, more resistant) boundaries than does the minority ethnocultural system as a whole, it is less exposed to majority society, its language use is more ritualised and more sanctified, and its whole tradition is more tradition-and-stability oriented. (Fishman, 1989: 229; my emphasis)

In Chapter 10: Urdu and Chapter 11: Mirpuri-Punjabi, I will show that the '2-front' (or '3-front') struggle taking place at present within the community of this book is being clearly won by the religious classical to the disadvantage of the vernacular languages.

Scope of this Book

This book will begin by situating itself within a tradition of literacy studies that understands literacy to be, above all, a social practice (Street, 1984; Gee, 1990; Lankshear, 1997; Lankshear & MacLaren, 1993; Barton, 1994). It will explore the nature of literacy practices as social acts and attempt to locate the practice of liturgical literacy within the broader definition of multiple literacies (Street, 1999; Gregory & Williams, 2000). However, the complex nature of liturgical literacy will also require an acknowledgement of the complementary fields of, firstly, literacy as a cognitive skill and, secondly, literacy in its pedagogical embodiment, both of which have important things to say about liturgical literacy as it exists today. For example, the grasp of the alphabetic principle, which Liberman and Liberman (1992) declare is a necessary cognitive precondition for learning a script, finds significant support in pedagogical principles based on phonics employed in those institutions responsible for teaching liturgical literacy whilst the 'look-and-say' method of teaching reading is rarely encountered (see Chapter 5: Teachers).

The social setting for the present book (an urbanised, ethnic minority in circumstances of economic deprivation) also brings into focus the marginalised nature of many groups living in Western countries that have a strongly developed liturgical literacy. Many, if not most, of the literacy studies that emphasise the social nature of literacy practices have chosen to explore the literacies of the marginalised, of those whose literacies are not recognised in dominant discourses. For example, Barton and Hamilton conducted their research within a working-class inner city community in the north of England among people whose literacy practices were traditionally less visible:

> [W]e are trying to reveal and question the traditional assumptions which frame literacy, to expose the ways in which it is ideologically constructed and embedded in power relationships[.] (Barton & Hamilton, 1998: 4)

Nothing is straightforward. In its wider social context, the liturgical literacy in this book is positioned marginally with respect to the prevailing dominant literacy. However, in a narrower social context, that of the mosque (the institution) and the imam (privileged elite), the congregation is often disempowered through lack of access to the meaning of the texts in use and obliged to yield to the authority of their imam, who may, or may not, or may claim to, have the knowledge necessary to mediate the text (see Chapter 5: Teachers). This is, of course, not unique to Islamic liturgical literacy, and there are ample examples in Christian history of similar situations. The Reformation was partly shaped by the pressure to render the Holy Writ more accessible and, therefore, not mediated by a powerful elite. Yet, at the same time, it was important that Protestant authorities maintained a close control over the 'correct' interpretation of scripture lest their congregations had ideas of their own. Gee (1990), discussing scriptures now translated, as a result of the Reformation, into vernacular languages, reminds us that this per se does not lead to informed and individual reflection and interpretation:

> The people are given the text for themselves, but then something must ensure they see it 'right' (not in reality through their own eyes, but rather from the perspective of an authoritative institution that delimits correct interpretations). In this case, the individual reader does not need any very deep comprehension skills, and surely doesn't need to write. (Gee, 1990: 37)

The Alaskan study mentioned above (Reder & Wikelund, 1993) describes the disappearance of the need for literacy specialists because of the shift from Old Church Slavonic to English. That it is possible for a literacy to be both dominant and *dominated* at one and the same time, and in the same context, is a topic to which we shall return later in this book.

Community Literacy and its Study

As in Barton and Hamilton's (1998) work amongst the working class communities of Lancaster and as in Gregory and Williams' (2000) study of East London literacy practices, this book will include a very necessary historical account of the community involved and this, in its turn, will involve us in struggling to define the true nature of community. This particular community, perhaps like all communities, does not present us with a neatly-rounded entity, situated as it is at a particular geographical and chronological juncture that faces both backwards and forwards in time as well as sideways across borders and national frontiers. When describing the use of literacy in such a community, we need to keep one eye on the community's links to its point of origin and the use of literacy there – both in the past and in the present – and another eye on the use of literacy in similar communities matched for beliefs, culture and language.

There are few studies directly concerned with liturgical literacy in the sense outlined above. Studies that have focused on religion and literacy have tended to concentrate on monolingual settings (Kapitzke, 1995; Zinsser, 1986; Johansson, 1977; Fishman, 1988), whilst others have had wider, or sometimes more limited, aims. For example, Wagner (1993), although focusing in a significant way on the liturgical literacy provided by the Moroccan *kutaab*,[7] sought also to elucidate the wider literacy practices, both religious and secular, of modern Morocco. More finely focused, Bledsoe and Robey (1993) explored the potential for 'secrecy' among Sierra Leone's Mende created by the use of Arabic liturgical literacy among non-Arabic speaking people. Baker (1993) wanted to focus on the significance of proper nouns in the practice of Arabic liturgical literacy in Indonesia, hypothesising that this grammatical category served as an important function in the apprehension of meaning for those not understanding Arabic.

The multidisciplinary nature of examining literacy as a social practice makes for a very complex and, at times, confusing field of study. The challenge is to come at one's chosen topic in such a way that always allows for new and different perspectives to be formed. The methodology selected needs to be as transparent as possible in order to allow for specialists in many areas to interpret the data presented within their own particular frameworks.

This book has used, in the main, ethnographic techniques (see Chapter

2), and has adopted for its guiding theoretical orientation the six proposi-
tions outlined in Barton and Hamilton's *Local Literacies*:

- Literacy is best understood as a set of social practices; these can be
  inferred from events that are mediated by written texts.
- There are different literacies associated with different domains of life.
- Literacy practices are patterned by social institutions and power rela-
  tionships, and some literacies become more dominant, visible and
  influential than others.
- Literacy practices are purposeful and embedded in broader social
  goals and cultural practices.
- Literacy is historically situated.
- Literacy practices change, and new ones are frequently acquired
  through processes of informal learning and sense making. (Barton &
  Hamilton, 1998: 7)

This is, of course, an overwhelmingly qualitative research paradigm, for
we are interested in what occurs in real social settings in real time.
Decontextualised tests and experiments can play little part in such a
description. However, there are certain data revealed by quantitative
methods that do provide relevant insights. For example, tests of reading
that account for reading accuracy as well as reading comprehension show
that young children who have experienced Qur'anic literacy on a regular
basis also develop into very competent decoders of other scripts, including
English. It has been shown that there is significant transfer of reading
behaviour between mosque school and mainstream school, and that a
significant problem faced by these young learners is the gap between
reading accuracy and reading comprehension (Rosowsky, 2001).

Liturgical Literacy as a Social Practice

Five significant studies in the tradition that Street (1999) names the New
Literacy Studies are Street's own *Literacy in Theory and Practice* (1984),
Wagner's *Literacy, Culture and Development* (1993), Heath's *Ways With Words*
(1983), Barton and Hamilton's *Local Literacies* (1998) and Gregory and
Williams' *City Literacies* (2000). What these studies have in common is a
view of literacy that insists that literacy cannot be understood without close
consideration of the lives, beliefs, values and customs of those whose
literacy practice is being described.

Street (1984, 1993) stresses the link between literacy and authority and
explains that literacy never exists as a neutrally available skill for all those
who desire it:

It is not sufficient, however, to extol simply the richness and variety of literacy practices made accessible through such ethnographic detail: we also need bold theoretical models that recognise the central role of power relations in literacy practices ... [T]he ideological model of literacy ... enables us to focus on the ways in which the apparent neutrality of literacy practices disguises their significance for the distribution of power in society and for authority relations: the acquisition, use and meanings of different literacies have an ideological character that has not been sufficiently recognised until recently. (Street, 1993: 2)

In this book, the ideological character of liturgical literacy is revealed in two ways. Firstly, it is obvious that liturgical literacy as described here is a marginalised and invisible literacy practice when set against mainstream schooling and schooled literacy. Secondly, within the community itself the authority commanded by those who are employed to teach, and by those who employ those who teach, plays a not insignificant role in the potential for change within those institutions charged with transmitting liturgical literacy to future generations (see Chapters 5 and 6).

Wagner (1993), whilst not totally at ease with literacy as social practice per se, still concedes the necessity to incorporate social and cultural background into any description of literacy practices. His work is characterised by a series of *vignettes* depicting everyday literacy practices in Morocco:

Because literacy is a cultural phenomenon, adequately defined and understood only within each culture, it is not surprising that definitions of literacy may never be permanently fixed. Whether literacy is thought of as including computer skills, mental arithmetic, or civic responsibility, for example, will vary across countries, depending on how leaders of each society define this most basic of skills. Researchers can help in this effort by trying to be clear about which definitions they choose to employ in their work. [O]ur work considers literacy to be both a social and an individual phenomenon: social in that social practices are shared among members of a given culture, and individual in terms of the specific set of attitudes and learned behaviours and skills involved in encoding, decoding, and comprehending written language. (Wagner, 1993: 11)

I have chosen to follow Wagner's example and have included vignettes at the beginning of selected chapters (see Chapters 3, 4, 5, 6 and 7) and in the midst of another (Chapter 10).

Heath (1983) describes the particular literacy practices of different communities and shows how literacy is very much a matter of socialisation and not merely a matter of formal instruction. Indeed, the formal instruction element to literacy practices fails or succeeds on its awareness of these socialisation processes:

> Both Trackton and Roadville are literate communities and each has its own traditions for structuring, using, and assessing reading and writing. The residents of each community are able to read printed and written materials in their daily lives and, on occasion, they produce written messages as part of the total pattern of communication in the community. (Heath, 1983: 230)

The young Muslims described in Chapter 3 going to the mosque on a daily basis are very much involved in the process of socialisation and the formation of their own social, cultural and religious identities.

Barton and Hamilton (1998), through a 'thick' (Geertz, 1973) description of literacy practices in Lancashire, show us that literacy practices exist through people, with these literacy practices shaping their lives and, in turn, people shaping the literacy practices:

> Literacy is primarily something people do; it is an activity, located in the space between thought and text. Literacy does not just reside in people's heads as a set of skills to be learned, and it does not just reside on paper, captured as texts to be analysed. Like all human activity, literacy is essentially social, and it is located in the interaction between people. (Barton & Hamilton, 1998: 3)

In Chapter 5: Teachers, and Chapter 10: Mirpuri-Punjabi, I share two significant examples of literacy practices responding to changing social and linguistic conditions: the use of Roman script in the teaching of liturgical literacy and the need of young people to transcribe religious songs and poetry.

Finally, Gregory and Williams (2000) incorporate the anthropological perspective of syncretism into their model for studying literacies. In multilingual communities that have a number of literacy and language practices it is not uncommon for learners to draw on their knowledge and experience in one language and literacy context when learning in another:

> This view states that young learners are not entrapped within any single early childhood literacy practice. The families in the study certainly reveal a complex heterogeneity of traditions, whereby reading practices from different domains are blended resulting in a form of reinterpretation which is both new and dynamic. (Gregory & Williams, 2000: 13)

Part 2 of this book presents a number of examples of how learners draw on their knowledge of schooled practices to inform their learning in the mosque and at home (see Chapters 3 and 4). There is also discussion at the end of Chapter 3 of how learned practice in the mosque influences literacy learning in the school. Integral to the present book is the importance of literacy practice and cultural identity.

The roles of the adults and children participating in liturgical literacy are determined by historical, cultural, linguistic, power and economic influences. For example, a Pakistani child in a northern UK city who is learning the Arabic script of the Qur'an is also, at the same time, acquiring a crucial element in her sense of identity, a 'this is what we do' sense of place and role. She is also becoming, linguistically and cognitively, differently literate[8] to many of her monolingual non-Muslim peers. She is learning a script that places extra demands on the child's cognitive ability (Wagner, 1993: 229) and increasing her awareness of languages beyond that of the home and the school. In the institution where she learns, the mosque, there are models of power and privilege which she has to recognise. The teacher will instruct in a manner noticeably different in style and content from that of her teacher in school:

> There is an immediate contrast between Maruf's community classes and home reading sessions, and his English school. Unlike Maruf's Qur'anic, Bengali and home reading sessions, there is no common pattern or ritual of repeating words correctly after the 'teacher' ... [W]e begin to see that Maruf will need to learn a whole variety of new strategies if he is to learn what counts as reading in his English class. (Rashid & Gregory, 1997: 114)

She will also be aware that the teacher may also have a privileged role in the hierarchy of the mosque, and her own position in the mosque will also need to be learned. In most Pakistani-administered mosques, women have little or no role in the day-to-day running of affairs (Anwar, 1985). The girl will almost certainly spend more time in the mosque as a child than she will as an adult. The written language most closely akin to her spoken language will, if there is no tradition of Urdu literacy in the home, perhaps be encountered for the first time in the mosque. In the case of Urdu, this will be another learning task, for the linguistic and stylistic differences are such as to present significant comprehension difficulties (Linguistic Minorities Project, 1983). As most of the children and adults attending the mosque either for instructions or for devotions are from the same community many aspects of their acquired social, cultural and religious identity are confirmed here.

At the same time that a child is acquiring this identity through active learning and imitation, his/her identity is shaped, equally importantly, by what he/she is not, a 'this is what we are not' sense of place and role. The dominant literacy and culture of the school are contrasted with those of the home and the mosque. Physical manifestations of the dominant literacy, such as script, are all-pervasive and, as we will show later (Chapter 12: English), encroach, colonise and even replace the less privileged. The child, and his/her parents, is aware of the power relations between the school, the home and the mosque. The school has a legal weight denied the mosque. The high stakes qualifications that allow admittance into economically and socially privileged career paths are won in the former. It might be argued by some that there are equally high stakes being presented as rewards in the mosque, albeit these are other-worldly ones.

The language of school and the language of the mosque contrast in a number of ways. The language of instruction in both cases can be alien, acting as a barrier to full admittance until it is learnt. As touched on earlier, there are four languages, at least, in the Pakistani mosque. There is the formal Classical Arabic of the Qur'an which dominates nearly all instruction and devotion. The Urdu of the imam may be evident in his Friday sermon or on the occasional wall poster. When not learning or listening, the congregation may speak in Mirpuri-Punjabi. The younger members may be conversing in English. In the English school, Standard English is the language of instruction, and colloquial English is spoken elsewhere among pupils and staff. Pakistani pupils may converse with one another in Mirpuri-Punjabi, English or a mixture of the two (Baynham, 1993). However, there is little place for the privileged languages of the mosque (Arabic and Urdu) in the school. The fact that often only Pakistani children study Urdu in secondary schools[9] sends a clear and uncompromising message to the rest of the school about its linguistic and cultural merit (see Part 4). This marginalisation is compounded by the current use of the term 'community language' in schools and other social settings, rather than the more prestigious term 'modern language'.

The literacy practices so far described can be considered signifying practices (Lankshear & MacLaren, 1993) that determine what and who are privileged in society. An important aspect of critical literacy lies in its attention to the link between knowledge and power and to identifying where power is located. Through these practices it might be argued, and it is, that marginalised groups are actively silenced through the nature of their restricted literacy practices. The various subjectivities engendered by these complex interactions between people, literacies and institutions prevent us from ever claiming an autonomous perspective for literacy. The multiliteracies that exist mainly in our urban centres are always competing or, at least, contrasting (Gregory & Williams, 2000). The all-pervasive weight of the dominant literacy is always making inroads into the complex and variegated picture of 'multiliteracy'. As mentioned above, any community would wish to preserve and maintain its literacy heritage as well as develop a new one. This cannot be achieved without a full awareness of the power relations involved in maintaining, preserving and marginalising literacies.

The principal institution from which the Muslim community in this book derives its liturgical literacy is the mosque. Most of the Muslim children in the communities researched will attend the mosque on a regular basis and become proficient, to a lesser or greater degree, at reading the holy text of the Qur'an. To understand what role this institution plays in the life of the community it is necessary to look at the structure and history of the mosque both as a building and as an institution. The personnel, the finance, the administration, the physical structure and arrangement of the mosque are examined in order to show how the community interacts with it, shapes it and is, in turn, shaped by it. Only then is it appropriate to ask questions about the literacy practices that take place in the mosque (see Chapter 7: Mosques).

The above description of the mosque as an institution necessarily involves discussions about power relations and cultural identities. The interface between the literacies practised in the mosque and the literacies encountered in the wider dominant community will be examined in the home, the school and in the world of work. Here, the issue of power relations turns not only on dominant and dominated literacies, but also on communities, institutions and stakeholders. It also demonstrates that the apparent neutral technology of a particular script plays its part in the complex picture created by different literacies.

Five Studies in Liturgical Literacy

There are a small number of significant short studies that address, to a lesser or greater degree, the subject of liturgical literacy. Most of these come from the anthropological tradition sharing the ideological model of literacy (Street, 1993). All acknowledge the intimate link between literacies and power, and address the issues thrown up by this relationship.

Bledsoe and Robey and the Mende (1993)

The Mende of Sierra Leone (Bledsoe & Robey, 1993) are a Muslim people and, as such, use Classical Arabic as a liturgical language. In the theoretical background of this study is the longstanding debate regarding literacy and orality, or what has come to be known as 'the Great Divide'. Those (Goody & Watt, 1963; Goody, 1968, 1977; Ong, 1982; Olson *et al.*, 1985) who have advocated a fundamental sea change in societies that become literate consider literacy itself to be an autonomous cultural development that has important social, economic and political implications for the society in which it happens. Literacy in this sense is neutral and technical: a discrete set of skills to be mastered through schooling and is uni-dimensional, literacy. Street (1984) opposes this with his ideological model, suggesting that literacy is always context bound, value laden, culturally influenced and is multi-dimensional – *literacies*. Moreover, in the autonomous model, literacy brings with it cognitive consequences, so that abstract thought is more readily communicated, clarity is more attainable in writing that is free from context and logic and thought itself become more transparent and, therefore, more 'democratic'. An interesting aside to this debate is that one of the more vociferous supporters of the autonomous model claimed all these benefits for Western Greek-based literacy exclusively (Havelock, 1976). Semitic literacy, as exemplified by the major alphabetic languages of Hebrew and Arabic, missed out. It is argued by some that only the Greek alphabet, which developed from Phoenician, had the capability to serve the advances in philosophy, science and culture brought by the Greeks, and that, other alphabets, also developing from Phoenician, such as Hebrew, Aramaic and Syriac, and early forms of Arabic, were somehow inferior vehicles for such intellectual development. This, of course, at one foul swoop, dismisses, or denigrates, the cultural achievements not only of all those cultures using Semitic-based languages, but also of all cultures based on languages with non-Phoenician-derived alphabets, and also of all civilisations and cultures with a non-alphabetic writing system such as Chinese and Japanese.

Of importance in the Mende study is the notion that, in terms of the autonomous model, written language tends towards clarity and 'truth' and spoken language facilitates 'obfuscation and lying' (Bledsoe & Robey, 1993). However, the usage of written Arabic for purposes of liturgy among the Mende Muslims reveals the potential of written language for concealing ignorance and promoting secrecy and thus contradicts the idea that the written word, and therefore literacy, is in some sense naturally given to more lucidity and is a promoter of abstract thought.

Written Arabic, or Qur'anic Arabic, is strictly the preserve of an educated elite who are able to use the prestige of this literacy to privilege their knowledge and their position within the Mende community. Indeed, what is happening is that instead of the Mende passively accepting the 'package' of literacy and being transformed by the experience, the Mende utilise and re-interpret aspects of literacy and mould it into their own cultural systems. Thus the Mende apply the literate skills to suit their own purposes and needs. Later we will show how this attitude to literacy is found among young Muslims in northern England when they freely adopt Roman script to transliterate Urdu and Punjabi poetry and songs (see Chapter 11: Mirpuri-Punjabi).

The use of literacy as the language of an elite and the book as secret and artefact is not unique to the Mende. The use of Latin in medieval Europe, as Cazal (1998) notes of Catholicism, restricted literacy to the few, and often restricted literacy itself to decoding, rote learning and calligraphy:

> *Société chrétienne, elle réserve à un petit nombre de ses members, l'élite professionelle et intellectuelle des clercs, l'apprentissage de l'écriture et l'accès au savoir. Elle leur délègue surtout le soin de conserver un ensemble clos de textes hérités – à la première place desqueles figure le texte sacré de l'Ecriture sainte – composes dans une language, le latin, maintenue comme norme linguistique et outil conceptual, en dépit – et contre – lévolution et la diversification naturelles des langues parlées.* (Cazal, 1998: 10)
>
> [Christian society restricts the right to teach writing and, hence, access to knowledge, to a small number of its members, the professional and intellectual clerical elite. It delegates to them the care of preserving a collection of inherited texts – the most important of which is the Holy Scripture – written in one language, Latin, which is maintained as a linguistic norm and a conceptual tool, despite – and contrary to – the evolution and natural diversification of spoken vernaculars.] (author's translation)

However, the Mende study begs the question, is literacy deliberately used for secrecy? It is possibly more likely the case that as the liturgical language is not the spoken language of the community, the liturgical literacy becomes willy-nilly an arcane language, privileged to the few and interpreted for the masses. It accretes to itself and its knowers status, privilege, power and authority. This is not as easy in the Arabic-speaking world where, despite the diglossic circumstances of classical and colloquial Arabic, the general congregation can have access to the meaning of the liturgical literacy to a greater or lesser extent. They very rarely have no access.

Below (in Part 2) we will discuss the very real issue in UK Pakistani communities of lack of access to the meanings behind the wealth of words commonly learnt and recited. There certainly is 'power through ritual authority' (Bledsoe & Robey, 1993), but added to that is even more power through linguistic, or liturgical, authority.

The secrecy factor is compounded by the nature of much Mende Islamic practice which tends, in Bledsoe and Robey's study at least, towards the mystical branch of the faith. In its more extreme and, in Islamic terms, corrupt forms, the mysticism found in some parts of the Islamic world exploits the ignorance of its adherents by nurturing an atmosphere of secrecy around the religious teacher, who may have an inner circle to whom he allegedly initiates into arcane and secret knowledge. The liturgical literacy assists these teachers in preserving their authority, as only a select few are instructed in literacy.

This study relies heavily upon the *moriman* – or magicians – of Mende society with the result that the liturgical literacy used, often in the form of amulets and secret formulae, itself becomes an arcane form invested with secrecy and esotericism. This form of liturgical literacy is equally at home in some UK Pakistani communities where the elevation of religious teachers such as *pirs* can sometimes lead to exaggerated claims of their esoteric and magical capabilities.

Of more significance to this present book, however, is the observation made by the Mende study that even the privileged elite are often poorly equipped to deal with the meaning of the words they are, in every other respect, quite comfortable with.

> Some Arabic teachers never reach meaning because they can only decode at the phonetic or surface semantic level. (Bledsoe & Robey, 1993: 123)

This is where the sensitive issue of bluffing comes in. In many parts of the non-Arabic Islamic world, but particularly among communities that are marginalised and lacking in education, it is relatively easy to become sufficiently 'literate' in the liturgy of the faith and therefore acquire a status that is open to abuse (see Chapter 5).

Weinstein-Shr and the Hmong (1993)

The study of the Hmong (an immigrant community originating in Laos in South-East Asia) in Philadelphia (Weinstein-Shr, 1993) poses some universal questions about literacy among migrant groups. How do social relationships within the community shape and influence the way that literacy is acquired and used, and, conversely, how does life in a literate environment affect or change social relationships?

> I will argue here that anthropologists have an important contribution to make in informing literacy instruction and educational practice as urban society becomes increasingly culturally diverse. (Weinsten-Shr, 1993: 274)

One of the central case studies featured Pao Youa Lo, who used literacy to connect to the past and to Hmong tradition without ever engaging with the language and literacy of the host community. In his interface with the institutions and representatives of the dominant literacy his role often appears unfocused and disempowered. Such is the lot of many members of marginalised communities, but this persona of Pao Youa disguised the significant power and influence he wielded in his own community. Later (Chapter 5, The Teachers) we will see how personalities similar to Pao Youa are represented in the UK Pakistani Muslim community where similar authority can be not only local, but national and even international, with no recourse at all to the dominant host community (Mufti Siddiq in Chapter 5).

Younger members of the Hmong community, more comfortable with the language, literacy and customs of the host community, adopt the newer roles required by interfacing with its institutions and representatives. The elder Hmong maintain more traditional roles within the community dealing with issues such as domestic disputes, marriages and traditional solutions to medical problems. Pao Youa, for example, favours preserving the shamanic tradition of the Hmong and is concerned about the Westernisation and secularisation of the younger generation. We will see later how religious authority is employed to bolster position in other communities (Chapter 5: The Teachers).

Zinsser and the Fundamentalists (1986)

Zinsser (1986) describes the use of scripture in a fundamentalist American Christian setting. Using participant–observer methods, her book shows the importance attached not only to the message of the scripture, but also to the book as artefact. It allows an interesting comparison to be made between the handling practice of these Christian children and their Muslim peers, albeit in a different social setting far away. Important to the community was the need for every member to have his or her own copy of the Bible. This is a practice that until very recently was common in many state secondary schools in the UK. In fact, I recall a tradition in inner London in the 1950s and 60s where pupils were given a Bible at secondary school which was then ceremoniously signed by all his or her classmates on the day the pupil left school. Some of the comments inscribed were often strangely inappropriate for a religious text! Nowadays for this custom, the Holy Bible has been usurped by the more mundane school shirt, blouse or sweatshirt.

However, the children handled the Bible, as an object, very casually:

A boy chases a girl before class begins. Both hold Bibles. The boy hits the girl with his Bible.

During assembly time a girl sucks on the end of a Bible zipper which has torn loose.

Required to join hands in a circle, a girl holds her small Bible in her teeth.

During aggressive play two boys shove a Bible back and forth across a table. A boy sits on his Bible so he can use both hands to perform motions to a song. (Zinsser, 1986: 58)

This contrasts dramatically with the use of the Qur'an as an object described below (Chapter 3: The Children) where all the behaviour in the examples quoted would be considered anathema. I recall visiting a Quaker community with a group of Muslim scholars from Turkey and remember witnessing their shock to find the Bible on the floor in the middle of the room. Muslim children are taught from a very early age that the Qur'an in its printed form is to be revered at all times. Thus in most Pakistani households the family copy of the Qur'an will be on the highest shelf of the bookcase often covered in an embroidered covering (Chapter 8: The Home). In the mosques the copies of the Qur'an used by the children will, like the Bibles of their Christian peers, be individualised, but will not be handled so casually. This practice goes so far as forbidding destruction of old and damaged copies of the Qur'an. This leads to the practice of collecting old Qur'ans and odd pages together in a cupboard somewhere in the mosque (Chapter 7, The Mosques). In fact, in the Islamic world as a whole the appearance of Qur'anic verses in print can be a problematic issue. Many newspapers often contain quotations from the Qur'an, and this can lead to the dilemma of what to do with the newspaper once it has been read. The ephemeral nature of newsprint presents an almost insurmountable problem. One device that is sometimes used to get round this problem is the use of numbers (numerology) to replace the ubiquitous '*Bismillahi arahmanirahim*' ('In the name of Allah, the Most Merciful') found at the beginning of many texts. All letters in the Arabic alphabet have a numerical equivalent, and the formula '786' can often be found at the beginning of printed or written public notices and announcements.

However, a common experience in the Bible school described by Zinsser was the emphasis placed on rote memorisation, where children were required to learn a verse each week, together with its citation. Unlike the Qur'anic school, stories were a staple fare of the curriculum, followed with much attention placed upon listening to stories. Here we notice a key link with the primary school practice experienced by these children. Listening to stories in the Bible school is not a million miles away from listening to stories in regular school (Heath, 1993). There is no parallel practice in the traditional Qur'anic school (though see Chapter 10: Urdu, for a description of a context where stories are used extensively).

Baker and the Tidorese (1993)

Baker (1993) addresses the issue of decoding as a cultural practice among the Tidorese of Indonesia. Devout Muslims, the people of the village studied, Kalaodi, read the Arabic Qur'an in a manner very similar to millions of Muslims around the world. Baker deals directly with the thorny issue of reading without apparent meaning and claims for this literacy practice a socially significant value transcending the literal meaning of the text.

> If at base we think of reading as an activity of interpretation that requires from the start some amount of language competence, then we would have to say that the uncomprehending recitation of written texts is something altogether different. But, if we also think of reading as the socially significant practice of taking up a text and going through the processes of actualising the inscribed words in a temporal sequence, *expending real time and personal effort in doing so*, then we have something essential to the activity of reading without yet concerning ourselves with comprehension and the interpretations that can follow from it. (Baker, 1993: 98; my emphasis)

Baker recognises that this literacy practice has a mnemonic function that links it diachronically with the practice of reading the Qur'an since the early days of Islam.

> The invariant manuscript of the Koran serves to assure the verbatim accuracy of what is being recalled aloud in liturgical performance. Indeed, much of what is recited in Arabic is done so from memory. And, even though many of the verses that are regularly uttered aloud are learned from hearing others recite, their invariance across local communities and language boundaries is assured by the one written source against which they could always be checked. In this respect a performance from memory is still a form of reading aloud. (Baker, 1993: 103)

Baker (1993: 108) draws a distinction between reading as a 'comprehending' activity and reading as 'apprehending' where apprehending means 'coming to grips with what there is to know without necessarily knowing how to subject it to predications, that is, to adequately comprehend it'. He also suggests that this apprehension has a lot more to do with substantive nouns than with verbs. He allows this perspective to direct the greater part of his commentary on the Kalaodi literacy practices, and singles out names as playing an important part in the apprehension of the foreignness of the Arabic.

Not understanding Arabic myself, I can attest from listening to recitations that proper names flash out as recognisable entities in a stream of pleasingly lyrical but uncomprehended utterances. (Baker, 1993: 110)

In the present book, it will not be claimed that oral decoding of the Qur'anic text holds meaning for the reciters in such a specific way, though some words, not all names, will resonate with meaning for some reciters (see Bashir in Chapter 4: The Parents). In fact, it is questionable whether the Kalaodi themselves consider their oral decoding to be merely an 'apprehension of names'. Arabic, like all Semitic languages, operates by modifying its roots. Most verbs and nouns are derived from a root pattern that can generate a 'family' of words based on the same root. When decoding the Qur'an without comprehension, reciters will sometimes recognise words that belong to a known root. For example, the Arabic word for 'book' is *'kitaab'* formed from the root pattern 'k-t-b'. Urdu contains many words borrowed from the Arabic, *'kitaab'* being one of them. A reciter will therefore probably recognise the word *'kitaab'* when orally decoding the Qur'an, and possible recognise other derived words such as *'kutiba'*, *'kaatib'*, *kaatiba'* without really understanding the nuances of meaning produced by such morphology. There are many examples that one can give of words which, because of their use as daily references to religious matters, might be recognised when the Qur'an is orally decoded. This, it is argued, is a form of comprehension that needs to be taken into consideration.

Wagner and Morocco (1982–1993)

Wagner (1982, 1993; Wagner *et al.*, 1986) describes the particular characteristics of Qur'anic schooling in Morocco.

> The study of traditional Qur'anic schooling would be of considerable social significance if only for the fact that tens of millions of children in many nations of the world attend them. This statistic indicates that Qur'anic schooling is one of the largest relatively homogenous forms of preschooling in the world today ... (Wagner, 1982)

In his major study on literacy in Morocco (1993), Wagner provides insightful data on the role of traditional Qur'anic pedagogy in a modernising setting. He argues against any malign effects of Qur'anic schooling and tackles head-on the common criticisms of such pedagogy that it leads to a smothering of the imagination (Hardy & Brunot, 1925), or that excessive memorisation displaces critical thinking (Miller, 1977). In a study that claims to be 'a project anchored in quantitative measures of language, reading and cognitive skills supported by several other modes of investigation', the authors consider Qur'anic schooling to be a form of complementary schooling that is a potential resource for development.

Wagner was able to compare the subsequent educational performance of children who had or had not experienced pre-school Qur'anic schooling as well as those whose first language was Moroccan Arabic and those whose first language was Berber.

Relevance of Previous Studies to this Book

Until comparatively recently, traditional Qur'anic schooling could be found only in countries with predominantly Muslim populations. With the migration patterns of the 20th century we now find many examples of traditional Qur'anic schooling in non-Muslim Western countries. The same issues that have arisen in countries such as Morocco regarding the interaction between state formal education and traditional schooling are now beginning to be explored. This book is a contribution to this field and seeks to shed light on the intricate relationship between, on the one hand, the Muslim communities and the institutions from which they learn their liturgical literacy (and, in some cases, their literary vernacular language) and on the other, the relationship between this literacy and the dominant literacy encountered and acquired at school and in the wider community.

Notes

1. Of interest is the support that Pope John Paul II gave to the revival of Latin in many aspects of the Roman Catholic Church (*Catholic World News*, 2003).
2. The verses traditionally understood to be the first of the Islamic revelation came to Muhammad whilst he was meditating in seclusion. The account relates how the Angel Gabriel appeared with a sheet in his hand and asked Muhammad to read. He answered, 'What shall I read?' and the command was repeated. This happened three times after which the first verse was revealed, 'Read in the name of your Lord, the Creator, Who created man from a clot of blood. Read, for your Lord is Gracious. It is He who taught man by the pen that which he does not know' (Chapter 96, verses 1–5, in Haykal, 1976).
3. These are known as collections of '*Hadeeth*' or 'sayings'.
4. Known by Muslims as the '*Fatihah*'.
5. Extra prayers said in congregation in the mosque through the month of Ramadan.
6. Verse 255 of Chapter 2 of the Qur'an.
7. The *kutaab*, in Arabic-speaking countries, is an elementary school, usually rurally located, for the teaching and learning of the Qur'an.
8. With thanks to Dr Elaine Millard as the coiner of this term originally used to identify the differences in boys' and girls' acquisition of literacy (1997).
9. There are some secondary schools in the UK that offer Urdu to all pupils. These more enlightened establishments are unfortunately in the minority.

Chapter 2

The Community and its Ethnography

Setting for this Book

This book takes as its field of inquiry one of the large number of Muslim communities now present in many cities of Western Europe, and, in particular, those communities of a south Asian, or Pakistani, origin that are found in many cities and towns, often in the Midlands, in the north of the United Kingdom and in some districts of London. The languages spoken by these communities are varied, and fully contribute to the reality of the United Kingdom as very much a multilingual society (Trudgill, 1984). The fact that these communities, in addition, all share a common liturgical language, or more exactly a liturgical *literacy*, means that their linguistic profile is a complex one. The importance of language and religion for cultural identity are well-researched areas (Kapitzke, 1995). Usually, they have been studied separately. Moreover, religion has often been treated as a cultural phenomenon not impinging too directly on the learning of students and pupils though there are, of course, many assumptions made and prejudices harboured regarding education both within and outside of these communities. For example, it is a commonly-held view that Muslim families discourage their daughters from pursuing higher education (Basit, 1997). This view will not directly enter this discussion, but is an example of commonly-held assumptions that indirectly affect the teaching and learning of young Muslims in schools that are there to serve these communities, and is certainly contradicted by evidence collected by this author.

The present book concerns reading. Whatever reading is in school, and here it is already an infinitely complex experience, it is not what reading is in the world in its entirety. The world of reading is much more complex than that which is represented in the classroom, where despite all the best efforts of teachers to be *authentique*,[1] only a limited range of experiences can be engendered and developed. This is not to belittle what goes on in the reading classroom, but rather it is to underline the infinite complexity of what reading is in the world outside of the school. Experiences of reading which take place out of school are no more real than those at school, for who can deny the reality or importance of reading and understanding a question in an examination, but the reading which takes place in the home, in the workplace, in the leisure place, in the place of worship, is a reading which is intimately linked with the reader's needs, duties, desires and feelings in a way school-based reading can rarely achieve. The present book concerns reading in a place of worship. This, of course, means that the dominant mode of enquiry will be an ethnographic one. Yet, from the outset, it will be stressed that the experience of reading being described is not, by any means, distant from and, therefore, unrelated to, the reading experiences of school.

The Community of the Present Book

The community depicted in this book has its origins in the Mirpur province of Pakistani Punjab and Azad Kashmir. From the 1950s onwards, men came from this province,[2] sometimes via the British merchant navy, to work in the steelworks and related industries in South Yorkshire. Wives and sometimes other family members followed later. The community settled in cheaper, inner city, mainly terraced housing in east Sheffield and either side of Rotherham city centre. Nowadays, most of the jobs that brought them to the UK have gone. Many males now work in the taxi industry. Others are unemployed. The national statistics for ethnic minority unemployment apply strongly in the area (ONS, 2003). Children attend local primary and secondary schools. In the late 70s, recognition of the educational needs of these children meant that additional resources were provided to Local Education Authorities (LEAs) in the form of Section 11 of the Commonwealth Immigration Act, which later became the Ethnic Minority and Travellers Achievement Grant (EMTAG, later EMAG). As the community has become more affluent, as UK society has become more affluent, travel to and from Pakistan has increased for adults and for children, with long spells out of the classroom affecting educational progress. However, it is also true that, with each new generation born in the UK, links with Pakistan and, as a result, reasons for travel are becoming weaker.

The language spoken by the community is generally Mirpuri-Punjabi, a dialect spoken in the corresponding region in Pakistan. The dialect has a written form that uses the Urdu script (which in turn is derived from Arabic script via Persian). However, this written form is rare and is generally encountered only in poetry. The principal literary language is Urdu, which is the literary language of the state of Pakistan, and before that was the written language of the Muslims in pre-Partition India. Hindi and Urdu are mutually intelligible. Not all of the community will speak Mirpuri-Punjabi as their mother tongue. There are also a number of Pushto speakers who originate from the Pathan province of Pakistan.

Among the younger generation, particularly the grandchildren of the first immigrants (third generation), there is much greater use of English at home, particularly when conversing with siblings, though it would be more accurate to describe this use of English as elaborate code-switching (Baynham, 1993). At school, Mirpuri-Punjabi is used freely among friends though schools (and teachers) vary in their response to its use, with some warmly celebrating the linguistic repertoire of their pupils and others feeling the need to restrict its use in the classroom. Urdu is now being offered to pupils, though again schools vary in their provision. Some are very imaginative and offer the language as a second language to all pupils regardless of ethnic background. Other schools aim the language only at 'relevant' pupils and thus underline its marginalisation.

It says something about the community and its religion when it is obvious that it invests considerably more time, and money, in developing literacy in the Qur'an than it does in developing literacy in the most appropriate literary language, Urdu. Although Urdu is taught in the mosques (though not in all), it is always subordinate to Qur'anic Arabic (see Part 3 for a fuller discussion of the languages used in the community).

As a researcher sharing the same faith, and who has worked within the community in question for many years, I have been able to access the homes and institutions relatively easily. The 10 families chosen for detailed investigation were self-selected on the basis of convenience inasmuch, as they had children at the school where I worked and, in two cases out of the ten, were related to a longstanding friend of mine who had died. I also ensured that the 10 families had a link to the two mosques described below. Each family has or has had a number of children go through the local primary schools and the local secondary school. In this latter context I taught some of them myself, but not all of them. The children had had various careers at school, with some succeeding academically and others not. The children were interviewed at home, at the mosque and at school. Before the research took place, I was on 'nodding' terms with eight of the fathers and a friend of the other two (though strictly speaking I had been a friend of their dead brother). I had met some of the mothers at parents' evenings at the school. The main method of collecting data from the family was by an initial questionnaire followed up by a group semi-structured interview with the whole family, as far as that was possible. All names of interviewees, respondents and community members have been anonymised. Permission for all interviews and conversations were arranged through direct approach or, in the case of children, through their parents.

The name of 'Midbrough' is fictional, as are many of the other place names within Rotherham , but here and there (in plates, for example) it has been impossible to avoid references to real place names. I have done my best to minimise these references.

Although I share the faith of the community, I do not live within it and share neither its language nor its cultural profile. But I do share the same liturgical literacy and it is this social practice that allowed my role of researcher as participant. Yet, as the researcher, I was still an outsider. During the course of the fieldwork I was aware of my growing involvement with the life of the community, but was still cognisant that there would have to be a withdrawal at some stage – what Bruyn (1966) has called being an 'imminent migrant'.

The awareness of contrasting experiences is reflected in this book by the attempt to legitimise the opinions of the various stakeholders within liturgical literacy. In the role of researcher as participant, I could relate to the parents through a considerable amount of shared experience and practice. My experience as teacher was also a key element in the establishment of common ground between myself and the imams.

A significant part of this book has been inspired by the Gregory and Williams' (2000) longitudinal study of the Spitalfields area of London. Although not sharing the more ambitious longitudinal aims of that study, this book also uses documentary and picture evidence to provide a mini-history of the community and its institutions. Another difference is that this book necessarily focuses sharply on one particularly under-researched literacy practice. Nevertheless, many of the ethnographic methods used in the Spitalfields study have been employed here: participant observation, interviews, life histories and the use of historical documents and images. I feel I share their aim:

> [O]ur aim [is] to investigate the role, scope and nature of literacy in people's lives as well as in the histories and traditions of which these are a part. (Gregory & Williams, 2000: 14)

This book has its origins in my own professional experience. Until recently, I had spent most of my career teaching English in UK secondary schools with significant numbers of pupils who have English as an additional language and, significantly, who are Muslim. As a teacher of reading, I noted quite quickly that these pupils were able to decode text in English very proficiently, in a manner well in advance of their comprehension ability, and often in advance of their chronological ages or even of their monolingual non-Muslim peers. Initially, I naively put this down to a successful programme of bilingual support provided by a team of Section 11 peripatetic teachers. For instance, in the mid-1980s it was still quite common for LEAs to have a separate centre where English as an Additional

Language (EAL) pupils followed an intense programme of English away from their peers until such a time as it was considered appropriate for them to be admitted to mainstream classes. However, when this method of support fell from favour, in the interests of inclusion, these pupils were managed within the secondary school through a balanced programme of in-class support and occasional withdrawal. As the perceived advanced decoding continued to manifest itself in the reading behaviour of these pupils, I had to re-assess my original conclusions as to where this superior decoding was developed.

Alongside this professional experience, I was also able to draw on my own experience of learning to read in other languages, and more significantly, in different scripts. Having learnt Russian, and therefore the Cyrillic alphabet, at secondary school, and Arabic whilst teaching in Egypt and as a consequence of embracing Islam, the written Arabic of the Qur'an, it became apparent that mastery of a code was a linguistic skill often easily developed in isolation from other skills such as reading for meaning. If you also add to this exotic mixture my self-taught musical notation which allowed me to 'read' music (that is, to follow scores), without being able to create it in any form whatsoever, then it became equally apparent that it was possible to develop a highly developed skill which, for cultural or religious reasons, was often detached from more meaning-laden aspects of language such as creativity and comprehension.

Furthermore, teaching practice in the mosque, which I observed in the course of my own visits, and also, in my own experience of teaching adults and children to read the Qur'an in an informal manner at home or in other settings, led me to reflect on the nature of learning to read the Qur'an for the pupils in the school who shared this religious practice. This led to a small-scale quantitative study undertaken to demonstrate the advanced decoding ability of Muslim secondary school pupils when reading texts in English, and the discrepancy between it and the same pupils' comprehension ability (Rosowsky, 2001).

It was clear that a probable reason for this advanced decoding ability was the intense decoding activity experienced by these pupils on an almost daily basis from the age of six until 13, albeit in a language other than English. It was also clear that the liturgical literacy learnt in the mosque, in the eyes of the dominant community, was a marginalised and under-reported social and educational practice that deserved a more just and detailed description. As a form of community education, it had provoked little research, either in terms of community culture and identity or in terms of its relationship with other, including schooled, literacies.

This book, therefore, addresses four related questions:

- What is liturgical literacy, both generally and in this community?
- What role does it play in this community?
- How does it interact with and relate to other literacies?
- What is the significance of liturgical literacy for the study of literacy and the linguistic future of this community?

In any ethnographic study, the sources of data are varied and multifaceted. A rich description of a literacy practice will include examples of texts utilised, but will also attempt to provide a description through photographs of locations, people and artefacts as well as other graphical aids such as maps, leaflets and posters (Wagner, 1993; Gregory & Williams, 2000). I ensured such a 'rich' mixture by incorporating spoken, written and visual documentation.

The two institutions that feature in this book are the two mosques that serve the community whose children attend the local schools. There is a doctrinal difference of opinion regarding certain matters of faith which has no bearing on this book but which keeps the two congregations separate, though at school, at least, this makes for no disagreements. Socially, too, the two congregations seem to cooperate. Both mosques organise regular Qur'anic instruction for both children and adults. The imams of the two mosques are responsible for leading the prayer and Qur'anic instruction. They also prepare and deliver the Friday sermon. Data collected from the institutions include interviews with imams and assistants, trustees and secretaries of the two mosques, observed teaching sessions, prayers and sermons, and occasional gatherings.

Further data are provided by the artefacts of this form of liturgical literacy (Wagner *et al.*, 1986: 254). Homes, mosques and rooms are described, together with the personal manifestations of the liturgy on jewellery and in wallets. The use of amulets and the use of the written word for supernatural purposes are also included.

This book is intended to shed light on the complex role that liturgical literacy plays in the life of a community and the way that literacy practice contrasts (Gregory & Williams, 2000) and interacts with other literacy practices in the community. This overarching question is addressed by means of an ethnographic case study involving individuals, families and institutions. This case study is a qualitative investigation that aims to give the reader a detailed insight into the place of liturgical literacy in this community.

A researcher can have more than one epistemological position and, although this book will reflect, in the main, the interpretive position of qualitative research, it will also, in places, adopt a more critical position.

Although it is recognised that the literacy practice that lies at the heart of this book is much misunderstood and under-researched and that, therefore, there is a necessary and worthwhile job to be done in a 'thick' description of this literacy practice, it is also recognised that this is a literacy practice that is marginalised and, in some sense, threatened, and thus the social conditions in which it finds itself needs critique.

This critical perspective, therefore, needs to place the particular social event being described in the context of a wider social environment. The interpretive researcher can sometimes be accused of operating only at the 'micro' levels of society, and is not disposed to applying what s/he describes to wider social structures. As Travers opines,

> For the critical researcher, context is conceptualised as the workings of society as a whole, and the aim of the analysis is to show how the actions and beliefs of people in particular situations are shaped by wider Durkheimian social structures, which exist separately from individuals. This is often conceptualised in terms of making a distinction between 'micro' and 'macro' levels of society [...]. The interpretive researcher, on the other hand, is only interested in how people understand what they are doing in any social setting, and does not accept that there is a 'macro' level of analysis, or that the analyst knows more about society than the people he or she is studying. (Travers, 2001: 123)

In making that step from describing the world to engaging in critique, this book moves from a description of the role played in the community by liturgical literacy to the issues of marginalised and endangered literacy practices, the lack of state support for language and literacy maintenance and, in this particular community, issues around Othering and islamophobia (Said, 1985).

Threading its way through the presentation and discussion of the data will be the premise that there is no 'neutral' method of 'describing' literate behaviours. Issues such as language rights and empowerment must always be to the forefront when describing literacy practices lest we be implicated in preserving the status quo regarding monolingual and monocultural literacy. Literacy is always entwined with a cultural struggle. Pennycook (2000) reminds us that language death does not happen in privileged communities, and that language, and literacy, maintenance is a matter of social justice. As this book will show, there are already signs that the linguistic hegemony of the English language is making inroads into the cultural heritage of recently-established non-Anglo-Saxon communities in the UK, particularly in terms of preferred scripts.

Themes of this Book

There are, therefore, a clearly identifiable set of eight themes that emerge from the discussion above:

The importance attached within the community to liturgical literacy

There is little doubt that the community in question values highly the acquisition of its liturgical literacy and expends considerable effort in this respect to ensure its continuation through successive generations. We will see how this manifests itself in both institutional structures and personnel and in notions of cultural capital that informs identity.

The attitudes in the community towards other literacies, including the mainstream one

The value placed upon liturgical literacy has to compete with a range of other literacies that are also deemed important. The relative weight given to each literacy practice is revealed in the amount of time, resources and energy given to it by the community. In an ideal situation, each one would complement the other but, as this book hopes to illustrate, there are limiting factors affecting each literacy practice.

The capacity of the community to support and nurture its own language and literacy

Linked to the above is the complex picture emerging of the home language, in this case Mirpuri-Punjabi, and its past, present and future role in the linguistic and literate development of the community. In this instance, the situation has much in common with mother-tongue mainte-nance in any recently settled community within the UK. However, its lack of an orthodox literacy adds to its precarious position.[3]

The link between literacy and authority as manifested in the relationship between the imam and his congregation

The teaching of the liturgical literacy is intimately linked with the role played by the imam in the Qur'anic school. The authority inherent in the relationship of pupil and teacher is extended to the congregation as a whole. The close link between liturgy and authority is partially derived, and maintained, through the complex relationship between the languages involved: Arabic, Urdu, Mirpuri-Punjabi and English (see Part 4).

The role of liturgical literacy in the formation of identity

The religious identity of the community is also partially determined by its common use of the liturgical language. It is one of the unifying elements that this community shares with the Islamic world. In terms of embodied cultural capital (Luke, 1996) it is an aspect of literacy that shapes people's lives for both those acquiring it and those who have it. To watch a young Muslim boy or girl reading Roald Dahl in the school library, and then observe the bodily movements associated with reading the liturgical language in the mosque is to realise quickly how literacy can be 'embodied' (Rosowsky, 2001).

The physicality of liturgical literacy texts

An important part of this ethnographic study will be devoted to what Wagner terms the 'material culture of literacy' (Wagner, 1993) and what Luke (1996) calls 'objectified cultural capital'. The literate environment of both the home and the mosque are telling factors in any consideration of the role played by liturgical literacy in the community. The books, plaques, posters, artefacts and decoration described form part of the backdrop in front of which liturgical literacy takes place.

The precarious position of Arabic-Urdu script in the teaching and in the use of liturgical literacy

In discussions with parents and imams it is quite apparent that traditional forms of Qur'anic education are being questioned. One significant development is the erosion taking place of the central role played by the Arabic-Urdu script. This manifests itself both in the use of Roman script for mother tongue and Urdu texts, and in the increasingly more common use of Roman script in the mosque to facilitate learning the liturgical language. This is a relatively recent development, but can be interpreted not only as an aspect of the complex tension between home literacies and mainstream literacy, but also as a local example of the more general linguistic move to prioritise the English language, and in this case, its Roman orthography.

The critical attitudes towards quality of education provided by the mosque

The opinions expressed in interviews regarding the quality of education provided by the mosque reflect a similar anxiety linked to linguistic issues. Although generally satisfied with the success of the mosque in teaching its young people liturgical literacy, a widespread concern emerges with the lack of understanding both of the liturgical language and of Urdu, or even Mirpuri-Punjabi, in instruction and in the general ritual. There is a growing demand for the use of English in the mosque.

The structure of the remainder of this book aims to illustrate the aforementioned themes by describing and analysing the experience of liturgical literacy on the part of community members. This is Part 2 of the book, which deals with Children, Parents, Teachers and Organisers (Chapters 3 to 6). Part 3 is devoted to the settings within which liturgical literacy takes place and comprises Chapters 7 to 9, on Mosques, Home and School. Part 4 is given over to a more detailed account of the four principal languages employed within the settings of liturgical literacy, namely Urdu, Mirpuri-Punjabi, English and Classical Arabic (Chapters 10 to13). Finally, Part 5 seeks to draw some conclusions and to identify implications for the central findings of the research this book reports upon.

Notes

1. The term Eric Hawkins (1981) uses to denote the use of real-life texts (newspapers, magazines, tickets, labels, etc.) and objects in the classroom.
2. Abdullah Hussein has written an interesting fictional account of this experience in *Emigré Journeys* (2000).
3. Time will be found within the body of the study for a discussion of an interesting UK development to promote Mirpuri-Punjabi literacy using Urdu script (see Chapter 11: Mirpuri-Punjabi).

Part 2

The Community and its Liturgical Literacy

Chapter 3

Children

Vignette: Sageer

Sageer is 13 and is in Year 9 in his mixed comprehensive secondary school. He wakes at around 8:00, gets ready for school and sets off from his house in Midborough at about 8:30. His house is in a road dissected by a busy dual carriageway leading into the town centre. This dual carriageway was not there when his grandfather bought the house in the 1970s. His walk to school takes him past the 'University Road' mosque, which he will attend later that day, a small park where he plays football and cricket and across another busy road, up a steep hill to the school, an early 20th century brick-built main building with a 1970s extension. His day is spent following a timetable of English, Maths, PE, Geography, lunch, for which he goes home, Science and Art. The school day finishes at 3:25 and he has been given homework in Science and English. He walks down the hill and gets home at about 3:45. His mum has a small meal ready for him and he watches television until 4:45. He goes to the bathroom where he undertakes his ritual ablution in preparation for going to 'University Road' mosque for 5 o'clock. He must make sure his private parts have been washed with water and his hands, mouth, nose, face, arms, head, ears, nape of neck and feet are then washed three times with running water. He collects his skull cap, or topi, from the table where he left it the previous night, puts it on and walks the three-minute route to the mosque. He enters the mosque and finds a place to sit and begins to read from the Qur'an that he keeps in a cloth cover on a bookshelf in the corner of the mosque prayer hall. Before him there is a low long floor table which supports the holy book and those of the boys sitting to his right and to his left. He begins to read from the second to last siparah (30th part) of the Qur'an. He reads aloud, but not too loudly, and begins to gently rock backwards and forwards on his haunches as he reads, matching his rocking with the regular rhythm of the uttered Arabic words. Much of what he reads he does not understand, but he is aware of the beauty of the sound of the words and he knows that he is engaged in an important aspect of his religion, Islam. Occasionally, he will utter a word that he does recognise. This will generally be a proper name such as Allah or Musa (the Arabic for Moses – the prophet named most often in the Qur'an). The ustaad, or teacher, asks Sageer to come and sit by him as he checks his recitation. Sageer reads fluently and accurately. He is nearing his third complete recitation of the Qur'an and will soon no longer be attending in the evenings. Some of his friends will stay on because they have been identified as boys who have the capacity to memorise large parts of the Qur'an. Some of his friends have already stopped attending, their parents having decided they have learnt enough. Sageer is good at recitation but finds it hard to memorise beyond a few pages at a time. His teacher praises him for his reading and he returns to his place. At 7 o'clock, he replaces his Qur'an on the shelf and, as it is September, and the sunset prayer is at 7 o'clock, he joins in the congregation who have gathered in the mosque. He stands with his friends near the back and completes the prayer. By the time he gets home, it is 7:15 and, although he would like to watch Eastenders, he knows he has to do his Science and English homework. By 9 o'clock, he has finished. He watches television for an hour or so with his parents and goes to bed at 10:30.

Plate 1 Sageer in the mosque

Introduction

The routine just described is a routine familiar to thousands of boys and girls, along with their parents, all over the UK. In most towns in the Midlands and in the north of England, in certain London suburbs, as well as in the urban areas of Scotland and Wales, the presence of large numbers of Muslim children is an increasingly obvious fact of life. As communities have established since the early 1950s, and the communities have grown more numerous and more settled, the need has arisen for the essential aspects of their religious and cultural identity to be passed on to the future generation. The mosque, and the education provided by the mosque, is the subject of this book. This chapter deals exclusively with the experiences of those most closely involved with the acquisition and transmission of liturgical literacy, namely the children who attend for two hours a day five days a week from the age of around six until the early years of secondary school.

This chapter will begin with a detailed description of the manner in which children are acculturated into the social practice of liturgical literacy, and will allow the reader an insight into, on the one hand, the rich and vibrant cultural activity that liturgical literacy represents and, on the other hand, the strain and pressure placed upon these children as they attempt to juggle such important aspects of their lives and identities in the context of finite time and resources.

Secondly, through liberal recourse to the words of the children themselves, it is hoped that the reader will grow to appreciate the role that liturgical literacy plays in the lives of these young people as well as allowing an insight into the complex relationship that exists between it and the other languages and literacies they use.

Finally, this chapter will shed extra light on yet another crucial relationship – that of learning in the mosque and learning in the school. We will see how both locations of learning can and should complement each other, though, at present, little is done or said that might facilitate such a coming together.

Readiness for Liturgical Literacy

From a child's perspective, the initial acquisition of liturgical literacy which takes place mainly in the mosque or mosque school is linked very much with his or her own acculturation as a Muslim child growing up and developing an identity and being initiated into the principal cultural characteristics of his or her community. In most Muslim communities, whether they are south Asian in origin, Middle Eastern, or even native converts, the acquisition of the liturgical literacy based on the Arabic Qur'an is a key element. A young Muslim child, regardless of the language spoken at home, will soon develop an awareness of, at first, the pervasiveness of Qur'anic Arabic – the environmental print of a Muslim community will invariably be permeated by Arabic script and Arabic language. Again the spoken language of the community is intimately linked to Arabic, where even the daily greeting of '*Salaam alaykum*' is Arabic in origin. A knowledge of Arabic, however basic or minimal, will accrue as a child is initiated into the cultural practices and language of the community. By the time a child is ready to attend the daily two-hour lesson in the mosque, there has been enough linguistic spadework to allow for an effective readiness for learning to read in Classical Arabic.

Bashir, a father of two boys and two girls, is happy to leave the job of teaching his children liturgical literacy to the teachers in the mosque. He sees no need for him to provide any sort of foundation before they begin at the age of five. He is, however, despite himself, doing an extremely important job in making sure his children are familiar with aspects of their religious practice and language by serving as a role model within the home. He will recite his evening and dawn prayers audibly when he is not at the mosque and his children from an early age will be exposed to the sounds and cadence of this different tongue. His home has many artefacts, printed materials and wall designs that feature Arabic script. His spoken language is punctuated reasonably regularly with words and phrases that are Arabic. When he sneezes he says, '*Alhamdulillah*' ('Praise be to God') and when he talks about doing things in the future he will say '*Insha' Allah*' ('If God wills it to be so'). Bashir is only doing what his parents did for him:[1]

> **Bashir:** ... I used to copy what my parents did when they were reading *salah* (prayer) ... but what I actually acknowledged as what was actually read in between, for the first time, was in the mosque ... so I knew my salah, *al hamdu lilllah rabbi-alameen*.[2] I knew my *salah* ...

At about the age of five, the same age as when they go to school, the Muslim children begin to attend the mosque school. They will either walk there with their parents, or more often, with their older brothers and sisters. Occasionally, they will be driven there if they live on the other side of town and their parents have a reason for them attending a mosque other than the local one. As families move outside of the area, being driven to the mosque is becoming more common, although, at the same time, more mosques in other areas of the town are being opened as well. In 1980 there was only one mosque in the town. There are now seven.

Interestingly, this pattern of attendance is not one necessarily copied from Pakistan where attendance at mosque school, as commented on by a number of parents who were born in Pakistan, was not as diligently insisted upon as it is here and now:

> **Munir:** At that time, the children used to go the mosque, but our father used to work at sea, on a ship, and nobody in our family told us that going to the mosque was very important. It's like now, the children go the mosque and they go to school as well. And at that time, we weren't bothered about it. And now I am grown up and I understand this is very important, you know, reading the Qur'an. Very, very important.

The daily routine of two hours after school, five days a week, was not one necessarily copied from back home. It was often the case that Qur'anic instruction took place in the mornings before school and for only two days a week:

Where did you learn to read the Qur'an?

Munir: Mosque. In Pakistan.

Not at school?

No.

Every day like here?

Couple of days like. After school. Morning time go school. I then come back.

At what age?

About 10.

Same for your wife?

No, at home. Private teacher used to come. At about 12.

Now that's much later than here, isn't it?

Here the children go earlier.

It is interesting also to note that many parents, particularly fathers, learnt to read the Qur'an principally in the UK, where the local imam would provide lessons for adults as well as the children. It was also very much the custom that girls in Pakistan at that time learnt to read the Qur'an in the house of a teacher rather than at the mosque. In this extract a mother and a father reflect on where they were taught how to read the Qur'an:

Where did you learn to read the Qur'an?

Morneeb: [consults wife] In Pakistan. In the ... like they doing here.

So it was separate to school?

Yes, separate. In somebody's house.

Same for you?

I learnt it a bit in Pakistan in somebody's house but when I came here, 'Church Walk' [mosque].

So if you went to somebody's house, does that mean you didn't go to the mosque, like they do here?

Not really, no. The girls couldn't go to the mosque anyway.

The boys?

Er, yes. In the towns maybe, but not in the villages. In the village you had to go to somebody's house I think. From what I can remember. I had to walk a few miles to go to somebody's house, to read.

In the UK the mosque has two jobs, a place of worship and a place to teach the children the Qur'an. That's not always the case in Pakistan?

No, it's not the case. It's just for prayer. I think most mosques ... It was at 'Church Walk' mosque that I learnt it.

It is worth noting that the picture painted by parents of their experiences learning the Qur'an back home in Pakistan contrasted significantly with the experiences of their own children. On the one hand, there did not appear to be the same level of urgency and commitment to this practice when they were children, and, on the other, there was no set age at which children would begin attending the mosque school. To a large extent, this can be explained by the presence of a state education system, however rudimentary, which also supported some instruction in Qur'anic recitation. However, it is also possible that the community is demonstrating the cultural phenomenon of intensifying its own culture once faced with the prospect of being far from home and alienated and marginalised by the host community. The acquisition of liturgical literacy, if it is to be achieved in such a perceived hostile environment, cannot be left to chance and the community accords it such an important part of its cultural capital that it invests a great deal, in terms of money and time, in the maintenance and preservation of this cultural activity.

Children and their Language Use

Muslim pupils, all with the same Mirpuri-Punjabi background, attending the local secondary school were interviewed in order to gather perceptions about themselves as Muslim children attending the local mosque schools, as speakers and users of a range of different languages and literacies, and as readers in a general sense.

The 20 children (six girls, 14 boys) interviewed were all in Year 9 (13 or 14 years of age) and attended the interview in small single-sex groups of three or four. With the exception of one boy, all pupils came from large families with at least four other siblings. Only one pupil was not born in Rotherham and so the majority had spent their entire education in the UK. The range of employment of fathers in the sample was very narrow. Two owned takeaway restaurants, four were taxi drivers, two were car mechanics, and twelve were unemployed. The children indicated that their mothers were either unemployed or housewives. They had all been to Pakistan on at least one occasion, but had never been to any other country.

When asked which languages they knew (see Table 1) and what they were called, all pupils named Punjabi and English, though two pupils omitted English – no doubt thinking the question concerned languages other than English. All pupils used the term 'Punjabi' for their home language and seemed unaware of the more linguistically-correct 'Mirpuri'

Table 1 Pupils' claims for language use

Child	Punjabi	English	Arabic	Spanish	Urdu
A	X	X		X	
B	X	X	X	X	
C	X	X	X	X	X
D	X	X	X	X	
E	X	X		X	X
F	X	X		X	
G	X	X		X	
H	X		X	X	
I	X		X	X	
J	X	X	X	X	
K	X	X		X	X
L	X	X	X	X	
M	X	X		X	
N	X	X			
O	X	X		X	X
P	X	X		X	X
Q	X	X	X	X	
R	X		X	X	
S	X	X	X	X	
T	X	X	X	X	X
Total	20	17	11	19	6

X indicates some personal knowledge

or Mirpuri-Punjabi'. Just over half claimed knowledge of Arabic. Worryingly for the long-term future of the community's main literary language, only six pupils claimed to have knowledge of Urdu. However, this may be down to the pupils' confusion over terminology. Even when talking with adults, there is sometimes a tendency to blur the distinction between the two languages, Urdu and Mirpuri-Punjabi, and some of the children may also have this imprecise distinction between their spoken variety of Punjabi and knowledge of Urdu.

Almost all pupils claimed to have knowledge of the language taught at school, Spanish.

When pupils were asked about their pattern of language use, all pupils claimed to be using both English and Mirpuri-Punjabi at home. This seems to be the present pattern in similar homes in the town. There are, however, signs that in the larger conurbations such as Birmingham and Manchester, particularly in families where parents were born in the UK, English is beginning to be predominant. Bashir reveals his sensitivity to sociolinguistic change when discussing his extended family in Birmingham:

> **Bashir:** I have got some family members who don't even know how to speak what I would call my mother tongue ... they've got a basic understanding, like I have of French ... of Spanish ...
>
> *Are they just English speakers then?*
>
> The great majority of the time they are English speakers ... I have a large family in Birmingham ... and they go the local mosque ... they acquaint themselves with Asian children ... but the majority of everything they speak is in English ... they don't have a mother tongue like we do. If my wife spoke in English I don't think my children would know as much ... of Urdu ... This is what I am seeing with my family members in Birmingham ... where their children have been brought up with this atmosphere and background where both parents speak English ...

Even in families that go to great efforts to maintain the mother tongue, there is evidence that the overwhelming propensity of the host community language, English, to usurp the community language, is changing patterns of language use in the home. In the following exchange the principal speaker is a Pakistani mother, Fameeda, who has spent considerable effort in ensuring the preservation in the family of both Urdu and Mirpuri-Punjabi. The additional comments are made by her 20-year old son Munir, and are a striking example of the fluid changes that are happening across the generations in respect to language use:

So, for example, if you were arguing with your brother, you'd be doing it in Punjabi.

Fameeda: No, I'd be doing it in English! [laughter]

So when is English used in the house? When do you use English in the house?

I don't use English in the house. I only speak English when my English friends come or people who do not understand Punjabi. Or Urdu. Then I speak with them English. With the girls I strictly at home speak Urdu. Because English I know, my kids know. Everybody knows.

So who speaks English at home?

(**Munir:** Actually, we speak among ourselves in English.) Sometimes they do. (**Munir:** A lot of the time.) Oh, yes. But when we speak with the children we speak Urdu. I mean, my daughters, they speak very good Urdu. And now I am teaching my grandchildren to speak Urdu. And I taught all of them to speak in Urdu.

When the pupils were asked to refine their answers by thinking about specific audiences, it was clear that Mirpuri-Punjabi was used when conversing with parents and grandparents, though two pupils still mentioned using English as well as Mirpuri-Punjabi in this context. With Mirpuri-Punjabi-speaking friends, conversations were almost exclusively in English (40%) or in English and Mirpuri-Punjabi (60%).

Locations are as important a factor in language use as audience and the four locations mentioned in the questionnaire were: home, school, mosque and youth club (see Table 2).

Table 2 indicates a clear distinction made between the languages spoken at home and the languages spoken at school. The majority of children at

Table 2 Languages and locations and language use

Language/Location	Home	School	Mosque	Youth club[2]	Total
English		12		12	24
Mirpuri-Punjabi	2		10		12
English & Mirpuri-Punjabi	18	8	4	6	36
English, Mirpuri-Punjabi & Arabic			2		2
English, Mirpuri-Punjabi & Arabic			2		2
Urdu & Mirpuri-Punjabi			2		2

school use English exclusively and a significant minority use both. Obviously, one has to take into consideration the considerable amount of code-switching (Baynham, 1993) that takes place with this type of language use. However, the exclusive use of Mirpuri-Punjabi is rare, with only two pupils claiming exclusive use of this language at home. In the mosque the picture is less clear and reflects an interesting linguistic picture. No child claims to use only English in the mosque although a number of pupils use English alongside Mirpuri-Punjabi. Although reading Arabic is the central focus for time spent in the mosque school, only four pupils claim to use Arabic in the mosque. Again, the fact that only two pupils indicate use of Urdu in the mosque reveals the present precariousness of this language within the community.

Although the membership of the youth club is predominantly British Asian and the leadership of the club is made up of British Asian youth workers, the principal language of choice is English.

Some 50% of the pupils claim to have learnt English at home before starting school whilst the rest acknowledged school as the location for the acquisition of English. However, it is clear that in families with a number of siblings the acculturation into school practices as well as rudimentary learning takes place regularly at home regardless of the principal spoken language in use. As Gregory (1998) reminds us, it is sometimes the role played by siblings in an individual's acquisition of literacy, and schooled practices, that is crucial. Bashir is acutely aware of the role his sister played in his acquisition of English literacy:

> *How and where did you learn English? Any formal education in English?*
>
> **Bashir:** English? I learnt it from my uncles, I learnt it from my older sister. She started school as soon as she came to England. We all basically came at the same time. She started teaching me what she was learning straightaway at school. I was two years of age, two and a half, and she'd come home and tell me everything that she was taught. My older brother, he didn't tell me anything. My sister, she was very very good in teaching. She taught us a lot before we actually started school.

Despite the indication that they rarely used Urdu, 12 pupils claimed to be able to read in Urdu, often qualifying their response with 'a little bit' or words to that effect. Of those who claimed some knowledge of Urdu, most said they had learnt it at home from their parents or even grandparents. Only two pupils said they had learnt Urdu in the mosque. As we will show later, the teaching of Urdu and where it happens is a significant issue for the community as it seeks to preserve and maintain its cultural heritage. In Part 4, we will explore in greater length the position of Urdu, as well as other languages, in the community.

Children's Perspectives on Literacy, Liturgical and Secular

Children were also asked questions about the mosque designed to elicit responses that might highlight the centrality of attending mosque and learning to read the Qur'an in the lives of these young people. It is revealing to note that in all interviews conducted during the work on this book, I found no child who had not attended an intensive course of Qur'anic instruction in the manner described herein.

Most pupils started attending the mosque when they were five or six years old, with only one pupil starting at as late as nine. They all named the mosque imam as their teacher, though three girls omitted the name of their teacher for they attend a house for Qur'anic instruction rather than the local mosque. They all attend five days a week for an average of two hours. Some start at 4pm and finish at 6, others start at 4:30 and finish at 6:30, and others from 5 until 7.

These pupils were all aged either 13 or 14 and, therefore, in terms of Qur'anic instruction were nearing the time when their mosque education would end. In fact, with the exception of a few boys who were going on to memorise, most of this group would no longer be attending the mosque by the end of the year. It is no surprise that these boys and girls had made significant progress with the Qur'anic recitation. The question 'How far have you got?' is one that seeks a quantitative reply, for children of this age will often express their progress by indicating how many times the Qur'an has actually been read. The more times the Qur'an has been read, the greater the child's perception that he or she has made good progress. When Kamran declares that he has 'finished nine times', he is indicating that he has read the Holy Book from cover to cover, out loud, correctly, nine times. The number of complete recitations of the Qur'an recorded by this group ranged from twice to nine times. When asked about memorisation, most children claimed to have learnt by heart significant portions of the book. For example, Wakas had memorised the 'first and 30th *siparahs*',[4] which amounts to approximately 50 pages of large type Arabic script. The 30th *siparah* is the last *siparah* of the Qur'an and is made up of a number of smaller chapters and is traditionally memorised by Muslims as it provides a good supply of shorter chapters that can be recited in the prayer. Many children also claimed to have memorised some *naat*, which are religious poems and often recited on festive occasions. These would not be in Arabic, but in Urdu, and occasionally in Punjabi, and sometimes even in Persian.

Most pupils claim to read the Qur'an at home sometimes and most pupils will pray either 'sometimes' or 'at weekends' or 'only in Ramadan'. All pupils claim ownership of a Qur'an and can describe where it is kept either in the house or in the mosque:

Ashraf: I keep it very high.

Wakas: In the mosque and at home on top of a wardrobe.

Akbar: In a basement where nobody can get it.

Ferzana: I leave it in the basement. Nobody can touch it.

Amjid: In a cupboard.

Samina: I leave it in the mosque but my auntie leaves hers in the drawer very high.

Rukshana: I have got my own Qur'an on the high shelf.

Rashid: I keep the Qur'an in the mosque.

Ghazanfar: I keep it as high as possible. It is on the top of the cupboard in the front room.

Noreen: On top of the wardrobe.

This illustrates the importance of the book as artefact and in all Muslim societies copies of the Qur'an are revered and carefully handled. Moreover, children are taught from young age that they must not handle the Qur'an if they have not undertaken the ritual purification described at the beginning of this chapter. This leads to copies of the Qur'an being placed in cloth covers and on high places so that they will not be inadvertently touched or handled.

Another set of questions was asked concerning reading; these questions were designed to elicit any common experiences the children might have in respect of reading. When asked about their thoughts whilst reading Classical Arabic in the Qur'an, the assumption is there that children do not, in this context, read for meaning. The responses to this question can be categorised in three ways. Firstly, there are those responses that might be termed 'thought by association' though there is the distinct possibility here that some of these responses, if not all, are prompted by feelings of wanting to give the right answer or of trying to guess what the questioner is after. Here are some examples of the first category:

Ghazanfar: Allah, His Prophets and the life after death.

Rukhsana: Allah and Prophets.

Jameel: Allah and His Prophets and the Day of Judgement.

Shakeel: Allah and good things.

The second type of comment pupils made focuses on thoughts that may occur whilst reading relating to the child's daily life:

Samina: I think about what is going to happen on that particular day.

Razaq: I think of my future.

The third category of comment is linked to the reading act itself:

Noreen: I think the reading is ok and I am doing it right.

Ferzana: I think about what I am going to be reading next.

Interestingly, similar questions were asked about reading in English, and where we might expect there to be more focus on the meaning of the text being read, there was evidence of the above three categories in the responses of the children.

There was the expected focus on the text with comments such as:

Ferzana: I think about the characters in the book.

There is the focus on school and competency:

Ghazanfar: I think about school and my level.

Amjid: I think about school and my skills of reading.

More surprisingly, there were comments that are, as with the reading of the Qur'an, linked to the everyday lives of the children, and may be considered as thoughts detached from the reading process. Here, the reading process creates a space for the reader to think and reflect on events unlinked to the text being read:

Akbar: I think about food, drink and school.

Noreen: I think about food.

Rashid: Drinks and food.

Fiaz: I think about what's happening at home and about football.

This lack of attention to meaning during the reading act can and does result in pupils in school being perceived as having problems with comprehension. Many of the pupils featuring in this sample demonstrated a significant disparity between their reading comprehension and their skills as decoders when they were in Year 7 (age 11–12). It is quite possible that this lack of attention to meaning which occurs whilst reading in English is influenced by the regular practice of reading without meaning in Arabic.

I have reported elsewhere (Rosowsky, 2001) how many pupils with a similar background will demonstrate a significant divide between their reading comprehension and their reading accuracy (decoding):

> There is one element of the cultural experience of these particular pupils which, on the one hand, promotes a specific reading skill, and, on the other, serves to depress the necessary accompanying skills needed for reading effectively. The reading accuracy scores of these children are almost certainly affected by their reading experience in the mosque Qur'anic schools. It is easy to discover that, in comparison with the time spent learning to read and reading in school, much more 'real time and personal effort' is spent learning to read and reading of the Qur'an. Teachers who have similar bilingual pupils in their classes will have noticed that the reading behaviour learnt in the mosque can often over-spill into their classrooms and libraries. Because of the poetic rhythm of the Arabic text, and as an aid to recitation, children, and adults, when reading the Qur'an, will often rock the upper part of the body backwards and forwards as they read. Many of these children do this when reading their English books, particularly in the library, if there is no need to sit at a desk or a table. The physical manifestation of the transfer of a reading behaviour such as this suggests that this is surely not the only transfer taking place. The fact that graphophonic reliance in the reading of Arabic is so heavily stressed cannot but affect the place of graphophonic reliance in the reading of English. (Rosowsky, 2001: 68)

Although children had claimed knowledge of reading Urdu in response to an earlier question, they all omitted to respond to the question on their thoughts when reading Urdu.

The range of books and other reading materials reported in the home was limited. The most commonly-cited newspaper was the free _Rotherham Record_. Only one pupil claimed to have the Urdu-language newspaper, _Jang_, in the house. Half the group estimated the number of books, of any kind, in the house to be less than 10. Some of the boys mentioned body-building magazines. Books read were school-based and included either typical Year 9 class readers such as _Buddy_ and _The Machine Gunners_, or personally-chosen titles such as _Killer Mushrooms Ate My Grandma_, _The Twits_, _The BFG_, _Pokemon Strikes Back_, _Football Fever_, or just simply, 'my library book'. More than half of the pupils claimed to have no Urdu books at home.

The link between availability of reading materials at home and progress in schooled literacy has been made on many occasions. Suffice it to say in this particular context, the apparent lack of reading materials would not support the acquisition of English, Urdu or Arabic in the home, and to some extent reflects an attitude to learning that while positive, locates learning outside of the home into the institutions of learning such as the mosque and the school.

> *Have you ever helped your children?*
> **Wajib:** Erm, I have not actually taught them ... anything in Arabic.
> *You left it to the mosque?*
> I have left that to the mosque ...

Acquisition of Liturgical Literacy: The Process

Children were also interviewed in the context of a family interview. The range of ages was wider than for the groups interviewed in school and included older boys and girls, sometimes young men and women, who were asked to reflect on their experiences as children going to the mosque.

At various times in this community, there was no female teacher in the mosque to teach the girls. This resulted in families making other arrangements for their daughters, usually involving a teacher coming to the house or the daughters attending lessons in the house of a female teacher. It was certainly not evident during the course of the interviews that parents thought it any less important for their daughters to complete the usual course of Qur'anic instruction. The main issue was the appropriate facilities in the mosque. This was either a case of there being no female teacher or, in some cases, dissatisfaction with the behaviour of the other children and the teacher's inability to control them. Below is an extract from a family interview where the main respondent is a young woman, Fameeda, who had recently left full-time education. The other comments are from her father, Jabbar:

> *What age did you start learning the Qur'an?*
> **Fameeda:** I started at about 8 or 9.
> *Where?*
> We went to this lady. We never went to a mosque to learn because at home from our parents, we had a lady teacher.
> (*Jabbar:* Neighbours, good neighbours.)
> *Is that because they didn't have a girls' class at the mosque?*
> Yes, that's the reason.
> *Would that be the case for most of the girls?*
> Yeah.
> *They wouldn't go to the mosque but would have someone come to the house?*
> Yeah.
> *So did you learn as a group then?*

Just our brothers and sisters, you know.

(*Jabbar:* Just at home like, you know)

So your brothers didn't go to the mosque either?

Coz they don't read it properly there. My parents didn't, you know ...

(*Jabbar:* I don't like ...)

All they do is mess about. But she was a good teacher and we learnt from her.

All the time?

Yeah, every day. From, like, 3 to 5 – 2 hours.

For how many years did you learn like this?

Two or three years.

So less time than if you had gone to the mosque?

Yeah. They don't have enough time for each child in the mosque. And us, she used to really push us forward. Each child.

A number of issues arise in this exchange. Firstly, we learn that in this family a decision was taken to instruct the children away from the mosque and this resulted in them starting a little later than the norm. The reasons given were that, for the girls, there was no suitable female teacher at the mosque, and for the boys, that there was dissatisfaction with behaviour. It is clear that the family valued these alternative arrangements for they allowed the children to complete their course of instruction in far less time than would be normally required in the mosque. The teacher–student ratio was so low in the mosque that the family felt their children would not be receiving the appropriate level of attention. Their alternative teacher allowed for the children to be pushed further and more quickly in their learning of the Qur'an.

However, it should be stressed that this arrangement did not imply that there was any break with the mosque in any other sense. The father and his sons regularly attended the mosque for prayers and the daughters eventually became teaching assistants in the mosque itself, providing classes for younger girls.

All children interviewed were asked about the way they were taught how to read the Qur'an. The same method was employed whether or not the child was taught in the mosque or in a private house:

> **Rukhsana:** She used to say the word first, tell us what it looked like and we used to repeat afterwards. And then she used to mix the words up and ask us which word was which. So not reciting things without knowing which word you're reading.

Rashida: You start with the *photi* – which is like equivalent to learning the alphabet. The *alif, bah* ... [5]

Is this a book? Or a sheet?

It's like a sheet, yeah. You start there with the alphabet and then go onto the *Qaidah*.[6] Which helps you pronounce it, like as a full word. Putting it into words. It's a guide book towards reading the Qur'an.

Fiaz: A new person goes to the teacher and learns to pronounce them. The teacher says it and you then repeat it. Keep on saying till I get it right. Alphabet and then you go like, same but different [short vowel sounds with the letters].

Shaheeda: We used to be in groups and then we usually had to come up to a bench where the imam's wife used to teach us. And one by one, we used to read a bit to her, and if we got it wrong she'd ask us to read it again ... and correct it.

But how did you actually start?

I can't really remember. We learnt the *photi*, like the alphabet, we learnt that first and then went higher ... You had to learn 5 *photi* to get to the Qur'an, by then you knew how to read it ...

Noreen: The imam's wife read it and we had to repeat it and keep on saying it ...

Farida: We had the letters first. The teacher said them and we said them after her.

The basic method for Qur'anic instruction was based on a phonics-based 'look-listen-repeat' model of learning. The children begin with the 26 letters of the Arabic alphabet and learn these firstly as names. For example, the first letter of the alphabet is called 'alif' and the child begins by learning the name 'alif'. The name sometimes has only an indirect connection to the sound the letter might represent. Children will then go on to learn the sounds represented by the letters so that 'alif' becomes [a], [i] or [u] depending on the vowelling that accompanies it. Unlike the English alphabet, the Arabic alphabet (Plate 2) is made up of consonants or semi-consonants and vowels are indicated by diacritic marks above or below the letters. A child will learn these consonants and then proceed to learn each letter with, initially, the three basic vowel sounds, [a], [i] and [u].

Again, each child will repeat and memorise the letter–sound correspondences until the teacher considers them ready to move onto the next stage. This will be to combine these consonant+vowelling units with others to form syllables. This stage is then followed by words, which can be real or

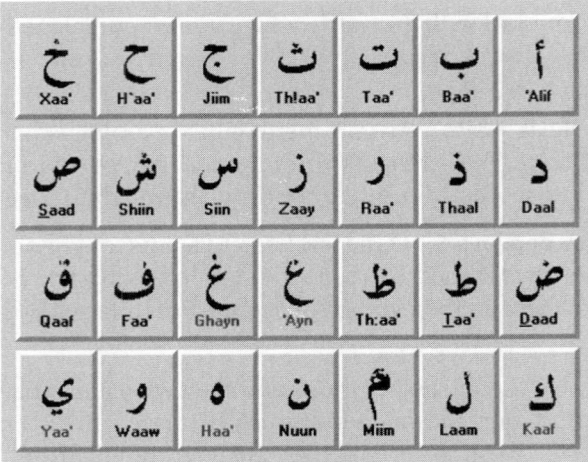

Plate 2 The Arabic alphabet with Roman script transliteration

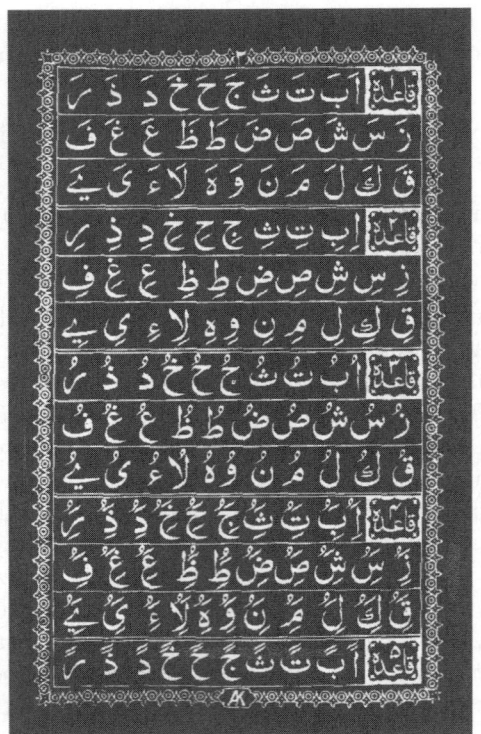

Plate 3 Arabic letters with vowelling

nonsense words. This then leads to reading phrases, which by now are all potentially meaningful and recognisable from the Qur'an or other parts of the scripture, such as the *kalimahs*. The *kalimahs* are a series of established utterances that encapsulate the fundamental beliefs of the Muslim (rather like a credo) and along with learning the words of prayer and recitation of the Qur'an constitute the main learning activity in the mosque. The central *kalimah* is *'ash-hadu a-laa ilaaha ill-Allah, ash-hadu ana Muhammada-r-asool Allah'* which means 'I bear witness that there is only one God and that Muhammed is the Messenger of God'. The final stage in this preparation for reading the Qur'an itself is the reading of complete verses which occupy the last few pages of the *Qaidah*.

The *Qaidah* is a short primer of the Arabic reading system. It usually contains between 10 and 40 pages and begins with the alphabet on the first page followed by subsequent pages that follow the sequence described above. Occasionally, children are given a single page containing the alphabet only, the *photi* (Punjabi for 'sacred book'), and this can be obtained in plastic so that the page remains intact after generous use by young hands (Plate 5).

These plastic pages are very reminiscent of the hornbooks that were still being used up until the 19th century in both Britain and America. These were also a page long and always included the alphabet in upper and lower case letters along with the Lord's Prayer. They were called hornbooks because a layer of horn, which had been boiled and beaten until transparent, was placed over the page to preserve the life of the page (Manguel, 1996).

The teacher makes the decision as to when a child is ready to move onto the appropriate next stage. Children are aware and sensitive about where they might have got to in their learning of how to read the Qur'an, and are always ready to declare, or boast, where they might have reached. Similarly, the teacher will decide when a child has reached the end of his or her course of instruction and will either inform the parents that there is no longer a need for their son or daughter to attend or that he or she would benefit from a more advanced course in memorisation which always comes later. There is a very 'quantitative' dimension to the following responses:

How much progress have you made? (whole Qur'an, so many siparahs, etc.)

Ghazanfar: I know it all but I don't know it off by heart. I can easily read it ...

Do you know any of it by heart?

I do know the last ten (chapters) of the thirtieth *siparah*. ...

Who decides when you have done or learnt enough?

Fameeda: It's the teacher, when she knows you can read all the Qur'an

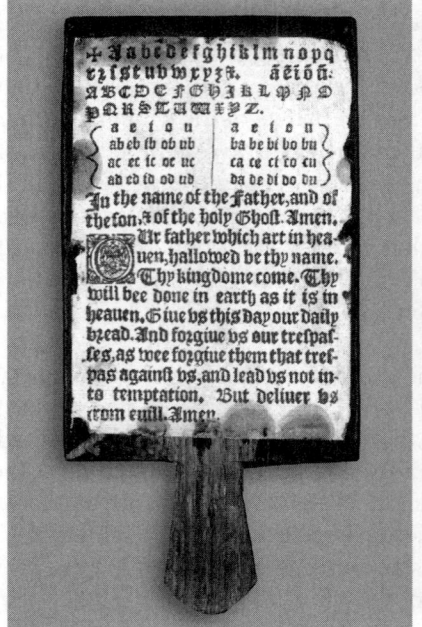

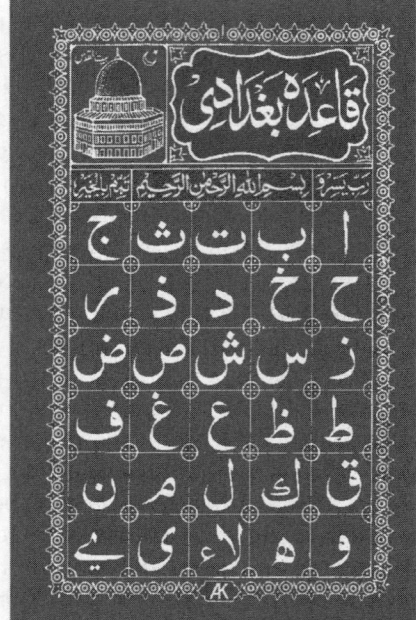

Plate 4 17th-century English hornbook
(*By permission of the Folger Shakespeare Library*)

Plate 5 Plastic *Qaidah* or *photi*

by yourself, you read it to her and she considers you can read it now and that's it.

At what stage are you when you stop going to the mosque?

Rashida: Well, I finished the Qur'an twice.

What does that actually mean?

Well, you just get to read it through from the first chapter until the end. And while you do that you get to memorise parts of the Qur'an, *surahs*, starting from the back, the last 30. There are 114 in total and I managed to learn the last 30. And you get to read the *kalimahs* in Urdu. Basically, when you have got to a stage where you think it is quite acceptable at the mosque you read that ...

Who decides, you or the teacher?

You decide personally, and go off to read at home ...

Who monitors how much or where you have got to?

The *ustaad*[7] at the mosque, which in my case, was Maulana Shabbir.

What about you? [to Rashida's younger sister, Robina]

Robina: I read it three times. And now I am learning the 30th *siparah*. I have learnt 27 *surahs*.

As in the interviews with children in school, the number of times one has read through the Qur'an serves as a measure of progress. Children are also encouraged to memorise as much of the last *siparah* as possible. This exercise will also help identify those children who demonstrate an aptitude for memorisation for it is at this age that children either leave the mosque school or continue with 'hifz' (memorisation) of the Qur'an.

Abdul Ghafoor and his brothers have all memorised the entire Qur'an and are therefore entitled to be called 'Hafiz' of the Qur'an, a very prestigious title within Muslim society.

What age did you start learning the Qur'an?

Abdul Ghafoor: About 13 or 14.

So when you said 14 or 13 you meant hifz ... Who taught you?

My dad. At home.

How much progress have you made? (whole Qur'an, so many siparas, etc.)

Hafiz of the whole Qur'an ...

How long did that take?

About two years ...

And your brothers?

They are all *hufaaz* [Arabic plural of *hafiz*] of the Qur'an.

Is two years normal?

Sometimes it takes longer ...

What is the best age for doing hifz?

Young. At about 8 years of age.

Once you have done this and learnt the Qur'an, how do you keep it?

You keep on reciting it ... Every day you should read it regularly ...

What do you do every day?

One *siparah* ...

And do you do it in order?

Yes.

So every month you go back to the beginning ... Do you have to keep going back to the text to check?

Yes. Or you read it to someone, a teacher ...

Do you help each other, your brothers?

Yes.

This aspect of learning in the mosque or in the Muslim community is a common one. Although Abdul Ghafoor and his brothers are rare in that most children do not go on to memorise the complete Qur'an, many children will memorise significant sections of the Qur'an beyond that needed for the performance of prayer, where all that is needed is the opening chapter of the Qur'an which is seven verses long and one of the shorter chapters from the last 30th, which could amount to no more than three or four verses. Nafisa tells us that she has memorised the chapter called 'Yasin' and Tasleem and Sajidah tell us they have memorised most of the 30th *siparah* (approximately 25 pages).

> *What about learning the Qur'an by heart? Did she encourage you to do that?*
>
> **Tasleem:** No, because, you know ... for that you have to go to a special school ...
>
> *Yes, if you want to do the whole thing. I mean learning 'Yasin' or something like that. A siparah for example.*
>
> **Sajidah:** Yes, we did that at home, the first *siparah* ... the second.
>
> *How much do you know by heart?*
>
> I only know the first page and enough to do my *namaz*. And 'Yasin' by heart.
>
> (*Jabbar*, their father: *Surah Yasin* is the heart of the Qur'an. The most important. You have to read it every morning after the *Fajr* [the dawn prayer]).

Liturgical Literacy: An Example of Syncretism

As we will see in more detail in the chapter devoted to teachers (Chapter 5), the curriculum of the mosque school is centred on learning how to read the Classical Arabic of the Qur'an. What other learning takes place varies from mosque to mosque. Teaching about Islam and its fundamentals and, in communities similar to this one, the teaching of Urdu are the two other dimensions to the curriculum that are possible. The extent to which these dimensions feature will depend on a range of interrelated concerns such as the availability of teachers, the wishes of parents and the choice of language of instruction. Discussion regarding the presence or absence of these dimensions takes place in Chapter 4: Parents and Chapter 6: Organisers and also in Part 4. At the time of writing, the curriculum of the mosque school has become an object of significant state interest. This is a consequence of the heightened securitisation that the state in the UK and elsewhere is seeking to impose upon the Muslim community and its institutions in the light of the events of 9/11 and 7/7. Government ministers and their advisers have spoken of the need to provide controlled standards for the recruitment of imams and to widen the curriculum to encompass such things as the teaching of citizenship (Choudhury, 2007; DCLG, 2006). In the same climate, British Muslim groups themselves have also called for greater regulation of those employed as teachers in mosques (The Muslim Parliament, 2006). It is too early to judge the impact of such interventions though, despite the frequently heavy-handed approach adopted by the government, many of the concerns regarding language usage and the broadening of the curriculum are shared by parents as we will see in the next chapter.

In this chapter, however, it will suffice to mention how the children experience any existing additions to the curriculum. In one of the two mosques there was a significant period of time when there was no female teacher available for teaching girls. During this period two sisters were approached and asked to run the two-hour sessions for the girls. These two girls, who were members of one of the families interviewed, had no experience of teaching except as recipients of teaching both in the mosque and in school. What they managed to achieve is noteworthy inasmuch as they were able to fuse some of the techniques they had experienced in school with the teaching objectives of the mosque school. This is an example of what Gregory (1998) refers to as syncretic literacy practices, or what has been described alternatively as a 'fusion' of different kinds of literacy (Millard, 2003). Here Nafisa describes how she and her sister went about teaching younger girls in the mosque:

> **Nafisa:** No. Can I just say something. You know, me and Nahida, we taught in the mosque. You know, Jamia Mosque in 'University Road'. We thought it was important to teach Urdu and Islam. I had the little group and she had the older group. We used to teach them Islam. And the girls we taught a lot and they were really interested in it. And we had lots of girls coming, like 50 or 60. Because they were really interested in Urdu. And Islam. They enjoyed it and we had comments from the parents, you know, the kids really liked what we did. And he [their father] brought some books from Dewsbury, some Islam books, and gave them out to the girls for free to learn something because they hardly knew anything. Most parents don't know anything. They are illiterate people, they don't understand Urdu or English. And when she [their mother] goes to houses, they still remember us. Saying 'they were the best teachers in the mosque'.
>
> *What did the community think?*
>
> They thought it was really good. They didn't want us to leave and

kept on calling us back. But we couldn't go back. There were too many girls to handle and only two teachers ... What we did, like, we put all the little girls in little groups, and we taught them one word first, and moved onto the next one. We had lots of kids but we put them in little groups and it was much easier for us. And we said we'd give them something if they learnt it.

Did they help each other?

Yeah, the older girls that my sister had, we put one of them in each group to help the little girls. The 5 or 6 year-olds. And then we all used to sit together and repeat what they had done. And ask them what they had been learning. And whilst they were in the groups we used to go round from group to group helping them as well. On Friday we used not to read the Qur'an. We just used to do Urdu for two hours. Because they used to get bored just with the *Qaidah* and reading. Keep on being fidgety. So on a Wednesday there was an Islam class, the girls who wanted to do an Islam class so we did that. And on Fridays Urdu.

In this mosque the girls were placed into groups by their two young teachers and older more advanced girls were used as guides for the younger ones. A reward system was introduced and the curriculum was varied with the teaching of Islam on Wednesdays and Urdu on Fridays. The sheer number of children attending the mosque school clearly necessitates some imaginative use of group work. It was clear here that the two 'teachers' were using their experience from school in the context of the mosque.

There were other ways in which the girls were advantaged by having teachers who knew not only something about school-based teaching and learning styles but also who shared in the their experiences, particularly in respect of language:

Was anything said to you when you introduced teaching Urdu into the mosque?

Nafisah: They really liked it.

Was that your choice? Did you have to ask anyone's permission?

No. We just did as we wanted. We were like the Heads there! We did whatever we wanted to.

Did you get paid?

Yeah. But we didn't really bother about that. We were only interested in getting the kids ...

So how did you get involved then?

This lady had left, she was on holiday somewhere, and they needed new teachers. And I used to go to school then and went straight to the mosque and he [the imam] asked if we would be interested and we thought it would be good fun. My dad said yeah it's a good job rather than going somewhere else. And that's the only job we've done since we left school.

Why did you stop? Is it because you got married?

My big sister got married and I couldn't carry on my own.

So what happens now?

There were two other ladies and it's a total disaster! Whenever I see the two ladies they say why don't you come down some time? But I haven't got any time now. It's because we were near their age and we knew English ...

So these two ladies don't know English?

They just know their own language and tell the children to shut up and do this and do that! And they won't listen. We used to speak English, and Punjabi and Urdu, we used to speak mixed, and they could understand and sit down. We used to give them choices, if you want to read, read, if not go home. Things like that. I used to copy like what the teachers at school would do.

There was obviously a conscious attempt by the girls to adopt teaching techniques from school and this, together with the ability to communicate to the girls in English as well as in Mirpuri-Punjabi led to the success of the short-lived venture. The ability of children to imitate teaching methods encountered at school and use them in a different context appear, within this community at least, to serve very useful purposes (see Gregory, 1998). Earlier we encountered Bashir who was reluctant to interfere with the teaching of the mosque. However, Bashir was also initiated into the ways of school and the English language by his elder sister who would teach him at home by imitating school learning:

How and where did you learn English? Any formal education in English?

Bashir: English? I learnt it from my older sister. She started school as soon as she came to England. We all basically came at the same time. She started teaching me what she was learning straightaway at school. I was two years of age, two and a half, and she'd come home and tell me everything that she was taught. My older brother, he didn't tell me anything. My sister, she was very very good in teaching. She taught us a lot before we actually started school.

It is clear that part of the cultural capital of this community is its ability to transmit language and culture through the imitation of institutional models of learning and their application in the contexts of home and mosque. It is also clear that, in this instance at least, it is often females who are more comfortable in adopting this school-based model.

Liturgical Literacy and Reading for Meaning

Learning to read the Classical Arabic of the Qur'an, nevertheless, remains the principal learning activity of the mosque school. The method of teaching is a very traditional one that differs very little from the manner in which all Muslim children are taught to read the Qur'an irrespective of their language or cultural backgrounds. There are *Qaidah*s for Arabic-speaking or Turkish-speaking children that are practically identical to those used in mosques where the congregation is Mirpuri-Punjabi-speaking. Often the main difference will be in the type of script employed, where communities originating from the Indian sub-continent will be more familiar with a more cursive script than those communities where Arabic is spoken which use a more angular and characteristically Arabic script. The principal reading skill taught is decoding and authentic recitation. One of the central characteristics of this form of teaching is its apparent lack of reference to the meaning of the words. Children, as we saw earlier, when asked what they might reflect on whilst reading can manage, at best, only a vague reference to religious values and concepts without making any linkage to the discrete meaning of words, phrases or whole texts.

The most-commonly recited chapter of the Qur'an for a Muslim is the '*Al-Fatihah*', or 'The Opening' which is, in fact, the opening chapter of the Qur'an and is seven short verses long. A Muslim, if praying regularly, will read the '*Fatihah*', at the very least 17 times a day, and will, usually, recite it many more times than this. It is as ubiquitous in a Muslim's daily routine as the Lord's Prayer might be in a Christian's.

All children were asked if they could explain the meaning of these verses to a non-Arabic speaker and non-Muslim. Apart from a general sense that the words were an important part of their faith, the children struggled to communicate a meaning for the words.

The part of the Qur'an that a Muslim reads the most is the Fatihah. The most basic and well-known chapter and, if you prayed five times a day, something you'll be saying every day about 17 times. If, for example, your friend, an English, non-Muslim, asked you to explain it, could you tell them what it is?

Jabbar (father): Yeah, we can explain it a bit, yeah

Nafisah (daughter): No, I'm not sure. I read it somewhere in English. But I've forgotten it now.

Jabbar: God bless you, blessings.

Could you translate the Fatihah for somebody, an English non-Muslim who didn't know and asked you what it meant?

Bashir: I wouldn't be able to go through it either line for line or word for word, but I'd be able to give a basic representation ... where *'alhamdulillah'* means ... I mean I wouldn't be able to give that as in full, but if I read *'alhamdulillah rabbi-alameen ... '* in complete I'd be able to tell the other person this *surah* which I have read to you actually means or has got equivalent understanding that ... 'I'm asking God at all times for him to put me onto the Straight Path ... ' ... er ... it goes on to say the *duas* which are included in it ... *'siraat ul mustaqeem'* which is part, which it says 'to the straight path' ... I'd have to probably read it over and over again to get all the rest of the words out, but this is ...

What about the Fatihah? You know the Fatihah? The beginning of the Qur'an ... the very first chapter ... the one you always say in namaz ... we say that at least 17 times a day if you're praying regularly ... So it's probably the most important part of the Qur'an for a Muslim ... Would you be able to explain it to a non-Muslim friend ... ?

Ghazanfar: No, we don't know what it means ...

You know the Fatihah? Just seven verses. What do they mean?

Munir: I'd have to go and look it, and read it.

Where would you read it?

In a book or something.

Do you know the Fatihah? The first surah of the Qur'an?

Amjid: Yes.

As you know, we recite it many times in regular namaz and we also say it on very many occasions outside of namaz. If you had to explain to a non-Muslim, what it meant, after all it is the most important verses any Muslim knows, would you be able to explain its meaning?

No. No.

Don't worry about that. I'm finding it's a general thing. If you were going to know one thing in English it would be that.

The intention behind the question was not to embarrass the young boys and girls but to seek the confirmation that the meaning of words and verse was not included as an essential ingredient of the reading curriculum. If the meaning of any section, chapter or verse of the Qur'an was to be known then it would have to be this collection of verses. The fact that such a regularly-recited chapter is not comprehended by the majority of the respondents[8] in this book underlines the importance and value that exclusive decoding has as a cultural and religious practice within this and other Muslim communities.

Children's Attitudes to Liturgical Literacy

The final set of questions for the children focused on their attitudes towards attending the mosque. This was an attempt to elicit responses that might reveal common values and understandings of this most intense of cultural experiences. There is no doubt that attending the mosque creates tension for the young believers and their parents. Sageer, whom we met at the start of this chapter, has to balance the demands of school, home and mosque as well as seek to have some sort of social life outside of these institutions. The community, however, is far from being able to alleviate these competing pressures. The two hours between school and home are acutely valued by the teachers who know this is the only time available to them to teach their young students. They know they cannot demand more time for fear of alienating both students and parents.

Maulana Shabbir: The limited time is two hours – that's what the community gives for their children. Five days a week. Two hours is little. Three hours – then you break the barrier of children's relaxation time and their leisure time and everything. So the 5 to 7 time is just balanced in between.

All children were asked about the importance of attending the mosque. As one might expect, all gave very positive responses. However, the clarity of their responses demonstrates that they do have opinions about one of the most defining aspects of their identity. Any critical comments were based on perceptions of student behaviour in the mosque rather than on negative attitudes towards the act of attending mosque itself.

All agree that attending the mosque was essential for their lives and themselves as individuals:

How important is it for you to go to the mosque?
Akbar: Very important. We finished school at 3.30 and went to the mosque at 4. Monday to Friday.
Did you find it hard to do all those things – school, mosque, homework?

Yeah. But once you start doing it you get used to it ... It is hard at first, you know when we were at 'Barbhill' (junior school), it was OK, because ... but when we were at 'Fieldworth' (secondary school) it used to be really really tiring, because you would get more homework and things and walk all the way home – ten minutes – get ready – go to the mosque – come back home – homework ...

Rashida: Because it is our religion it is very important.

Tasleem: It's our religion, innit? That's what we've got to do. We have to learn about our religion. It's very important.

Nafisah: As a young child, it is quite exciting, as you go a bit you learn how important religion is to you. And how you've got to bring it into everyday life. So it does become very important. And you get encouragement from there. It builds your confidence.

Ferzana: I think it is important, very important to learn about Islam and Arabic. That's if they are learning it there, but if they are not, what's the point of going if all they are doing is messing about. It's better if they just learn at home with their parents, if they can do it, or go to a better mosque school.

When asked about the principal activity in the mosque, learning how to read the Qur'an, children remained equally positive, if a little imprecise:

Why do you learn the Qur'an?
Amjid: Because we are Muslims and it is part of Islam ...

Rukshana: Because it is something to do with the religion.

However, once the discussion turns on meaning, the child is obliged to deal in generalities and can only refer to the overarching value of reading the Qur'an.

When people say 'learn the Qur'an' what do they actually mean?
Rozina: Learning how to read it. And to understand what it all means.
That doesn't seem to happen so much, does it?
As you go through reading it, the *ustaad* points out little things that are important and introduce them to your everyday life. It's not something you would probably remember for ever ... You can't go back to it and say 'I know what that means'. You remember the general idea. And about how to incorporate it into your life.

Finally in this phase of the research, the children were asked if they perceived any differences or similarities in the manner by which they had been taught to read at school and at the mosque and were invited to suggest ways in which the manner of learning to read at the mosque could be improved.

Their answers are characterised by considerable candour and thoughtfulness revealing again the seriousness this aspect of their lives has for them.

Is there any difference between learning to read in the mosque and learning to read in school? How might you explain this difference?

Samina: No, I think they were both the same. She used to teach in schools as well. She did it the same way. From the alphabet.

Fiaz: I think mosque was more stricter and, like school you have to go ... no matter what like ... because the government says so ... but the mosque was just family thing ... and that is why it was much stricter and didn't let anybody mess about ... but in school teachers couldn't be too strict with you ... so you used to mess about much more in school ...

What about the way you were taught to read, rather than the way you behaved? Did you know how to read before you went to school?

Munir: The age you went to nursery was the age when you went to the mosque ... I don't know about the difference because you always start with the basics and then you move on ...

Sujad: For the Qur'an we had to do everything in our heads, whereas in school we could also write things down on paper. In some mosques they still use the cane like in the old days.

What might you get the cane for?

For not learning. Instead of getting detention, you'll get the cane instead.

Ameer: Personally, I don't find any differences. If in English there's a word you don't understand, you can get a dictionary, but you don't have Arabic dictionaries, but in school you just get the dictionary.

How could learning to read the Qur'an be easier or better? Or learning about Islam?

Nafisah: What we did, like, we put all the little girls in little groups, and we taught them one word first, and moved onto the next one. We had lots of kids but we put them in little groups and it was much easier for us. And we said we'd give them something if they learnt it.

Munir: If the Qur'an was written in English, like a word is in Arabic but written in English for the Arabic words (i.e. Roman script) it would be easier.

Tasleem: I'd like there to be more English books. About Islam. Let children read them.

They've got English books in the mosque, in the bookcases, haven't they?

Yes, but they don't open them. Maulana Shabbir used to do it every day. We used to get more cleverer, more about Islam.

The last word in this chapter will go not to a child but to the teacher mentioned in the last quotation who, although no longer employed by the mosque which featured in this book, left a lasting impression with many of the children he taught. He will feature more prominently in Chapter 5: Teachers.

I asked him about the children's attitudes to learning in the mosque given the other demands upon their time and his response was the following:

> *Maulana Shabbir:* Because of the difficulty that they are facing at the *masjid* (mosque) they tend to make excuses of not attending the *masjid*. In other words, try to cut corners, or stay at home. Then you have those who are willing to come and those who are willing to come but not learn anything at all just try to sit there. And you have those who just come and learn and learn ... I think children's attitudes you can't really say something concrete ... because they are just in a mood of their own. You might have a problem with a child for one whole week where he is not learning anything whatever and the same child next week might turn around and be top of the class. And you might have a child who's been coming first every time and then he just switches off ... And I think it's always just, as it says in the *hadeeth* [sayings of the Prophet], the *iman* [faith] always goes ... increases or decreases, I think it is the same thing with children ... it increases or decreases ...

Summary

This chapter has attempted to provide an insight into the practices, thoughts, feelings and attitudes of the young people involved in the acquisition and practice of liturgical literacy. It has sought to demonstrate the rich, but complex, nature of the latter and to stress the fundamental and central role it plays in the lives of these young people. An important theme in this book is the way the different generations of the community relate to and interact with liturgical literacy. The next chapter seeks to add to this book on liturgical literacy by describing the parents' practices, thoughts, feelings and attitude

Notes

1. This quote and others come from a series of semi-structured interviews conducted by the author with members of the community. The author's questions, prompts or occasional responses, when they occur, are in italics. The quotes are quasi-verbatim, with only occasional repetitions and infelicities edited out.
2. This is the opening line of the first chapter of the Qur'an, *al Fatihah* – 'Praise be to God, Lord of the worlds' (my own translation).
3. Two pupils had never attended the local youth club.
4. The Qur'an is traditionally divided into smaller parts of equal length to facilitate regular recitation. The most commonly used division is into thirty parts, called in Arabic, *'juz'*, and in Urdu, *'siparah'*. However, there are other divisions such as the division into 60 parts, called *'hizb'* both in Arabic and in Urdu.
5. The first two letters of the Arabic alphabet
6. The *Qaidah* is the basic (and universal) primer used for learning Qur'anic Arabic in all mosques.
7. *Ustaad* is an Urdu word derived from Arabic, 'master', and denotes a teacher.
8. I asked the same question of most parents, and although their number is too small to draw a secure conclusion, their responses lead me to conclude that the lack of understanding of this chapter is common to all generations.

Chapter 4
Parents

Vignette: Munir

Munir is over 60 years old now and is retired. He was born in a small village in Mirpur, part of Azad Kashmir. He spent the first 16 years of his life in the village where he went to primary and middle school. His father worked on ships and he saw him quite rarely. He arrived in this country with his two brothers in 1963, having followed their older brother who had arrived in 1957. They all lived together in one house with two other cousins. Apart from a few evening lessons to learn English held at the local college, there was no opportunity to continue studying. Anyway, this was not the reason for coming to the UK in the first place. Rotherham, at this time, was a good place for those seeking employment. The steel works that surrounded the town centre at Templeborough or at Parkgate, the railway marshalling yards at Tinsley and the glass manufacturers, Beatson Clark, whose plant loomed large over the town centre, all were ready takers of the large numbers of young labourers coming from the small rural province of Mirpur. Munir first started work in a factory called Steel Products and stayed there for 10 years. He finished there and moved to the British Rail marshalling yards at Tinsley where he spent five years. He then moved to Beatson Clark where he inspected mathematical bottles. Here he stayed for 26 years. He took early retirement when he was 57 on the grounds of ill health. He married in 1971 in Mirpur and retuned with his wife shortly after. He has had six children and now has three grandchildren. In the 1960s, he and his brothers used to return to Pakistan in order to visit their parents. They could afford to spend long periods of time out of work back home because they knew there were always going to be jobs waiting for them when they returned. The economic downturn in the 1970s meant that an extended stay back home might result in losing employment. This economic reality, together with the fact that their parents passed away, as well as the steady arrival of children, has meant that the need to return has diminished. He also knows that his children would find it very difficult living in Mirpur, so the dream of returning, which was there with him and his brothers when they first came, has now disappeared. In the early days they were young and concerned principally with earning enough money to live on and send home. There was little time for thinking about their culture and its maintenance. In a sense, at the beginning, the men thought their sojourn in the UK would be a limited one and they would return home. As they began to put down roots, most markedly by having families, the need to preserve something of their culture and religion asserted itself. Throughout the late 50s and 60s, if Munir wanted to pray, as he did on a Friday or at Eid twice a year, he would take the bus to Darnall in Sheffield and pray at the nearest local mosque. As the community became more conscious of its religious and cultural needs, a mosque opened near the town centre in 1971. This would be a place that served the needs of the community in terms of prayer, but would also allow the children to be taught a basic understanding of their religion and how to read the Qur'an.

Vignette: Akhtar

Akhtar came to this country when he was 10. His father had come earlier in the early 1950s and Akhtar came with his mother and younger brother in 1970. He attended the local school for four years and left with a number of CSEs. Although very bright, as his later life proved, because of his limited English he was put in a stream at school that did the lower-status CSEs. He left school and went straight into an apprentice scheme at British Steel. Here he worked for five years before he was able to purchase a shop and since that time has been a successful small businessman. Like many of his generation, Akhtar still suffers the frustration of having arrived in the UK at an age that meant he missed UK primary education and, because of the lack at that time of additional support within schools for non-English speakers, struggled his way through secondary education leaving with few qualifications and, therefore, could take up only a low-paid job. His father worked 16 hours a day, six days a week, and Akhtar is determined that his own children will enter the professional class. His eldest daughter has just been accepted to study law at Leeds University. Akhtar has strong opinions about the education provided by the mosque, but cannot be too vociferous in the community because his uncle is the mosque's chairman.

Introduction

There are three generations of parents at present in the community. The older generation is made up of those men who first came to the UK in the 1950s and early 1960s. They were either already married before they came, or they went home to marry and their wives remained in Mirpur. Any children that were born were the result of visits home which, in the early days, could last for up to one year or more. Eventually, with the economic realities and immigration acts of the 1970s upon them, these men took the decision to bring their wives and any children they had to the UK. They moved out of homes shared with other men and began buying houses for their families. This is Qurban reflecting on his visits home in the 1960:

Qurban: I have been to Pakistan many times. First time was in 1966, then I come back again. I went in 1966 for one and a half years.

Because our parents were alive, you know. We used to go there for the sake of our parents. And now our parents are passed away, there is nobody, no close relative, so we don't go there now. Because children have grown up here. And also when children have grown up they don't want to go there, don't want to live there. It's difficult for them, you know, to live there.

The second generation of parents interviewed for this book are those who were born in Mirpur but were brought here by their fathers in the late 1960s and early 70s as the first generation began to realise families had to be reunited and that visits home were becoming less likely and less desirable. These children had often spent much of their primary education in Mirpur and arrived in this country with little or no English. They either spent a year or so in primary schools or went straight into secondary schools, depending on their age on arrival. By the start of the 80s these young people began to marry, often with relatives from Mirpur, and from the mid-80s onwards their children began to pass through the local schools. These children, therefore, were born in the town and attended all phases of compulsory education. Here, Hanif describes his arrival and experiences of school:

Hanif: Yes, I came in 1969 with my mum and dad. And my wife came in 1981 when we got married.

When did your father come?

Maybe early 60s.

Did he come alone?

Yes, in those days you came on your own and you had to bring your family later. And, like I said, I was primary level. Here, I went to 'South Ash' School, not comprehensive, I got some CSEs, that's about it, I didn't go to college. Started work in a garage. I left at 15, no 16, that was the year it changed.[1] 1974–75. I wasn't urged to go into the academic side in those days for some reason. I still remember the careers adviser, he goes ... into the academic side, more told to work, don't know, some reason, I could just remember right if I get another chance I might have gone into college, or university, but those days, no. I started as a motor mechanic, for a long long time. Then I did taxi driving for a bit and then back into motor mechanics.

Is it your business?

Yes, it is. It is my business from the beginning more or less. I started it from scratch.

The third generation of parents in the community were, of course, the sons and daughters of the generation just described and, as such, were the parents of very young, pre-school, children. These were not specially targeted for interviews although some of the 'older' young people who gave perspectives in the previous chapter were just embarking on the journey of parenthood. Their own experiences and those of their children are crucial for an understanding of the future role of liturgical literacy in the community. However, their role as third-generation parents is not fully examined in this chapter (but see Chapter 11).

Attitudes and Concerns

In respect of the education provided by the mosque, the parents interviewed had very interesting views. All the fathers attended the mosque either on a daily basis, more likely with the first generation who were now reaching retirement age, or on Fridays. All had sent their children to the mosque for some time. However, there were some families who elected to have their children learn how to read the Qur'an outside of the mosque. This was usually down to dissatisfaction with levels of behaviour in the mosque school or with the lack of individual attention available with such low teacher–student ratios.

Nafisah: My mum says if there's a good teacher then they will learn, otherwise they go there just to mess about.

Jabbar: There's too many children. 60 or 70 children. The Moulvi (imam) just does the *Qaidah* and that's all.

When asked a general question about the quality of education provided by the mosque, most parents from both generations were candidly critical of certain aspects of either the organisation or the curriculum. It is important to mention, however, that all were satisfied with the principal learning objective of learning how to read the Qur'an. There is no doubt that the methodology adopted for instructing the children in the accurate decoding of the Arabic text is an extremely effective and highly efficient one.

There were two main bones of contention in respect of the education provided by the mosque. Firstly, it was felt by many parents that not enough time was allowed for children to develop a better understanding of their religion beyond the learning of the basics of ritual and liturgy. In addition to learning how to read the Qur'an in Arabic, children were always taught how to pray. This consisted of instruction in bodily movements as well as memorisation of the correct wording, also in Arabic. They would also be taught how to conduct the ritual ablution needed before prayer and handling the Qur'an or entering the mosque. These elements of the ritual comprised the 'basics' as some parents and imams termed them. Yet parents admitted that they felt this was inadequate as a religious education for their children and, as a consequence, their children were growing up ignorant of much of the fundamentals of their religion. As noted in the last chapter, government advisers would add to this that there is a need to provide a space in the mosque school curriculum for lessons in citizenship. Parents might respond by saying, let's walk before we can run.

Akhtar: You should learn Islam as well as reading ... They don't do that in many mosques. They don't do it at all.

Nafisah: But in the mosque there, there is no good imam, you see. She says that in the bigger cities and places they can learn Islam. (*Jabbar,* her father: Birmingham, Manchester.) But in Rotherham there's none. In Manchester and Birmingham there's Islam lessons and things like that. In Rotherham not many, it's a small community, 20 years they have none and the children have missed all their education. My mum says that we have lessons, stories things like that, she reads books and tells us things. (*Jabbar:* Urdu books from the library and all this.) She tells us at home.

So a lot of your knowledge about Islam comes from home?

From books which tell of the prophets and all that.

Wajib: I think a lot more could be done to improve it. I think we're lacking. I think that's one of the things we're falling behind on. Because the Qur'an is recited and memorised in the mosque ... I don't think that's good enough, just memorising the Qur'an. Especially this society that we are living in. These days. We need to go deep into the ... I don't know if we can do that the amount of time the kids have in the mosque it's limited time as well, isn't it? They only have two hours, maybe an hour and a half afternoon every day five days a week. I think we need to go deeply into the teachings of Islam because that's where we're lacking as well.

Qurban: That's the problem. They've got books. Nowadays, it's very hard. Unless there's something in the community you can go to, like in big towns they'll have places, but apart from the mosques we have nothing here in Rotherham. There's nowhere to go. There's a gap there. Where youngsters can go and learn about Islam. Nothing in Rotherham.

Languages in the Mosque

The second major concern for parents in their dissatisfaction with the education provided by the mosque was the lack of use of English. And here, parents' views do coincide to some extent with those coming from outside the community, though not with the same motivation. Indeed, many of the worries about the lack of a general knowledge of Islam by the children could be dispelled if the complex language situation be resolved. For the elders, and those in the community who had learnt a reasonably proficient level of Urdu, much of the general teaching about Islam takes place in the Friday sermons and at the occasional religious gatherings held at various times of the year. The language for all these events, at present, is in Urdu. In the two local mosques serving the community, both imams have a very limited knowledge of English and, although very proficient in terms of religious knowledge and in the teaching of the reading of the Qur'an, always deliver their sermons in Urdu. With the increasing absence of Urdu knowledge among the young people, the value of this language for enabling and shaping religious knowledge is becoming more limited for the future of the community. In my visits to the mosque, and in particular, my attendance at the weekly congregational prayer on Friday, I could not help noticing the number of boys and young men, some of whom I had taught, forming the last two or so rows of people at the back of the prayer hall. I suspected a language problem:

> *What about all the boys who come to Friday prayer and sit at the back?*
>
> **Munir:** I told them, and in the month of Ramadan, the imam from Eastfield Mosque, they used to come to *tarawih* [special prayers in Ramadan], and try to explain in English, but I think it is very very important, that our young boys, of 20 or 26 years old coming to the mosque, but our imam is only speaking Urdu. And it should be in English. Then they can understand what Islam says. They are coming there and just sitting there.
>
> *So the speech is in Urdu not in Punjabi?*
>
> Well, our imam his speech is in Urdu, about Islam, you know, what Islam says, for people my age, they don't know about Islam, and people are without qualifications, without education. In the mosque. But the imam does not come from our area, that place is Kashmir ...
>
> **Munir:** The only problem is about our children. For example, you said a lot of children go there, and sit at back ...

However, the parents also indicated that English should be used much more extensively in the mosque, including during the teaching of the Qur'an. Since the events of 9/11 and 7/7, UK governments, encouraged by the media, have been able to advance the image of non-English-speaking imams playing a vital role in the creation of young radicals and their mere lack of English has been sometimes interpreted as a key component in the radicalisation of young British Muslims. A key study on the radicalisation of this group (Witkorowicz, cited in Choudhury, 2007: 28) draws attention to this factor, but adds that the rejection of the teachings of local imams is not solely down to the language issue. It is also tied up with the rejection of the mores and values of their parents' religious practices which they have come to see as quaint, old-fashioned and, importantly, private, unable to address their own particular identity issues. There is now in place a set of standards for the testing of foreign-born imams that, in theory, verifies their suitability for employment in British mosques. Despite a more recent government introduction of checks on a 'knowledge of ... British civic life, including and understanding of other faiths' (Ministers of religion, n.d.), the emphasis still placed by some on the appropriate level of English for these imams risks missing the point that language is only one factor out of many responsible for the encouragement of radicalisation. As Birt notes, the one definite consequence of such a policy is to further the influence of the Deobandi tradition in British mosques 'which alone of all the theological tendencies in Britain, provides sufficient numbers of home-trained imams, producing some 80% of British-trained imams in 17 seminaries' (Birt, 2006: 695). The parents interviewed for this book were unanimous in their view that English was essential for learning in the mosque and in the mosque school. However, their greatest worry regarding their own children was not that they might be radicalised, but that they might neglect or reject their religion altogether and 'go off the rails', drop into the drug culture or, perhaps, choose a thoroughly Westernised lifestyle.

Akhtar: The biggest gripe I have with them is that they won't preach in English ...

Is it because of the language?

Wajib: Yes, because of the language as well. Because most of the kids, they are very fluent in English and were born here and most of the kids speak English and some of them have difficulty understanding Mirpuri or Urdu. Even Urdu. Mainly Urdu they have difficulty understanding it. I mean if they don't understand it how are they going to learn? So what I have been suggesting is that the teachers can communicate well with kids and they get the message across. This is why we're falling behind.

Munir: I think myself, if children go to the mosque, they should read in Arabic and also in English as well. They should understand what is the meaning of this word. I mean, if they are reading that, and they don't understand, don't know what is the meaning of this, they are just wasting time. We want proper teachers, qualified teachers, who can teach these children born in this country.

Qurban: Mosque education is just all right for reading. They can just read. But a little bit more, what I am feeling, if they give an education by through meaning, what Arabic means, the language, everything. They give with English. Then I am more happy, because it is easy to understand for children as well. What means everything like.

Akhtar: There's a guy, Mr Shabbir, who's got a private school. He's doing excellent work. Because it's in English! This is what you've got to do ... They're preaching in Urdu ... Urdu is not our language ... Urdu is not the language of my children ... although it is a beautiful language ... beautiful language ... and I regret not keeping it up ...

This poignant last comment about Urdu reflects a general view towards the use of Urdu which is the subject of a later chapter (Chapter 9). Suffice it to remark at this point that the expressed desire for the greater use of English in the mosque school was not matched by a similar desire for the rigorous teaching of Urdu to the young.

The teacher, Maulana Shabbir, mentioned in the last quotation was previously employed by one of the local mosques and, indeed, achieved considerable success with parents and students, by teaching and preaching in English (a product of a UK-based Deobandi seminary). He was, however, dismissed by the mosque committee after a dispute and has now started his own mosque and teaching institution in another part of the town.

Parents and the Institutions of Liturgical Literacy

The administration of the two mosques was another issue that evoked comment from the parents interviewed. It is interesting to note that at present the administration of the two local mosques and other mosques in the town to which they are linked, by and large, is the preserve of men from the first generation of settlers. The committee of 'Church Walk' mosque belong to that group of men who came alone in the 1950s and early 1960s, as does the chairman of the 'University Road' mosque. The time and, in many cases, considerable money invested in the establishment of these places of worship have given these men the authority to maintain the status quo in terms of the education provided by the mosque. It is, of course, not that long ago that there was no mosque in the town, and their presence now and the education provided for the children, whatever its nature, must appear to these men as a significant and great achievement.

The parents, however, who vary from those being on the fringes of the administration of the mosque to others having little or nothing to do with their respective mosque trustees, have plenty to say on the way the mosques are run:

> *Akhtar:* I think the mosques are letting our kids down ... I think they are helping to diminish Islam. I think they are little empires ... Run by little men who are little despots ... And that goes for all of them ...
>
> *Wajib:* Ah well, I help there. I do the collection on Friday, the money collection, and count the money, that's all I have. I do give some advice ...
>
> *You're not a trustee then ...*
>
> No, I'm not a trustee at all.
>
> *How do you become a trustee?*
>
> I think you get invited, people choose you as well. Bit of both. Mostly invited.
>
> *And how often does this happen? I mean, have the trustees you have been trustees for a long time?*
>
> Oh yeah, a long time. My father was a trustee. But he's dead now. In 1997. He was a trustee and a founder of the mosque.
>
> Yes. He's [the chairman of the mosque] got the power. I mean ... I don't think he's personally interested in that matter [use of English in the mosque]. I have mentioned it in front of him and I have mentioned it in front of other people as well that we're lacking and I think it's like knocking my head against a brick wall. I've given up on it now.

The apparent conflict between these two stakeholders is closely linked to the difference that can occur across generations. It is noteworthy that no representative of the second generation of parents described above is a trustee at either of the two local mosques, despite their being middle-aged and relatively successful financially.

> *Hanif:* Yes. The old people, oh God, they are the biggest barrier ... I've mentioned it a couple of times that we should have it in English, 'Oh, what about our own language?' They confuse Pakistani culture with Islam. They are two different things ... Islam has nothing to do with ... there are things we do in Pakistani culture people think is Islamic ... it's not ...

Qurban: Main thing, for example, in our mosque committee is my cousin, you know, he is the secretary. He has a language problem. He can speak English, but he speaks broken English. He can't speak full English. He can't explain what is our problem. If anyone goes to the council meeting from the mosque, we should have a good representative, he can explain what is our problem. A person who speaks broken English, he can't ... it's difficult. We want a qualified person. Who knows English, and can explain to people on the council committee. Then they can help. If they don't understand how can they help?

Munir: And this committee is absolutely rubbish. I think myself. Because they do not give a chance to other people who are interested who want to do something about this generation.

What about in the mosque? Do you have any role there?

Akhtar: No. The reason being my uncle is the chairman of the mosque. Qurban Hussain.

He's somebody I need to speak to ...

Don't mention you've spoken to me! [laughter]

OK, why?

No, seriously. He's an unelected chairman. He's the Mugabe of our mosque.

Because he has been there since the beginning basically?

Yeah ... well it helped. What it was...That's how it usually works ... He's alright ... he's doing voluntary work...he doesn't get paid for it ... There's supposed to be a trust ... supposed to be elections ... He doesn't believe in things like that ... I'm not saying anything because he's my uncle ... [laughter]

Parents' Acquisition of Liturgical Literacy

An unexpected outcome from the series of interviews conducted with parents was the information that many parents learnt how to read the Qur'an themselves in the UK at one of the local mosques. It is interesting to note how many parents used the education provided by the mosque to learn a skill they had either forgotten about, or neglected to learn, when they were young. There is a strong sense of many of these men equally engaged in activities that help forge cultural and religious identity. The education available to these men when younger, both secular and religious, was limited in the villages of Mirpur with little in the way of facilities and often a lack of knowledge or expertise on the part of the teacher or imam.

The parents were, therefore, able to bring an interesting perspective to the different ways liturgical literacy was acquired here and back home:

> *Jabbar:* No, here is different. There ... I think teaching is different. Here, the imam is more a graduate. And there is an imam who is in the village he is alright as a teacher but very different there to here. To teach. And these imams there have no qualifications.

One man, Munir, described a special class that was set up by the imam in the afternoons for those who wanted to improve or refresh their knowledge of reading the Qur'an. He remarked upon how the methods used by the imam were a significant improvement on those employed back home when he was a boy:

> *Munir:* I have learned in the last two years in here. I have tried to learn it for about two months. With the imam in 'Church Walk' mosque. And they teach very very different there than how we read in our village. He teaches us very different there ...
>
> *Does he teach you more accurate pronunciation?*
>
> Yeah, more accurate ... because the reading of the Qur'an is where the words come out from the throat, the nose. And he tries to explain that. It is not easy for us ...
>
> *Did he just teach you, or was there a group?*
>
> We were a group of 5 or 6. Same as my age. 50–55.
>
> *Once a week?*
>
> No, every day we did that. But only two months. Imam was busy.

Another man described how he studies with his sons and how their practice is quite different from how he remembered learning back home in the village:

> *Qurban:* Sometimes we sit together, me and children, and Wasim, and he tries to teach me as well, because he is learning from here, and he is good at reading the Qur'an. And Fasal he is very good too. And sometimes I get help from them. I learned to read 30 years before, and it was very different there to here.

Gender Role Models

Mothers were often able to provide more guidance for their children in the learning of the Qur'an than their fathers. As we will explore later in the chapters devoted to the different languages of the community, it was often the mother who served as the main role model, both in terms of Islam and in terms of the literary language, Urdu. Many of the fathers, whose origins were the rural villages of Mirpur and Azad Kashmir, and as a result, had had a relatively low level of education exacerbated by moving from home to the UK at crucial times in their lives, were married to urbanised, educated women whose knowledge of Islam and Urdu often exceeded that of their husbands.

> *Wajib:* I remember sitting down on the floor most of the time. It was a poor school. We used to, we could read and that. *The missus didn't have that background, a strong educational influence up there,* but there wasn't that many books and we used to write on the slate, with chalk and everything, and I remember we used to have assemblies. Teachers were good. They believed in corporal punishment and all that stuff. I learnt a lot from Pakistani education. Urdu wise. (my emphasis)

> *Hanif:* She was more in the town basis. And I was from the village side.
>
> *Is there a difference then?*
>
> Yes, there's a difference. Probably more resources. My wife's school had more resources. They probably sat down on chairs and everything. The school was near to the house as well. In my case it was a mile two miles maybe. My wife goes to classes, like, she reads the Qur'anic verses, at 'Rosehill' Community Centre.
>
> *Teaching?*
>
> Well, you can say teaching, she reads with the people, teaches them how to read. Poetry and everything. She does that every Friday. When she goes to this community meeting, a lot of ladies can't read Urdu, so she has to read it and tell them whatever.

> *Nafisah:* My mum speaks Urdu, she doesn't speak Punjabi, she speaks in a more mannered way. More than my dad
>
> *So do you all speak to your mum in Urdu?*
>
> *Jabbar* (her father): I only speak Punjabi, you see, I like my language. I like it.
>
> *Nafisah:* My mum speaks good Urdu so we all speak Urdu with her. So they come up with better language and that... [laughs]

Attitudes towards Secular Education

When asked to comment on their opinion about the education provided by the state school, most parents were very positive and generally expressed a very benign view of the education their children received. Sometimes this is negatively compared with their own experience when arriving in this country back in the 60s and 70s. These men consider that their children's experience of state schooling contrasts very favourably with their own experiences when they arrived with their mothers in the late 70s and early 80s.

> *Hanif* [consults wife]: I could have done more if the school had helped me ... in my school I could have done more but in those days school wasn't ... was ignorant of the Asian community. Those early days.
>
> *So there wasn't any extra help?*
>
> No, there wasn't. No extra help. You went to college to do anything academic. Right, that's my belief.
>
> *Because of the language problem?*
>
> Yeah, language problem. Probably, ignorance, more than likely in those early days. There wasn't as many Asian people in Rotherham probably. Nowadays, I mean, my daughter has gone to university, Manchester University. My son is at college. So more has been done for the Asian community now, I suppose.

> *Wajib:* That's why I was quite backward ... because I wasn't thick or anything, but I was quite backward because it took me so long to pick up the language. To learn the language. When it came to maths, I was always top of the class. Because that's the same. And when we were taught maths times tables up to 20 times tables off by heart, we had to learn them, before we were 5 or 6 years old. We learnt before we were 10 or 11. We had to learn them off by heart. Whenever it came to maths I was top. But it took me so long to pick up the English. I was lacking in other subjects. So, when I did CSEs I mean some of the questions I couldn't understand so if you don't understand the question, just one word even, you don't understand the question do you? So obviously, I didn't do very well. That put me a lot back ...
>
> *Is that typical? Of men of your generation?*
>
> Yes, it was typical.

Generally, the children of the community have achieved more educationally than their parents did. This, in a sense, disguises the real level of achievement of this group of pupils in the local schools. Parents, on witnessing the apparent academic success of this group of pupils, and unaware of the levels of educational achievement of other groups, will naturally look upon their schools in a favourable manner. However, that children from Pakistani heritage (Mirpuri) traditionally achieve statistically less than their mainstream peers is little known within the community.

Akhtar: I think by all accounts from my own experiences I think they do a very good job. .... as far as the educational standards are concerned, I can't really comment that much because my children have done very well at school. They have all done exceedingly well. They have not gone on to build on that, the two of them, the third one, God willing is going to be a barrister. She is doing very well in her A-levels.

Hanif: Nowadays, I mean, my daughter has gone to university, Manchester University. My son is at college. So more has been done for the Asian community now, I suppose. On a general level, yeah. Education wise yes. A lot has been done for the community.

Bashir: I think they're doing a good job. Most of my children did well. For themselves. So obviously I can't blame schools as regard that obviously. Pupils have to try themselves and parents have to force it ... I think we're lacking in that respect as well. Parenting.

Munir: I think they are good. No complaints. Education is good here.

When asking parents about education it is hard to prevent them dwelling on aspects of pupil behaviour as point of reference. This chapter remains true to this tendency by ending with a quotation from Bashir, who, in a way, represents that third generation of parents in the community mentioned at the start of this chapter. He missed being born in this country by two years, but he did spend all his education here. He was married at 16 and has two children, Aftab, 5, and Ferzana, 9. He attends the 'University Road' mosque and assists with handiwork and odd jobs. He is a fully qualified electronics engineer. His words tell a story of learnt wisdom and frustrated ambition. It is telling, and poignant, that he lays the responsibility for his frustrated ambition not upon any failure of the system, but rather upon himself.

What is your opinion about schools in UK? As a pupil, as a father?

Bashir: My opinion is – very nice atmosphere, although you do have your down side, which is always portrayed on the news with the bullying aspect. The actual differences that children come with into school, ie. colour differences, they will always be a part and parcel of children and as I know in adolescence as well, whether people accept others that are different will be there. Children do acknowledge it, but I never felt hurt about anything, I got called names, but I've never acknowledged any of that. From a teacher's point of view the only bad experience I ever received was at college. It wasn't at school. So obviously as yourself are aware, it's not necessarily a type of person, or type of colour of a child. If a child is going to be destructive which ours wasn't – I saw destructive children walking around the school. We had mixed classes in the comprehensive school, so you were mixing with children beyond your own form and you saw other children as well, you saw them out on the playing fields, you saw them outside on the playground, that is what will never be taken away ... whether it is a completely white school, whether it's a mixed school, or whether it's a predominantly Asian school, these issues are always there ... you still have your ... if it's a completely Asian school, then obviously they still abuse each other ... they still call each other names ... there's no getting away from that. A mixed school, it's still the same. And if it's a completely white school, which I've seen, I actually went to 'Midbrough' Infants, at that time there was just me and my cousin were attending the school. But we saw the children and how they played ... they didn't notice anything different between us and themselves ... so we always heard, 'your dad is this ... ', 'your mum is this... ' So coming from our point of view, it was all straightforward. These are the things that children will always say ... 'My dad's got a better car than yours'. So beyond that, no problems with teachers ... no problems with studying.

What about the academic side of things? Are you satisfied with the level of education you came out with?

I am satisfied, but I would have been more satisfied, if I did more.

Do you then put it down to yourself?

To a certain extent, to myself. Why I say this is I was promised a result in Religious Education to be an A or an A+. I got an E or an F. Why I got an E or an F is because the rest of the subjects at school, they were all end of year exams. The maths it was taken in stages. And I could have done the higher paper. But I was asked to come in after school. I didn't want to go in after school on a Friday, didn't want to go into school on a Thursday. Just to learn a little bit more in maths. Whereas my teacher, he said, I'm capable of a C if I go for the lower paper, but I would like you to go for A. You can get an A. And me thinking the way I was thinking, a child, 'Well, if I can get a C, and always all teachers tell you, that an A, B or C, basically are equivalent. In value. All employers accept them. All people wherever you go accept them. The thing behind an A is that you're accepted even more ... by, if you're going onto college, if you're going onto different forms of education. University and whatever. Me being a child, I didn't want to do homework, I didn't want to stay at school after school. That was it. Once the chance is gone, it's gone. You can't realise it as a child. If you had learnt these things slightly younger, then possibly I might have felt there is an advantage, but it was basically down to me. My lack of everything really.

Bashir touches on a number of issues here which, unfortunately, are not part of the central theme of this book. However, his experience, when put alongside the experiences of many of his contemporaries, paint a dismal picture of frustrated hopes, low expectations and, it would appear from his initial rationalisation of name-calling, rabid racism. Yet, the marginalisation of the literacy practice of liturgical literacy is a theme of this book. The community whose literacy practice it is, in the words of Bashir, is marginalised. It will be shown later (Chapter 9: School) how marginal liturgical literacy is positioned in relation to the privileged mainstream school system, and, by extension, how the community's marginalisation is thus exacerbated.

Summary

In this chapter the parents of the community have been given the opportunity to present their experiences, opinions and concerns regarding the theme of this book. Their experiences and opinions about liturgical literacy are vibrant and strong. The strength of feeling expressed in their words reveals the centrality of liturgical literacy to their lives and those of their children. There is little doubt that the cultural capital liturgical literacy represents for the community is a cherished and fundamental one regardless of its apparent lack of value outside in the wider society. Alongside this literacy practice, parents have also been keen to opine their thoughts and feelings regarding the other literacy practices that have a vital role within the community. In particular, they have adopted a relatively non-critical attitude towards state schooling as experienced by their children. Their words demonstrate a serious engagement with issues of both pedagogy and language. They have plenty to contribute regarding the teaching and teachers of liturgical literacy and it is those individuals charged with the teaching of liturgical literacy who are the subject of the next chapter.

Note

1. The raising of the school leaving age (ROSLA) last happened in the UK in 1972.

Chapter 5

Teachers

Vignette: Mufti Siddiq

Mufti Siddiq has lived in Rotherham for 20 years. He was born in the North-West Province of Pakistan where the people speak Pushto, not Punjabi. He was taught the Qur'an at the age of 10 and had learnt it all by heart six months later. He spent 20 years at the Dar-ul-Uloom (Faculty of Sciences) at the University of Karachi where he graduated in the 1970s and quickly followed this with an MA and PhD in Islamic Studies from the same institution. He was also awarded the title of Mufti, allowing him to make judicial decisions in cases of civil and religious disagreement. He came to this country in 1980, where he became imam of the only mosque in the town, and began his work in the Muslim community. After approximately 10 years, he had to relinquish most of his duties in the mosque as his other roles developed significantly. He is currently the holder of two important and prestigious posts within nationally-recognised scholarly societies in the UK. He regularly travels the country attending meetings and speaking at conferences. He most recently visited Denmark where he spoke at an international conference. New mosques, funded by the Saudi government were recently opened in Spain and Bosnia. Mufti Siddiq was one of the invited guests at the opening ceremonies. At present, he provides a weekly lesson for the elders in the mosque on a Wednesday afternoon and, when he can, delivers the Friday sermon in a mosque in a small neighbouring town. He is the father of seven children, six of whom attended the local schools. All his children have been very bright and demonstrated considerable ability at school. However, for three of them their arrival in the UK came too late for them to make the necessary progress in English that would enable them to succeed academically at 16. Mufti Siddiq himself demonstrates little knowledge of English though his understanding is suspected to be much greater than he lets on. As a parent, he very rarely visited the children's school, even when one of his sons was having behavioural difficulties. The schools have no awareness of the important role Mufti Siddiq plays locally, nationally and internationally. He lives in an end-of-terrace house in 'Derham' and his office is the front room of the house. The main wall opposite the fireplace is festooned with shelves laden with books. The books are mainly in Urdu and Arabic, but include titles in Persian, Pushto and English. The desk opposite the bay window is covered in papers, letters, notes, pens, pencils, envelopes with in-trays and folders containing other papers. The remaining wall space, above the fireplace and above the desk, features a decorative Islamic calendar, two pieces of

Islamic calligraphy and the ubiquitous photographs depicting Mecca and Medina. There is a coffee table in the centre of the room, which is also strewn with papers and books. This is undoubtedly the room of a man of letters. That the 'letters' are not in English means that the work of this scholar is unknown to those around him. Few, if any, of his non-Muslim neighbours know of his scholarly reputation and his international status. When it is necessary to interact with the UK world outside of his community, he relies on his eldest son to act as intermediary, both as translator or interpreter and as scribe.

Introduction

The history of the two mosques that feature in this book is described in a later chapter (Chapter 6). However, the role and function of the principal teacher in the mosque, the imam, shares a historical perspective. The appointment of a particular imam in the 1980s eventually resulted in enough community disagreement (provoked by the Deobandi–Berelvi tensions that are described in Chapter 7: Mosques) to provoke the establishment of a second mosque. A very successful English-speaking imam was dismissed from one of the mosques because of the authority of one of the elders who took a personal dislike to him. The teacher in a mosque is never 'just' a teacher. This chapter will show how the role and function of the teacher, the imam, are intimately linked to questions of tradition, authority and language.

Duties and Responsibilities of an Imam

The duties and responsibilities of an imam in a UK mosque vary from one establishment to another. In truth, these duties and responsibilities are determined by the committee or group of trustees charged with the administration of the mosque. It is also true that, until recently, the Muslim community has been left alone to determine these exact duties and responsibilities. Increasingly centralised regulation is making of the imam a much more public figure and, though there are those both outside and inside the Muslim community who would encourage a role that focused on a Church-of-England-inspired civic renewal (Blunkett, 2003; Institute of Islamic Scholars, 2002), there are important particular characteristics on the ground that might delay such an evolution. Despite the wishes of the Government, imams still remain ostensibly the employees of the local trustees of mosques. Whereas there is scope for the training and shaping of imams employed in the prison service and the NHS that would enable them to play a more civic role (Birt, 2006), simple economics preclude such a development in most UK mosques, with the exception of the few larger, well-funded, big city mosques. The imam is nearly always an employee of the trust that runs the mosque. In some cases where mosques have been set up by individuals, for example in a private house, the imam may well be responsible only to himself; but in most cases, where mosques have been established with the consent and support of the community, there is a trust that administers their affairs. Sometimes the imam is employed only to lead prayers, including preparing a sermon for Friday. This may be the case in larger cities where mosques are large and staffing is more extensive. In the two mosques of this book, the imam is employed to lead prayers, but also has the responsibility for teaching the children of the community how to read the Qur'an as well as the basic requirements for conducting prayer and ritual ablution.

> *If you had to summarise to someone the main responsibilities and duties of an imam, what would they be?*
>
> **Maulana Shabbir:** The main duty of an imam is they should have a good character, that's most important, obviously a beard as well ... his recitation of the Qur'an has to be perfect ... and he is mature ...
>
> *What are his duties, insofar as what he has to do?*
>
> Well, the imam ... it varies in every single mosque ... very much so ... In some mosques, the imam, his job is just to lead the *salat* [the Arabic word for 'prayer'] and that's it ... In other *masjids*, the imam has more duties, like he has to do the *salat*, he has to teach the children, he has to get involved with the community with its problems ... I think in every *masjid*, the committee it has a set contract , as far as I know, for the imam ...
>
> *What are your responsibilities in the mosque and in the community?*
>
> **Hafiz Shakeel** (translated by Hanif): Five times a day prayers, and also teaching the Qur'an to the children, and also *Juma* [Friday prayer].

Qualifications and Training

The teacher must be suitably qualified to carry out his duty in regard to the teaching of children. He must have attended and qualified from an institution that has a recognised reputation and that has covered the basic curriculum allowing him to teach in a mosque setting. These institutions have, until recently, traditionally been in Pakistan and imams have routinely been recruited from back home. However, it is not unheard of for the imam of a mosque with a predominantly Pakistani congregation to recruit an imam from India, as was the case for one of the mosques in

Rotherham until very recently. In addition, there are now institutions operating in the UK that prepare students for work as an imam. Mufti Siddiq
acts as an external examiner for their assessments. These latter, of course,
have the advantage that they prepare imams to work in the UK context, and
their graduates are usually fluent English-speakers. On the other hand,
they do not always carry the same academic reputation as their counterparts overseas. The four imams who feature in this book all attended prestigious institutions in Pakistan and in the UK. The present imams of the two
mosques attended the Faculty of Religious Sciences (Dar-ul-Uloom) in
Faisalabad and Islamabad. They entered these at the age of 11 and graduated when they were 21. An Islamic College of this nature begins at school
age and a student can continue to undergraduate and postgraduate levels.
The final qualification is roughly equivalent to a BA in Islamic studies
covering knowledge of the Qur'an, the *Hadeeth* (sayings of the Prophet,
their provenance and authenticity), *Fiqh* (jurisprudence) and includes
imamat (knowledge on how to be an imam). Both imams also carry the title
Qari which means they have completed a course on how to recite the
Qur'an correctly. One of them is also a *Hafiz*, which implies he has memorised the entire Qur'an by heart.

Table 3 Educational profiles of imams

Imam	Age	Arrival in UK	Place of origin	Place of education	Titles/ qualifi- cations	Mother tongue	Speaks English
Hafiz Shakeel	25	1998	Pakistan: Mirpur	Pakistan: Faculty of Religious Sciences, Faisalabad	BA Hafiz Qari	Mirpuri-Punjabi	No
Mufti Siddiq	51	1983	Pakistan: North West Province	Pakistan: Faculty of Religious Sciences, University of Karachi	PhD MA Mufti Hafiz	Pushto	No
Maulana Shabbir	35	Born here	England: Leeds	UK: College of Religious Sciences, Bury, near Manchester	BA	Mirpuri-Punjabi	Yes
Qari Mustafa	40	1999	Pakistan: Azad Kashmir	Pakistan: Faculty of Religious Sciences, Islamabad	BA Qari	Mirpuri-Punjabi	No
Maulana Zubair	58	1983	India: Gujerat	India: Faculty of Religious Sciences, Delhi	BA Qari Hafiz	Gujerati	No

Mufti Siddiq, as mentioned earlier, graduated from the Faculty of Religious Sciences of the University of Karachi and holds a PhD from the same institution. Maulana Shabbir is the only imam to have received his qualifications from a British-based institution, the Dar-ul-Uloom in Bury, near Manchester.

Being an imam is not only about having the correct qualifications. There is a traditional profile for an imam that is taught in the institutions and which must be fulfilled if an imam is to be appointed. He must be of good character, look like an imam (that is, dress following the example of the Prophet) and have an excellent recitation of the Qur'an.

> *Maulana Shabbir:* The main duty of an imam is they should have a good character, that's most important, obviously a beard as well ... his recitation of the Qur'an has to be perfect ... and he is mature ...

> *Hafiz Shakeel* (translated by Hanif): He reads the Qur'an well, he has the appearance of an imam, his life is within the *sunnah* (the word used to describe the example of the Prophet) ...

Training for Teaching Children

It is noteworthy that no mention is made of any particular quality for teaching children. The above qualities would no doubt serve the definition of an imam whose sole responsibility was to lead the prayers in the mosque. That most imams are also responsible for teaching children is a factor that the above definitions ignore. However, there is built into the teaching and learning model employed by these traditional institutions (such as the faculties of religious sciences, and the mosques themselves), an aspect of deployment that ultimately contributes to an element of teacher training. Chapter 3: Children showed how allowing older children to work with or supervise younger children was a practice well used. This was not only a reflection of necessity caused by the large numbers of children and the lack of teachers. It was also an example of that very traditional form of 'mentoring' involving the use of older children to instruct younger ones, which is not peculiar to Islamic settings, and is, perhaps, universal in one form or another.

Hafiz Shakeel of 'University Road' mosque was able to 'practise' his teaching of the Qur'an by working with the younger students in his college:

> *Do they have any opportunity to practise?*

> *Hafiz Shakeel* (translated by Hanif): They do it within the *madrassah*, because they have small children there as well, learning the Qur'an. And the same thing happens here as well, with older children who

have learned the Qur'an, as there are too many children here, so the imam tells them to go and sit with and teach some of the younger children. That's the way of learning.

Maulana Shabbir, who attended the UK-based college, went a step further. This, no doubt, contributed to the success he had both at the 'Church Walk' mosque and at present in his own establishment in another part of the town. Training for teaching, on his particular course, was an option that he chose to follow. It was not a compulsory element of the course, which still allowed its graduates to serve as imams without it. However, Maulana Shabbir, through personal choice, and possibly with an eye to the future, elected to take the optional course in teacher training:

Did your training involve pedagogy?

Maulana Shabbir: There is actually because I myself had teaching training ... whilst I was at the Islamic college ... but that is an optional thing you see ... I mean you get some people who, some students who go for that option ... and you have those who wouldn't ... so yes I have had some training ...

What did that training involve?

Well, basically it involves the method of how to teach the Qur'an itself ... that's one thing ... secondly, how to discipline children ... that's another thing as well ... that's most important ... mainly it's these two things ...

And do you get opportunity to practise whilst there?

Yes, you would do that with the younger students in the college. What would happen is for a period of two months under the supervision of a supervisor, you would have two months with a class of ten, and you would implement all that you had learnt there ...

Mufti Siddiq, as well, was employed to teach younger students in the college where he studied. However, in his case it was more akin to graduate teaching to undergraduates.

Mufti Siddiq (translated by his son, Abdul Ghafoor): I taught *hadeeth* and *fiqh* in certain Islamic schools, in Pakistan, in Dar ul Ifta [College of Law].

How these men were recruited to their positions will be dealt with in the next chapter (Chapter 5) but all these imams, by any account, are exceptionally well-qualified for the jobs they do. They are all highly respected within the communities they serve, and any negative comments that are occasionally voiced are purely down to matters of doctrinal difference which are not the subject of this book. Their authority is never called into question by the community members. The only negative comment came from the Mufti himself, when he was discussing the imam who had been dismissed from 'Church Walk' mosque and who was now operating a very successful teaching centre elsewhere. His comment, although terse, spoke a great deal about the differences in prestige between Islamic colleges back home in Pakistan and those in the UK:

Do you know anything about the school that has just been set up in Cliff Road?

Mufti Siddiq (translated by his son, Abdul Ghafoor): There has to be a qualified teacher to teach the kids ...

And he's not?

No he isn't.

He has got the advantage of English, but that's all?

Yes, the school itself ... because wherever there is a religious school, the Pakistani parents send their kids there ...

Wasn't he the imam of 'Church Walk' for a time?

Yes, he was.

The interviews upon which this chapter was based all took place after 9/11, but before the closer-to-home UK events of 7/7. In the light of what has happened in the UK recently, it is clear that the foregoing discussion appears a million miles away from some of the more heated discussions around 'good imams' and 'bad imams' fostered recently by some politicians and some of the media. Yet, for me, a passionate practising Muslim, as well as a so-called dispassionate academic, the reality of the past 30 years in the UK is much closer to what I have just written than it is to what we all hear almost daily on our television sets and read in our newspapers. The reality is always more banal than dramatic, more rooted in the everyday than making history, more accidental than planned. One of the imams of the community is described by some others as a 'taliban', whilst I know him as the father who is tearing his hair out because of his son's poor behaviour at secondary school. Another imam is accused of knowing no English – and therefore, according to the current orthodoxy, aiding and abetting the radicalisation of Muslim youth – but, at the same time, he is described as the sweetest and kindest person you would be likely to meet. The majority of imams in the UK, I would argue, have similar low-profile or unremarkable roles. The ogre of the radicalising, mind-poisoning non-English-speaking imam is not a long away from the hideous creations of orientalists writing in the 19th century about some of the British Empire's eastern subjects, or even from the monstrous caricatures of rabbis created by the Nazis.

The Methodology of Teaching Liturgical Literacy

The methodology of teaching the Qur'an does not differ across the mosques, neither in observed teaching sessions nor in the words of the teachers themselves. Their method may be termed as 'tried and trusted' in the true sense of the words as this is a method evident across cultures, national boundaries and time itself. Its simplicity and its reliability are its greatest strengths.

Although never referred to as synthetic phonics,[1] this method is obviously one that lies squarely in that particular school of thought regarding reading acquisition with its build up from smaller units to larger ones. The reliance on whole-word recognition and the subsequent breaking down of words into smaller units, analytic phonics, does not feature in the early stages of learning to read the Arabic of the Qur'an.

As this aspect of teaching the Qur'an is so important in the context of this book an explanation of this method will be left almost verbatim from the interviews conducted. Firstly, Hafiz Shakeel outlines the basics of the method as he uses it:

Explain briefly the process of teaching the Qur'an. Methodology?

Hafiz Shakeel (translated by Hanif): First of all, there is the alphabet. Afterwards, it is the Qaidah. Most of the words are from the Qur'an. But separately, you can see it written, how to learn those words, so they finish the *Qaidah* off, then they learn the Qur'an. From the first *siparah*.

What is the overall aim in the teaching?

Completing the Qur'an.

How long does that take?

Two years, but longer if he's a bit slower. And it's not much time ... just two hours a day ...

At what age do they start, then?

At about six years.

So if they are really clever, they could finish in two years?

If they are slower, it could be three years, clever ones less than two years.

But at the age of eight or 10, what do they do next?

They can read *hifz* [memorisation].

Does everyone do the hifz?

Yeah, if they are interested, some don't bother, they leave as soon as they have read the Qur'an. They stay and read it at home. They don't come to the mosque. Some, like my children, I ask them to go to mosque, learn more, about *salat*, learn more about the Qur'an. Learn in translation.

What is the best way to learn hifz?

First they teach them from last *siparah*. And small *surahs*.

And how many children are expected to learn the whole Qur'an?

Not much over here. People are not that interested. If they are, they will send him to a *madrassah* to learn every day. Here it is not much. I don't think so anyway. We might do one or two *siparahs*. We have got one kid here who is doing ... has done about seven *siparahs*. As Hafiz.

The Problematicisation of Script

Hafiz Shakeel, along with the other imams involved in the teaching of the Qur'an, has to face the problem of children being less and less familiar with Urdu, and, by extension, the Urdu script which itself is a variation of Arabic script. As a consequence, he is choosing to exploit the children's knowledge of written English in order to facilitate certain procedures in learning in the mosque. This is a development occurring in UK mosques that has both advocates and opponents among the teaching cadre. The former see the use of English, or Roman, script, as an efficient way to support the learning of the Arabic script. The latter interpret this development, particularly the use of Roman script, as potentially damaging, and could lead to children finding it harder to learn the Arabic script. In 'University Road' mosque, the imam, who speaks and understands only a little English, is a supporter of this method of transliteration:

Hafiz Shakeel (translated by Hanif): We have a book if you want it. Complete *salat*. You can read it in English. It is in Urdu, but written in English, words,

That's interesting ...

That we use to teach young children and older ones ...

Why are you using English letters then to transcribe the Urdu?

Especially for these young children, they can't easily understand Urdu, some children born here, hard to speak and read Urdu.

So would the child understand it if they read the transliterated Urdu?

Plate 6 Hafiz Shakeel's book of transliterations

(THE SIX DECLARATIONS OF FAITH)

(1)The First Kalmah, Tayyab (Sanctity)

Laa ilaaha il-lal Laahu
Muhammadur-Rasoolul-Laah.
(sallal laahu Alaiehi wa Sallam)

There is no worthy, of worship but Allah, Muhammad (blessing and salutation be upon him) is the Messenger of Allah.

(2) The Second Kalimah,
Shahaadat (Evidence)
Ash-hadu Al-Laa Ilaaha Il-lal
Laahu Wahdahu Laa Shareeka
Lahu Wa Ash-hadu An-na
Muhammadan Abduhu Wa Ra-
Sooluh. (Sallal Laahu Alaiehi Wa
Sallam)

I bear witness that there is no worth worshipped but Allah, who is One and without any partner; and I also bear witness that Muhammad (blessing and salutation be upon him) is His bondsman and Messenger.

(3) The Third kalimah,
Tamjeed (The glory of Al-Laah):
Subhaanal-Laahi Wal
Hamdu Lil-Laahi Wa Laa
Ilaaha Il-lal Laahu Wal-laahu
Akbaru Wa Laa Haula Wa Laa
Quw-wata il-Iaa Bil Laahil
Aleey-yil Azeem.

Plate 7 Arabic, English and transliteration

NEYAT FOR NAMAZ FOR MALES

All Sunnat neyat

Main neyat kiti is namaz ki partha hoon khaas vaaste allah tallah day (2,4) rakat namaz sunat sunat muthabay rasullalah wakat namaz (fajar) (zohar (asar) (magrib) (isha) moo mera tharaf khana ka'ba shrif.

Nafal neyat

Main neyat kiti is namaz ki partha hoon khaas vaaste allah tallah day (2,4) rakat namaz nafal bandge allah tallah day moo mera tharaf ka'ba shrif.

All farz neyat

Main neyat kiti is namaz ki partha hoon khaas vaaste allah tallah day (2 fajar) (4 zohar,asar) (3 magrib) (4 isha) rakaat namaz farz farz alaah tallah day wakat namaz (fajar, zohar, asar, magrib, isha) peechay is imaam saab day moo mera tharaf khana ka'ba shrif.

Witar neyat

Main neyat kiti is namaz ki partha hoon khaas vaaste allah tallah day 3 rakat namaz witar wajib is raat kay moo mera tharaf khana ka'ba shrif.

Plate 8 Transliterated Urdu

Yeah ... Like, when you read the first *salat*, like with the *jamaat*,
So the children know enough Urdu, to follow this?
That's right, yeah ... If they don't, they can read the English ...
Do you think this is a good idea? Or would you prefer them to be able to read the actual Urdu script? If you had the choice ...
Both. English is their mother language. It is their mother language now. Even when they come home they speak English. They don't speak much our own language. That is the only way to remind them, read something they can understand it ...

On the other side of town, the teacher who resigned his position as imam and teacher at 'Church Walk' mosque, Maulana Shabbir, outlines the method of teaching children how to read the Qur'an in the following way:

Maulana Shabbir: Well, basically, it all starts with *alif bah tah*[2]... you start the child with *alif bah tah* ...
What do you mean 'start the child'? What do they have to in order to learn it? What do you do in order to make them learn it?
I would say it is a bit similar to school, when a child goes into nursery ... and the only difference would be that there when you have something like a for apple, b for banana, and so on you wouldn't have that here ... the child has got a book, and we're talking about our place here, not talking about any other mosque, but the way we do it here ... you have a child who comes to you totally new at 6 or 7 years old ... a beginner and you have to teach him the Arabic alphabet ... the way we would do it is that the child would come and, obviously, start with *Bismillahi arahmanirahim*[3] ... that's the first thing we would like him to learn.
They would just learn to say that, not read it?
Yes, just verbally. *Bismillahi arahmanirahim.* Because in the *hadeeth*, it says, the Prophet said that as soon as the child, when he begins reading the Qur'an, and *alif bah tah* is the Qur'an, so the sins of the parents are forgiven straightaway ... so that's why it is a principle to teach the child *Bismallahi*, so at least the parents, they have all their sins forgiven ... so that's verbally *Bismillahi arahmanirahim.* That will be repeated every single day until it sinks into the child's mind. Then you start with *alif, bah tah* ... and you repeat that with the child with the book in front of them ... 'this is *alif, bah, tah* ...' Usually, what we tend to do is have a group, rather than just an individual ... If you have a group then they can all sit and learn together ... so they would go and

the teacher would repeat that maybe two or three or four times, then go back in a group and learn *alif bah tah* ... when they've learnt that, then the next stage and the next stage and so on. So with the beginners, obviously it is not always concrete that they would learn it properly, you would finish the 28 letters of the Arabic alphabet, and from the 28 they might know about 20 or 18 or 21 and the others they might forget or something ... so basically that's how it is done ... so just get them used to ...

So are they learning the names of the letters initially, not the sound?

They are doing two things. Firstly, what they are doing is they learn the name of the letter, how it is pronounced and where it should be pronounced as well ... because the method of teaching is the child follows the lips of the teacher ... so when the teacher says 'zha', the child will look at the teacher and say 'zha'. He doesn't have his head down and just say 'zha', because if he says 'zha', there is 'za', 'qaf' and 'kef'. So the teacher needs to explain that when you say 'qaf' the mouth has to be full, but when you say 'kef' the mouth has to be empty ... so just to get them used to pronouncing the letters correctly ... and that's the beginning stages and that would be implemented for everything ... for his prayer ... that's a basic rule ... for everything ... So the teaching method in the Qur'an is very very different to English in schools ...

If I understand it correctly, they go from a knowledge of being able to read and understand the alphabet to being able to read the sound with different tashkeel[4], so they know the vowelling and tashkeel, to syllables?

Yes.

Short sounds? Mixing up the consonants with the vowelling. Until you get to a stage where you combine it to make a word. Are the words always real words or is there sometimes use of what we call in English nonsense words – a made-up word just to allow the child to practise sound and consonant combinations?

Actually you have both. The reason for that is, firstly it's just to get the child used to spelling ... it's like children always learn better when they can learn to spell. So it's the same sort of concept in Arabic as well ... that once they have done the alphabet, then they go on to small letters, then when they start mixing up the letters together, they have to learn the *harakat*,[5] of how to spell the *harakat*, the *madda*, the *shadda*, how to spell all of that, the *tanweens*, so it's like in English, a child he would say, a-p-p-l-e. 'apple'. Similarly here in the Qur'an in the beginning stages, it's the same thing ... and this exercise is implemented through all of the beginning stages, even through to the Qur'an because it makes it very easy for the child ...

However, unlike Hafiz Shakeel, who is attempting to use English, or transliterated Arabic and Urdu, to short-cut the decoding process, Maulana Shabbir has strong views against this practice:

Do you use any shortcuts? I have noticed in discussion with others the use of Latin script, Roman or English script to help teach the Qur'an, or prayers or whatever. Now what is your opinion about that?

Maulana Shabbir: We are totally against it because we feel that we are missing the essence of Arabic ...

So you are aware of this going on. Why do you think it is happening?

I think it is done because a lot of teachers think that because children can relate to English much better, that's why if we have this type of scheme or system to help them but we are totally against it, we don't approve of it as well ... because we want our children to be fluent in Arabic reading and don't want them to ... .because the script is as essential a part of the Qur'an as the actual language of the Qur'an. And I think the other reason is maybe because children are not being explained the spelling purposes ... you see you have two things ...

Do you do any writing then? You talk about spelling, so do you get the kids to write at all?

We do make the kids do Arabic writing, but it starts at a later stage, at a very later stage ... but spelling, as I was saying, if a child has the ability to spell at the beginning stages in Arabic or any Arabic book with *harakat* (letters) would not be a problem for him, he could spell it out.

And I see, there's also a danger, that in the community itself, if the children are weaned off proper Arabic script for reading the Qur'an, it is also going to be a handicap if they want to start to learn Urdu ... because I know Arabic and Urdu are not exactly the same script, there is so much similarity that if you learn one, it is going to be a lot easier to learn the other ...

The use of Roman script to facilitate learning Arabic in the mosque is, therefore, a current issue for the mosques and their teachers. Bashir, one of the parents featured in the previous chapter, confesses that he actually learnt initially the Arabic of his prayers and the Qur'an from transliterated materials:

Can I just ask a question ... If the children are using this [a transliterated sheet] *... In a sense they are also going to learn this, aren't they? If you took* *away the English part, the English transliteration, they could learn the shape of the letter, alif, bah, tah and so on, and listen to the sound of somebody ... the English transliteration is just somehow a bit of an aid ...*

Bashir: Yes, it is a very good aid ... because most children even like myself ... I didn't start mosque when I was two or three ... I started the mosque when I was five ... so I had already started school ...

So you had some basics of English (reading)?

Yeah, basics of English ... what I read as my first acknowledgement of *salah* (prayer) that was at mosque ... although I used to copy what my parents did when they were reading *salah* ... what I actually acknowledged as what was read in between for the first time was in the mosque ... and even at the age of five I could read very very fluently in English ... this was down as I said earlier on to good teachers ... I used to help my cousin in the school ... while I was studying as well ... the thing is I read my first *salah* in English form ... it had no Arabic written there ... so I knew my *salah, al hamdu lilllah rabbi-alameen,* I knew my *salah.*

Did you learn that from something written down?

I learned that off by heart from a transliterated form ... there was no Arabic in the book at all ... no Arabic ... everything was in English form ... My Qaidah was in Arabic, it did have the transliteration of all the letters below so I knew what I read individually, but the place and time when it became slightly difficult was trying to understand the joining of letters. This was explained, but obviously my local masjid at that time didn't have anybody to speak in English and tell me. So whatever they said, basically, went. Because there were no transliterations of that form, where the letters and words are joined with the ... we know them as the *zebbahs,*[6] the *zairs,* the *pashas,* the *maads,* I didn't understand that point, because I had read in English format ... and I read in a transliterated *Qaidah.*

Whatever the advantages or disadvantages of using transliterated script to aid the learning of the Qur'an, there is no doubt that the community's recourse to Roman script operates in other important contexts as well. In Chapter 9: Urdu and Chapter 10: Mirpuri-Punjabi, I will examine how Roman script is now being used, particularly by the younger generation, to transliterate Mirpuri-Punjabi religious poetry and Urdu songs.

Use of English in the Mosque

The difference in attitude towards English use in the mosque expressed by the two imams is an interesting one. Whereas Maulana Shabbir is a

AN ORGAN OF MARKAZUL-ULOOM AL-ISLAMIYYA
33•35 Ridge Road • Rotherham • S65 1NS • South Yorkshire
Tel/Fax: 01709 835675 • 378832

Issue No. 8
Dec 2003 - 1424
Shawal / Zul-Qada

WHAT AFTER RAMADHAAN?

My dear brothers, my Muslim sisters, with the passing of Ramadhaan we have highlighted a number of points.
May Allah benefit us through them.

We bid farewell to the blessed month, its beautiful days and its fragrant nights. We leave the mouth of the Qur'aan, Taqwaa, patience, mercy, forgiveness and freedom from hellfire? So what have we harvested of its ripe fruits and extensive shade? Have we attained Taqwaa and graduated from Ramadhaan with the diploma of the God-fearing?

What have I gained from Ramadhaan?

My dear brothers & sisters, if you are from those who profited from Ramadhaan, achieved the attributes of Taqwaa and truly fasted only for Allah, then praise Allah and thank him, ask Him for steadfastness upon Deen.

Beware of unravelling the yarn after it has been spun - what would you say if a woman was to spin a thread and then sew a shirt or a thawb with it. Then, when she looked at it and it pleased her, she started cutting the threads and tearing them apart strand by strand for no reason.

what would people say about her?

This then is the condition of one who returns to sinning, immorality and shamelessness, and abandons obedience and righteous actions after Ramadhaan. After being favoured with the unlimited blessing of Allah within Ramadhaan, how can such a person return to sins and evil actions. How evil can it be that Allah is only known in Ramadhaan?

The situation after Ramadhaan

People discarding Salaah as soon as the announcement is made for Eid. The Masaajid used to be filled with worshippers for Taraaweeh Salah which is a Sunnah, we see the number of visitors to the Masjid decline for the five daily prayers which are Farz (compulsory)

Many other none Islamic and Haraam activities and things are practiced that it puts one to shame to see a Muslim fulfil them. So if a servant is truly thankful to his Lord, you will see him advance in good deeds and obedience and you will see him distanced from disobedience. Thankfulness (Shukr) is the abandoning of sins.

May Allah safeguard us from all types of sin. Ameen.

I asked ... Allah gave me....

I asked for strength....
And Allah gave me difficulties to make me strong.

I asked for Wisdom....
And Allah gave me Problems to solve.

I asked for Prosperity....
And Allah gave me Brain and Brawn to work.

I asked for Courage...
And Allah gave me Danger to overcome.

I asked for Love...
And Allah gave me Troubled people to help.

I asked for Favours...
And Allah gave me Opportunities.

I received nothing I wanted...
But I received everything I needed!

'So blessed be Allah, the Best of creators' (23:14)

Plate 9 English-language newsletter produced by Maulana Shabbir

fluent and confident speaker of English and advocates the use of English in the mosque when teaching about Islam or giving explanations about particular aspects of reading Arabic, he is clearly opposed to the apparent encroachment of English script as a shortcut to reading Arabic. Ironically, Hafiz Shakeel has little command of English, and struggles to communicate with many of his younger students. Yet he expresses no wariness about the introduction of the Roman script for his students, believing they possess a linguistic resource that can only assist them in their endeavours to read and learn Arabic.

We learnt of parents' concerns about their children's understanding of Islam in the previous chapter. On the whole, the parents were satisfied that the children learnt how to read the Qur'an well, but were concerned that children were not learning enough about their religion. They put this down, mainly, to language. Mufti Siddiq is well aware of the language problems that beset the mosque in its efforts to teach the children their religion:

What is your opinion about education provided by the mosque?

Mufti Siddiq (translated by his son, Abdul Ghafoor): It is good, but it is not enough in the mosque ...

What else is needed?

They learn to read the Qur'an properly, but they don't learn the main things about Islam ...

What is preventing that happening?

The first thing is language ... most teachers speak Urdu ... .and the children do not understand it ...

For example, after namaz [prayers, Urdu] just now in the mosque, you gave a short lesson, dars, you did it in Urdu. Do you mean that not all the community would be able to understand?

No, the elders do understand ... every time I give a *dars* I look for someone who can translate it into English, but there isn't anyone ...

Differentiation in the Mosque

In this chapter we also examine the children's progress during their learning from the perspective of their teachers. Although most children begin attending the mosque at the age of five or six, it is quickly apparent that some children make better progress than others. Therefore, the teacher who is sensitive to this matter has to have strategies ready to manage the different rates of progress among his students. Maulana Shabbir, who has very clearly articulated views on pedagogy, has a generally very sound opinion on differentiation:

What about the precocious child, the one who begins at 5 or 6 and makes very quick progress? Do they just go more quickly, or do they get extra things to do?

Maulana Shabbir: With them we tend to make them do the basics first before doing any additional stuff ... That's more important ... if a child is capable, get his basics out of the way. He's on that, he's ok, he's well established on the basics, might be moving on to different levels of education ... maybe additional things

Memorisation, where does that come in?

Hifz Qur'an again, is on the child's ability and aptitude ... .if a child is capable of being *hafiz* Qur'an, he's very clever, quick, intelligent, then we always get in touch with the parents, 'this is a gifted child, capable of memorising the Qur'an' and if the parents say 'right, ok' then he is set to work in a *Hifz* Qur'an class ...

That's a separate group?

That is a totally separate group. There is no age limit. We have children of the age of 7 and children of the age of 14. There is no set age at all. Once a child is capable, his recitation is very good, he's able and willing, he has ability ...

What about at the other end, with kids who find things hard?

With them there is a lot of leniency ... we tend to have a lot of leniency with them ... and most of all there's more support for them as well ... there's no pressure on them at all ... children always deliver if there is a bit of pressure on them ... we noticed in the mosques, children always deliver and parents want their children to deliver so do the *ustaads*, the teachers, and the ones who have this kind of problem there will be a lot of leniency for them. Whereas other children are doing something in two days, this child will be left alone at his own pace to do the same thing in one week until he catches up and does understand what he has done. So there is a lot of leniency I would say ...

Do they get extra help?

They do. That's why they are having the leniency ...

Is that extra help coming from you as the teacher? Or do you have assistants?

We have enough, I think it comes from both sides, the teacher, the assistant, from the children who sit next to him, as well as the parents ... so with someone like him, a child like that, the assistance will come from all around.

Hafeez Shakeel, though less expansive, employs similar strategies to those used by Shabbir:

What about catering for children of different abilities? Boys with learning problems?

Hafiz Shakeel (translated by Hanif): They just have extra time. And also give them help from older children. They give them extra help.

OK. What about the opposite? Children who are very good?

They are given extra things like extra lines, chapters. He can quickly finish the Qur'an.

Liturgical Literacy and the Wider Islamic Curriculum

Apart from learning how to recite the Qur'an in Arabic, the teachers were also asked about the rest of the curriculum and what it entailed. Given the comments from parents in the previous chapter, it is no surprise to learn how small a part in the teaching time is allotted to general teaching about Islam. However, the success of Maulana Shabbir's new school may be down to the increased and systematic time devoted to the Islamic religion in general. However, Shabbir is a realist and recognises the pressures on his young students. In order to incorporate a more extensive curriculum, that would include more general teaching of Islam, something would have to give. He is adamant that the mosque's primary duty is to facilitate the acquisition of the community's liturgical literacy. What he terms the 'basics', how to read the Qur'an, how to perform ablution and how to pray, are essential for a Muslim for the rest of his or her life. He is concerned that time spent on more general matters would be time lost for this more fundamental aim. He recognises that the young person is already giving two hours of every day to the acquisition of liturgical literacy, and is loathe to encroach any further on his or her time:

Apart from learning the Qur'an what else is taught?

Maulana Shabbir: Well, firstly, the common thing which I think is taught in every single mosque or *madrassah* is the basics ... *iman* [faith] ... *salah* [prayer] ... *taharah* [purification] ... *hajj* [pilgrimage] ... *zakat* [alms giving] ... the basic things of Islam ...

How are they taught these things? Is there a time set aside for this?

I think in every single mosque ... they always start off with the Qur'an recitation first, that is always a must at the beginning and once they complete their Qur'an recitation and they have learnt everything the teacher has taught them in that lesson, then they go on to the next stage of whatever the timetable has set for them ... so, for example, on Mondays they would learn about faith ... the 6 or 8 *kalimahs* that are known ... the important beliefs of Islam ... they would learn those and then the day after concerning *salah* ...

Is that as rigorous a part of the general teaching as the Qur'an in the mosques?

What do you mean?

In the sense that, one of the things I hear from parents is that they want more of that. They're not saying they want less Qur'an, but I don't see how you can do both to the same degree. More of one thing will result in less of the other ...

You see, with children, what you have to understand is that they remember something today and they forget it tomorrow ... it's just like a person becomes a perfect driver once they have their own car ... and he keeps on driving ... until they can do everything blind because they have had the practice day in day out – same thing with children, if you were to do the extra things that parents are saying, then these essentials which are part of life for them in the future, like for example, the memorising of *salah*, the *fatihah*,[7] the *surahs*, the *tashahud*, the *durood sharif*, the *dua*, the *dua in qunut* and all of these things ... if you were to just teach the child he memorises it and then you move onto greater detail for example the *tafseer*[8] or the translation of the Qur'an and leave it to one side, the child is going to forget, because the child is a child, and until you have it so that the child repeats it every day, like a driver, if he doesn't repeat it every single day, every day he is going to come up with a new mistake, because he is a child, so the essentials have to be repeated every single day ... Now the additional things which some parents suggest, can only be covered if there is time ... now that is one thing that the mosques don't have ... in hand. Time. To teach the additional things. Which are important as well. The limited time is two hours – that's what the community gives for their children. Five days a week. Two hours is little. Three hours – then you break the barrier of children's relaxation time and their leisure time and everything. So the 5 to 7 time is just balanced in between. The additional things can be done, are done up and down the country once a child has become fluent and capable of remembering his essentials ... the basic thing of *wudhu*[9] ... now once a child is explained practically as well verbally how to perform *wudhu'* and he does that every single day at home because his parents make sure he does his *wudhu* and because he is doing it every single day and mum and dad are with him or the teacher in the *masjid* ... is implementing that with him ... practically or verbally through books or taking them into the *wudhu* room, making them *wudhu*, so he knows that that this is what he has to do every day, wash my hands first, read the *dua*s, wash my hands, gargle the mouth, nose, so he knows this practice five days a week because he is doing it ...

Hafeez Shakeel, on the other hand, has less to say on this subject. His problem is possibly a language-related one. There is no doubt that he is a gifted individual and older members of the community testify to his eloquence and erudition when speaking on religion. He has at his disposal a veritable treasure-house of engaging and moving teaching stories and verse.

Sadly, for many of the younger members of the community, these riches are denied them by their lack of or imprecise knowledge of Urdu (see Chapter 9).

Traditionally, the Muslim community in all parts of the Islamic world would receive significant instruction on their religion by means of the Friday sermon. The eloquence and erudition of this imam delivered through a delightful sequence of teaching stories and poetry in the Friday sermon would, in different circumstances, serve as an ideal teaching context for the whole community. Unfortunately, as the language of the sermon becomes more and more detached from the needs of the congregation, so its teaching value diminishes and a viable meaningful alternative needs to be considered. The uncertain responses below reveal the sensitivities around this subject in the 'University Road' mosque:

> *How do the children get taught about their religion? Apart from namaz and wudhu and how to do it ... here in the mosque?*
>
> [Long discussion in Mirpuri-Punjab.]
>
> *What about teachings from the life of the Prophet?*
>
> **Hafiz Shakeel** (translated by Hanif): Yes, we do teach them ...
>
> *When does it happen?*
>
> Once a week, on a Friday ...
>
> *So there's a different programme on a Friday?*
>
> It is about *salat* ...
>
> *Does that mean you are talking to the children on Friday then?*
>
> Yeah.

It is perhaps this aspect of the mosque school, along with the question of language usage, that drew most vociferous opinion from my respondents. Again, it is an interesting coincidence that the mosque school curriculum has fallen under the gaze of the outside world, in particular that of the government and the media. Recent UK government initiatives have sought to intervene in discussions around appropriate curricula for mosque schools and *madrassahs*. The UK department, Communities and Local Government, has recently published a series of documents and policy statements seeking to stake a claim in the further development of mosque curricula and in the appointment of staff. With the general heading of 'Preventing violent extremism: Winning hearts and minds' it seeks to lay the ground for a policy initiative designed to tackle the issue of radicalisation among, in particular, Muslim youth (DCLG, 2006). A key document accompanying the series (Choudhury, 2007) identified a number of recommendations including a large-scale review of Muslim institutions:

The appeal of extremist groups reflects, in part, the failure of traditional religious institutions and organisations to connect with young people and address their questions and concerns. Religious institutions and organisations must be able to connect to young people, address their needs and concerns ... .This could be undertaken by a commission on faith and education in Britain, which could explore how religious education is delivered in all minority faith communities. Its remit could include the training needs and employment opportunities and conditions of those who provide religious education as well as the role of faith institutions and of faith and non-faith schools. (Choudhury, 2007: 32–33)

The document quite clearly places part of the blame for the development of radicalisation at the door of the mosque school. It contains no suggestion that mosque schools have been successful in anything, despite the fact that thousands of young Muslims are perhaps better decoders of Classical Arabic than they are of English; despite the fact that young British Muslims still identify themselves with their religion more readily than with their ethnicity, and as a consequence, have a different approach to socially demanding issues such as the drinking of alcohol, casual sex and the treatment of the elderly; and despite the fact that hardly any mosque school has ever sought or been allowed local government funding and most have relied heavily on the 'self-help' principle to get established and be maintained.

The document goes on to claim that 'a lack of religious literacy and education appears to be a common feature among those drawn to extremist groups' (Choudhury, 2007: 33) This is more understandable given the demands on the resources of those with the responsibility of teaching in the mosque school. Whilst the central aim of all mosque schools remains the acquisition of Qur'anic literacy, there will be no *time* for anything else. Though, to my knowledge, the 7/7 bombers attended mosque schools, the majority of their classmates did not follow in their footsteps.

Decoding and Understanding

When it came to understanding what is being read in the Qur'an, the teachers were clearly united. There was no time to teach the understanding of the Qur'an in the very little time that was allowed. Only by going on to a college of further Islamic education would it be possible to begin understanding the language of the Qur'an. And even then, it might not be that straightforward. In Chapter 2: Children, it was shown that the children interviewed had a rather rudimentary knowledge of the words they were reciting and none of them could explain the meaning of the most recited verses in the Muslim world, the *Fatihah*. Mufti Siddiq's five sons are all *hufaaz*[10] of the Qur'an (they know the entire 600-page Qur'an by heart). Yet were someone to ask even the oldest son to explain the meaning of a particular page or section, he would be unable to do so without the aid of an Urdu or English commentary. This lack of knowledge of the meaning of the Arabic words of the Qur'an, unfortunately, sometimes extends to those in the community who claim authority on its behalf. Many UK-based imams working in Pakistani-heritage mosques would also be hard pressed to come up with an explanation for a selected Qur'anic passage without recourse to an Urdu translation and commentary.

Where do you teach the understanding of the Qur'an?

Hafiz Shakeel (translated by Hanif): We just read the Qur'an. In Arabic. They don't understand it. It takes time to understand it.

In Pakistan, does that understanding come later?

Yes, afterwards. When they have finished the Qur'an.

For example, if I were to pick any page from the Qur'an, and asked you to explain to me what it is saying, could you do that?

Abdul Ghafoor (son of Mufti Siddiq): I won't be able to do that ...

What do you have to do, to get to that stage?

You have to go to the Dar-ul-Uloom ...

If I were to ask a normal imam in a mosque in Rotherham or in another large town the same thing, would he be able to explain it from the Arabic?

If the imam had good knowledge then he would be able to, but not many of them ...

There's no guarantee that he would be able to then?

No.

Would he need an Urdu explanation?

Yes.

Summary

In this chapter I have attempted, whilst giving an account of the personnel and methodology involved in the teaching of liturgical literacy, to suggest some of the tension that exists at this particular temporal nexus created by changing patterns of language use. Despite the time-honoured and reliable teaching methods employed for the transmission of liturgical literacy, more contemporary issues keep intruding to problematicise the process. The use of English in the mosque, and the related issue of Roman script, is a topic to which I shall return in Part 4: Languages. The need to equip young people with a more informed knowledge of their religion, as they seek to accommodate their faith within the wider social and ever-more secular environment, is exercising teachers' minds as well as those of the parents we heard in the previous chapter. The teachers, however, do not always have the final say in what is taught in the mosques. And, increasingly, there is intense interest from outside of the Muslim community about the nature of teaching and learning in the mosque school. It is still too early to evaluate the effect of the setting up of a national body for the accreditation of imams. Lord Ahmed of Rotherham has recently proposed a 'Mosques and Imams National Advisory Board' and it is, as I write, treading a wary pathway through the political and religious pitfalls that are bound to lie in wait for any such national body given the diversity and often sectarian differences characterising Muslim communities in the UK. In the next chapter I will examine the role that the administrators play within the mosque and the community.

Notes

1. Among the competing 'schools of thought' regarding the most appropriate way to introduce children to the written code when teaching initial reading, synthetic phonics is a method which relies on introducing ever-larger units of shape-sound correspondences (letter – name, letter – sound, letter + vowel sound, syllables, monosyllabic words and so on). This might be characterised as 'bottom-up' methodology. In contrast to this, analytic phonics relies on the teacher introducing meaningful units of sound (i.e. short words) to a child/learner and then breaking the word down into its constituent parts and, similarly, might be interpreted as a 'top-down' approach.
2. *'alif, bah, tah'* are the first three letters of the Arabic alphabet.
3. This Arabic phrase means in English 'In the name of God, the most Merciful, most Compassionate' and is the saying by which most Muslims begin significant actions, both religious and secular.
4. *'tashkeel'* is the system of diacritic marks that represent vowels and other features of pronunciation and which a reader must know in order to pronounce correctly words in the Qur'an.
5. These are different examples of *'tashkeel'*.
6. More examples of *'tashkeel'*.
7. This and the Arabic words that follow in this sentence are all examples of different prayers a child has to know in order to perform the daily prayer.
8. *'Tafseer'* is the science of understanding the meaning of the Qur'an.
9. Ritual ablution.
10. Plural of *'hafeez'*, someone who has memorised the entire Qur'an.

Chapter 6
Organisers

Vignette: Qurban Hussain

Qurban Hussain arrived in the UK in 1955 when he was 17 years old. He worked as a steelworker for 35 years and retired on grounds of ill health in 1980. He always sits in the same place in the mosque, to the right by the wall, against which he rests when not engaged in his prayers. He is an acute observer of the life of the mosque, attending most prayers, although his ill health has recently obliged him to spend periods of time in the hospital. He is the chairman of the mosque, though no one is quite sure how he came to this position. There were other trustees, but most have died and have not been replaced. When he speaks about the mosque he speaks with a passion that illustrates his intimate involvement with its past, present and future. His life, the life of the community and the life of the mosque are all interwoven and in order to understand one of these elements it is necessary to understand them all. For the first 10 years of his life in Rotherham, he had little time for praying and going to mosques. Twice a year he took the bus and travelled through the industrial areas west of Rotherham and east of Sheffield to the suburb of Attercliffe where Eid prayers were held in a converted house. Here he met up with friends and relatives who lived in Sheffield. And, twice a year, he thought it would be a good thing to have a similar place in Rotherham, but it would be 10 years before practical steps were taken to achieve this desire. By 1968 it was clear that the community needed a mosque, as much for meeting together as for a place of worship. However, at this time, though not yet an issue, the future Islamic education of the community's children was to become a deciding factor in getting things moving. What to buy and where to buy it was more of a concern than how. The community prided itself on the principle of 'self help' and rarely if ever asked the Town Council for help. On those few occasions when they had asked, a rejection was the usual response. Qurban went from house to house in the community, and on Fridays from town to town where mosques were already established, to ask for donations towards purchasing a place. A large non-denominational chapel had become available near to the town centre and the funds were available for its purchase. The building was purchased in 1968 and opened as a mosque the following year, in 1969. Qurban and those closely involved with collecting the funds for the purchase and upkeep of the mosque were now the trustees and they quickly appointed someone from back home to come to Rotherham to serve as its first imam. The next 10 years were exciting times for Qurban as he tried to balance his work at the steelworks with his responsibilities as the chairman of the mosque. Much of his time in the initial years was spent organising, funding and doing the considerable refurbishment the old chapel needed in order for it to function as a mosque. The heavy wooden pews had to be removed as did the large heavy wooden pulpit with its accompanying large wooden plaques emblazoned with Biblical quotations that would not be appropriate in the new mosque. The building would be being used at least five times a day rather than once or twice a week and so the heating system had to be replaced to cope with the greater demand. The two other sources of great expense and worry were the carpet and the ablution facilities. Qurban was able to arrange for a small extension to be built on the side of the chapel to accommodate the toilets and washing facilities. The mosque also benefited in the early days by a benefactor who, although not Mirpuri like the rest of the community, was of Indian descent and was a successful local businessman. He paid for the carpet. Qurban made sure a quality vacuum cleaner was purchased at the same time. Towards the end of the 1980s, the community was beginning to be affected by sectarian disputes. Qurban found himself in the middle of these disputes which at one time led to physical confrontation between members of the community and sadly a large part of the community felt the need to leave and buy their own mosque. In 1969 there was one mosque. By 2001 there were seven.

Introduction

Many mosques in the UK were established in a similar way. The men who were most closely involved with the collection of funds and the subsequent purchase of the building usually became the trustees. All mosques, if they are to benefit from charitable status, must set up a trust that acts as the body responsible for the mosque and its activities. The trust itself can vary in its power and authority. Sometimes the trust functions as a collegiate body which discusses and makes decisions jointly. This is certainly the case with one of the mosques in the community. Indeed, the trustees of this mosque went so far as to appoint a larger committee made up of other members of the community in order to incorporate a larger cross-section of views. The secretary of 'Church Walk' mosque wanted to widen participation in decision-making, partly as a means of warding off criticism:

> *Mahmood:* Well, it used to be the trustees responsible. Later on we realised, it is hard to satisfy everybody. Because of public involvement ... They will always be making criticisms ... Sometimes we have chairman, secretary, trustee, but at other times wider community involvement. So we always set up a small committee. Between 20 to 30 people. They keep the community happy ...

The other mosque in this study, in theory, has a trust. However, in practice, one man makes decisions, although he is assisted by a secretary and a treasurer. Here is one of the more charitable views about the mosque chairman:

> *Wajib:* Our mosque committee ... there's only one person who's the committee and everything ... Mr Hussain . He's a trustee ... and he's the committee ... He's the chairman, he's everything. At the moment.

The Role of the Trustees of the Mosque

It may appear, to those outside of the community and even to some within it, that these men have accrued to themselves a considerable amount of authority within the community. After all, they have the power to recruit, hire and fire the imam of the mosque and also decide how all the not-inconsiderable collected funds are spent. Yet for all their critics, these men spend a great deal of their own time working on behalf of the community. They are in the positions they are as a result of the work they did when their respective mosques were being established. Furthermore, the work they did in the collection of funds almost *ipso facto* resulted in their privileged position at the end of the process. Another vital factor contributing to their positions is that many of these men also invested considerable amounts of their own money, as well as time, in the purchase of the mosque

> *Wajib:* Oh yes. They put their own money. They put in quite a lot of effort. Obviously. We always used to go with my father to different towns to collect money, knock on people's doors, we're building a mosque. I can remember that. We went to Derby, Bolton, around the Midlands.

> *Mahmood:* In the beginning there were five trustees. And then some people, for some reason, wanted to be involved in the mosque. Outside people. And they always raised questions about the mosque, different things, so we decided, me and Pasha and some people, best way let these people involve some more in real terms, don't let them speak away from the mosque, better inside, so we added a few trustees, those active people, who speak all the time, sometimes in favour sometimes against. And then we were nine. At the moment, most of them, four or five have died. So we are three left. Because we are closest to buying the opposite land, now because we are all in our 60s, so we are thinking even in the process of appointing new trustees. Young men. More educated.

As the last few comments above suggest, there is a realisation among the trustees that the younger generation need some involvement in the running of their mosque.

Responsibilities of the Trustees

The main responsibilities of the trustees are to appoint the imam and to maintain and develop the mosque as a building and as a centre for worship and learning. The way in which they appoint, and the terms and conditions of employment for, an imam vary. In one mosque the latest imam was recruited from Pakistan through 'word of mouth'. The previous imam had accepted a post in another northern town and needed to be replaced.

Who appoints the imam?

Ghulam (translated by Hanif): Yes, the trustees.

How did you recruit him?

It is done by word of mouth. We have contacts. Maybe, someone in another mosque will say we have a very good imam and tell us. Our imam is from Pakistan, not finding in this country.

The imam before the present one was an Indian, wasn't he?

Yes. He was Indian. He had been here all fifteen years. He has now moved to Preston.

In the other mosque, the present imam was appointed after the dismissal of the previous incumbent, the English-speaking Maulana Shabbir.

Munir: Maulana Shabbir he left, he had an argument with my brother, you know. He used to go the mosque, not giving him education about Islam. He just go there, and he was doing something there against Islam, in the mosque, and Maulana Shabbir, is giving like a punishment, not giving an education, so Hameed went there and he said to him, why are you not giving him an education, he's coming to the mosque. So he had an argument with him, and actually, they all blamed Hameed, he expelled him from the mosque, and this is what happened. Everybody, says that Hameed he did that. And everybody was happy with Shabbir. But also Shabbir made up his mind that he wanted to move from here, he wanted to start his own place, a private, giving education.

How did you recruit the imam?

Mahmood: But we are lucky, you know, most of the time somebody always approached us wanting a job. I am not sure what the legal terms are, but I think most of our imams have been self employed rather than employed by the mosque. Even if given set wage, but because responsibility legal was so high, we are all volunteers. We are not getting penny out of this position. Purely voluntary work. So we decided, tax affairs, insurance affairs, other legal things, they know what they are getting, but they are responsible for their own selves.

The terms and conditions of employment of the imam are a sensitive issue with some members of the community. The trustees who employ the imam would argue that they are paying the imam a fair wage, particularly if compared to wages that would be received for the same job back home in Pakistan. If accommodation is also included in the package, as it is with one of the imams, their argument is a little sounder. However, in terms of the national UK minimum wage structure, these imams are being paid very little and it could be argued that these men and their families are living below the poverty line. For men with such impressive qualifications, as mentioned in the previous chapter, the mosques are getting a bargain. However, as happened with Maulana Shabbir, as it becomes more acceptable to recruit imams from UK-based seminaries such as the Dar-ul-Uloom in Bury or the Dar-ul-Uloom in Dewsbury, the trustees will have to re-examine the rates of pay they currently operate for their imams. As we also saw in the last chapter, there is the added factor of relatively well-paid salaried posts now available in the prison and health services attracting well-qualified imams, and, equally importantly, imams with knowledge and expertise of working with and within the local communities.

> *Mahmood:* ...but we can't get people. It's difficult to pay. Paying one year it's £50. This is the problem. People cannot afford, because the majority of the people they are without work, they can't pay this money. And the committee they are only getting from those people who have been paying for a long time. Only they who are paying every year, they only pay. And a lot of people are coming without money, and children also, they are getting education but they can't afford it, this is the main thing.
>
> They are paying £150 a week to the imam. Other teacher is getting £50. Those two are getting £200 a week. And they also have another mosque in Wordsworth Road, Eastfield. There are three teachers there. They are getting the same money. And it is a big burden for the community. The big problem is money, otherwise it's ok. They can get a qualified person.
>
> *Maulana Shabbir:* There again, it boils down to the committee ... what they set for the imam ... that is all I can really say on that ... it varies ... it depends on what type of duties they are doing and how they set the duties ...

Could I ask, for example, over the past 20 years, could I safely assume that those sort of things have improved?

No, they haven't improved ... I mean the imams, to be honest, like I said, this is a question for the committee, who can really answer it, to actually find out what the salaries are ... as far as I understand it imams are low paid ...

What do you mean by 'low paid'?

I mean they aren't paid the minimum wage, that's what we would say ... I don't know for what reason but that's the type of salary ...

Is it tradition for the mosque to provide accommodation?

Yes, it is.

Would that be free?

That again, I couldn't comment on that ...

But that sometimes happens? You get a house?

That does happen.

When you have an imam from Pakistan, do you have to find him somewhere to live?

Ghulam (translated by Hanif): Yes, for time being.

Is there accommodation in the mosque?

Yes. We have bought a house in Charles Street.

Once an imam is appointed, his contract is decided by the trustees. There appears to be rather a 'grey area' surrounding the status of the imam in respect of the mosque. In one mosque, the imam is 'employed' by the mosque only on a 'self-employed' basis. Whether this is to create greater flexibility for the imam or to avoid additional expenses on the part of the mosque remains to be seen, but suffice it to say that the current imam has little in the way of employee rights, were he to seek them.

Mahmood: I think most of our imams have been self-employed rather than employed by the mosque. Even if given set wage, but because responsibility legal was so high, we are all volunteers. We are not getting penny out of this position. Purely voluntary work. So we decided, tax affairs, insurance affairs, other legal things, they know what they are getting, but they are responsible for their own selves.

Running the Mosque: Self-sufficiency

This apparent avoidance of making the imam an employee of the mosque and all the legalities that that entails is linked to a more general tendency within the community to rely on itself and to avoid as much as possible legal agreements with officialdom and other outside agencies. Ballard describes how peasant farmers back home in Mirpur operate very much a similar practice to that demonstrated by the mosque trustees in Rotherham. This is one of the more positive aspects of the complex social system of kinship favours generally referred to as *biraderi*:

> Over and above a taken-for-granted awareness of the benefits that can accrue from collective activity – as, for example, in the extended family – peasant farmers are invariably strongly committed to self-sufficiency. Bitter experience has long since taught them that outsiders are not to be trusted, especially when they are the tax-gathering agents of rapacious landlords and rulers: peasants therefore invariably place an extremely high premium on independence and autonomy. In the context of a working assumption that outsiders will never have anything but their own exploitative interests at heart, peasants routinely mistrust everyone but their own immediate kin. (*The Impact of Kinship*, n.d.)

This is exemplified by the attitude of one of the trustees to seeking planning permission. A building has become available opposite the mosque and would be an ideal site for developing the mosque's facilities. One of their urgent needs is for a place to educate the girls of the community separately from the boys. However, at present, the site is a vehicle mechanic's and would need planning permission, if bought, to be converted into a place of worship or a place of learning. The chairman of the mosque trust feels they should purchase the place first and then seek permission:

> *Mahmood:* Because he is selling it (a yard across from the mosque), we decided that if we did not buy it we would lose the chance for progress. So we consulted our members and we decided that if we buy it, in the future, we might need some plans, we don't know, we can use it for many many things. We could extend the mosque. We could make the bottom part a car park and the top part for making *wudhu*. Or it could be a facility for girls. Muslim girls don't like to be taught with the boys ... And if we can do it, there is already a small building there ...
>
> *Have you bought it already?*
>
> Yeah [though I think there was some misunderstanding here].
>
> *Do you have to have permission from the council in order to do things with it?* ·
>
> We have not asked them because if we end up on the losing side of it,

we won't be able to buy it. But if we buy it as a garage, then they will go away.

Some officials are personally good. But as a policy, I don't think there is a good policy. And I don't want them involved too much, because sometimes it becomes too restrictive.

This reluctance to seek close contact with the Town Council in respect of the mosque is also fuelled by the council's own apparent reluctance to look favourably upon requests in the past. Both chairmen of their respective mosques are united in their disdain for the local council, and their lack of enthusiasm to support the local Muslim community in the town and often compare them very unfavourably with the councils of other major towns and cities.

Mahmood: As far as I know, there is no special relationship, but when we were in the past, the politician or MP, or local council leader, or the Mayor, these people asked to speak to our congregation, we always give permission. Otherwise, I don't see not much in this town. And this is my biggest complaint. Because I am not too clever, don't know how to approach it, in different towns the council is a lot better than in Rotherham. We have paid everything by the community, the land, the mosque, all the bills, even ...

There is no council grant?

No there is nothing. They don't even know we exist here or something. Even we asked the car park there for many many years. We never had a positive response.

Have you ever tried to get any help?

Ghulam (translated by Hanif): I have tried when I bought this one for a community centre. They offered me £145. And I rejected that. I said I don't want it.

£145?

£145. I remember because general hospital built it new, before that it was Oakwood Hospital. When they built a new property, I collected, I remember, £200 or something from my people and I gave it to council. For the hospital. And Keith Simpson, councillor in charge, he offered £145 to Ahmed ... . Ahmed told me. I said no. I asked everybody.

That wouldn't even pay for a carpet ...

Council gave me a headache. This extension. This extension has got a flat roof. It's leaking all the time. Three times the Council has rejected our claim. Planning permission to put pitched roof. We keep repairing, it keeps leaking, what can we do? Last time, when I applied again, John Holt, the architect, he keeps trying, to do half, pitched roof and half make extension. To change the toilet area.

So the Council has been difficult about it?

I don't know why. I am not saying. But the Council has never done us any favours. When I bought this mosque, they didn't give me planning permission. I got a solicitor and went to court. Glister. And when it went to court, Glister says, 'why are you not giving it to him planning for this place?' It is a residential area, they said. And that's why people need a place to pray! Not make a mosque in the jungle! That's what he said. Then the council couldn't answer. Then he said, 'You give him part three of this paper' ... because he pays rates, he pays taxes, for many years he is working, he is asking me in quite friendly way ... two people he ask the question, how long you been in this country, how long you been working here, do you pay tax, I told him, when I come in, working from the mill, 7 days, 6 day week, then I pay tax, insurance, I pay rates, the solicitor said why you ... these people ... plan ...

Qurban: Also we have a problem with a community centre. If you go to other towns, they have very good community centres, the local government has helped with this. But in this town, there is no help from Council. They have been struggling, when my big brother was alive, he had meetings with the Council ... but still we have a problem. Nobody is helping. Just this council in Rotherham. They don't do anything. For our community. I mean if anything happens like someone dying, everybody is coming here, but there is no big room. And people in other towns, if anybody passes away, they go to that community centre. They have everything there, all arrangements, like if people come from other towns, for eating, you know, and they do everything in the community centre, for people don't go in their houses, because there is no big room. It is our culture, we do that things. Custom, you know like. So this is very important – a community centre.

The Mosque and the Town

These strong feelings towards the Council reveal an aspect of the community that transcends any sectarian differences there might be within the community itself. Both mosques and their members, who have been involved with the running of their establishments since their inception, claim to have met nothing but resistance from official agencies. The community, existing as it does within a context of economic deprivation and social marginalisation, finds itself, even after 50 years, on the periphery of mainstream affairs. An illustration of this marginalisation can be found in a local history society's website (*The History of Rotherham*, n.d.) which in its survey of the industrial history of the town in the post-war years makes no mention of the Mirpuri community and the contribution it made to the steel industry and other important local industries such as Beatson Clark. Many of the older men interviewed for this study mentioned periods of employment in the enormous bottle-making factory just north of the town centre. Indeed, on a visit there to a pupil engaged in work experience during the 1990s, I was shown a prayer room created for the Muslim employees of the factory.

> *Munir:* At Beatson Clark. I went there in 1963. We had a prayer room upstairs, because everyone watching we decided we wanted a room. You know people were watching what we were doing and we said no. So that's why they gave us a room. In 1963, when I started there there was only one person who used to pray. And at that time the people, six people were working, on the machines there, sorting bottles, and when it was time coming for prayer, he finished and went upstairs, to read, to pray, then he come back because those 5 people keep working and he says it's my prayer time so he's left the job and gone upstairs … It's very very difficult because only 15 minute break tea time and half an hour you know snap so there was no time for prayer. I mean if anyone wanted to pray he can pray during the time. Snap time and break time. But there is only a few people there now. There is not any more Muslims there.

Adapting to New Times: Language

We saw in Chapter 4: Parents that there was pressure in the community for the mosques to adapt to the new situation of growing numbers of children attending the mosque with little or no knowledge of Mirpuri-Punjabi, making it difficult for the Mirpuri-Punjabi-speaking imams to communicate with their young students. There was also considerable pressure for the mosques to incorporate more teaching about Islam rather than a limited course of instruction in learning to read the Qur'an. Wajib is a parent who has similar concerns. He is not alienated from the mosque and works with the trustees carrying out certain duties. One of his duties is to make the collection before the prayer on Fridays. His father was involved with the initial purchase of the first Rotherham mosque in 1969:

> *Wajib:* My father was a trustee. But he's dead now. In 1997. He was a trustee and a founder of the mosque.

He has, however, approached the chairman with some ideas about changing the mosque's curriculum and introducing the English language.

Is there anything you would like to change?

Wajib: The teachers need to teach the basic teachings of Islam. This is what we lack.

In English?

Bilingual. Urdu and Potwari as well.

If this meant they would spend less time learning how to read the Qur'an, would this matter?

I have been saying that, for the past, since my father died, 10 years. I have been trying without any luck.

Is English used in the mosque at all?

I think one of the lads who is teaching he speaks English. The imam doesn't speak any English, might speak some broken English, might try and communicate in broken English, but it doesn't have the same effect, does it?

What would have to happen for it to change?

A lot. You tell me. [laughter]

Who's got the power in the mosque? Who can make things change? That chap you were talking about?

Yes. He's got the power. I mean ... I don't think he's personally interested in that matter. I have mentioned it in front of him and I have mentioned it in front of other people as well that we're lacking and I think it's like knocking my head against a brick wall. I've given up on it now.

Have you spoken with the imam?

The imam is in favour of it. The others are in favour of it.

What about parents? Would they support you?

They would support me, but I know for a fact that if the system I was thinking about was introduced and it started showing results sooner than later then the parents would support me as well because they need to see some results. Positive results for parents. You know what I mean? If there are no results, I mean, parents contribute towards the mosque ... the running of the mosque ... I don't know ... I don't think there is any extra income from outside the mosque ... from the government or anything like that ... if there is I don't know anything about it ... it's run on voluntary contributions ...

Wajib highlights here a significant gap between the generation of the trustees, all members of the first generation (described in Chapter 4: Parents) and the second generation, all of whom have children passing through the mosque school at the moment. The prevailing view of the trustees, as articulated by the respective chairmen, is that the present system is adequate and doing a good job.

Firstly, in respect of the language question, one chairman interviewed had very few concerns and appeared not to appreciate that there may be a problem:

> *Do you think it is important for the children to speak English in the mosque?*
>
> **Mahmood:** Oh, yeah. Can speak any language in the mosque. Mosque has never been restricted to a language.
>
> *What about the teacher or the teaching?*
>
> If the teacher can speak English we are very happy, but if he can't because there's no requirement ... if anyone wants to learn the Qur'an, English is not a requirement of it at all. You say, *alhamdu lillah*, not 'how are you?' Do you see, so the child, I want for Qur'an better Arabic teacher. With better pronunciation. Better ability. Who can convince the children this is the way to read. Can teach better. But for communication, English is our language today.

His main concern is that the teacher is extremely well-versed in Arabic and that, all things being equal, this was the *sine qua non* for effective instruction in the mosque. In a sense, he is correct because without the necessary command of Arabic the main teaching objective, learning to read the Qur'an, will not be met. Yet he is not too bothered that English is not used in the mosque.

Adapting to New Times: Curriculum

In terms of the mosque's curriculum, both chairmen are satisfied with the provision offered to students and parents:

> *What do you expect the imam to teach the children?*
>
> **Mahmood:** Because we are living in a non-Muslim society, my sole priority is to learn the very basics of Islam. That's my priority. That for a mosque we cannot expect more. It is not that institution where you can learn classical things. Very simple, everyone knows their *Al-Fatiha*, reading the Qur'an, recitation, what we teach in the funerals, you know, different things ... basic ... introduction of the Qur'an ...

How do you feel about the education for the children in the mosque? How important is that for you and the community?

Ghulam (translated by Hanif): Yes, we are quite happy. At least they learn the Qur'an. They know the *salat*. That's the main thing you know.

We see here how the aims of the mosque education and the choice of language are determined by the trustees. Until there is change in the membership of these groups within the respective mosques, there appears to be little likelihood of any substantial change. The fact that Maulana Shabbir was dismissed when he was the only imam using English regularly in the mosque is symptomatic of this attitude.

We end this chapter not with the words of a trustee, but with the words of frustration of a parent who, like Wajib above, has found expecting trustees to change a bit like 'knocking my head against the wall'.

Munir: I think each kid pays about £1.50 per week. But I was saying to Mr Hussain who is the chairman, if the results started coming through the parents would be willing to pay about 4 or 5 pounds a week. If they could see improvement in their kids because no parent wants their kids to go astray from Islam. They are not in favour of that. But we now, as a community, like I myself, and the majority of parents, know that their kids are going astray. And that's one of the reasons why they are going astray because they are not communicating very well, they are not taught. Because I myself personally don't know even the basics of Islam – how can I teach that to my children? If I don't know it myself. And that's why I feel that strongly about it. Because I think there should be more emphasis on that instead, as you said, you know ... I suggested that, you know, you can teach and recite the Qur'an two or three times a week, and the teachings of Islam, what Islam says, why are we fasting, why do we pray, what are the benefits of all these things? They don't know that. I don't know that. How can I tell my kids? The majority of the parents in my age group don't know that. So they can't communicate that to them. When in Pakistan, when the kids are in Kashmir or Pakistan, I mean you don't have to know really all parts of it because you pick it up from the people around you ... But over here what you pick up are bad things ...

Do the children understand the sermon on Fridays?

I don't think they do. They might be able to understand it, but not fully. The older people can understand it, but what's the point of ...

It's in Urdu, isn't it?

What's the point of trying, as they say, to teach old dogs new tricks?
What's the point of teaching the old people? They know most of it.
Why not have more emphasis on the children?

Summary

The tension suggested in Chapter 5: Teachers, is very much evident around the major stakeholders in this chapter. The vested interests of the ageing chairmen and trustees of the two mosques in this study are, at present, delaying any large-scale changes taking place in the structures supporting the maintenance of the teaching of liturgical literacy. In a sense, this is inevitable, and not necessarily a bad thing. The community as a whole has a lot to be grateful to these men for having had the prescience some 30 years ago or more to fund and establish the means to promote and maintain its heritage of liturgical literacy. Indeed, some of the elders involved availed themselves of the opportunity to acquire liturgical literacy for the first time in Rotherham (see Chapter 4: Parents). The model adopted for the institutional transmission of liturgical literacy was a tried and trusted one. The mosques of Rotherham employed imams from back home and they taught in the traditional way. For a time this was more than adequate, and, indeed, the chosen methodology of teaching liturgical literacy remains, and, I suggest, will remain the most effective one available. However, with the changing social and linguistic nature of the community, there is an evidently growing and more vociferous call for change in the mosque's structures. The call, on the one hand, for use of the English language, and on the other, for a more balanced teaching curriculum, is a difficult one for the Chairmen, trustees and other elders to withstand. Many of the issues around language choice and use that fuel these tensions are dealt with in Part 4: Languages. Before, however, moving there, it is important to move from people to places. In Part 3, I will examine the various settings where liturgical literacy takes place, beginning with the principal institution of transmission, the mosque.

Part 3

The Settings for Liturgical Literacy

Chapter 7
Mosques

Vignette: 'Church Walk' Mosque

Standing facing the Jamia Mosque in 'Church Walk' looking east, a constant flow of traffic is at one's back. The two lanes bear commuter and shopper cars, business vans and lorries as they negotiate their way around the town centre. The noise is constant and loud. The fumes are in the air and the air pollution must be high. On the other side of the road, past two more lanes of busy traffic going in the opposite direction, is a grass rectangle separating the road from a large furniture warehouse located in the former 'Midbrough' Independent Chapel and one of the area's most significant, but also neglected, historical monuments, the Walker Mausoleum. The independent chapel was built in 1777 as a breakaway from the main Wesleyan movement. Many of those who broke away were members of the Walker family whose name was closely associated with the iron and steel industry in the 18th century. To reach the mosque from that side of the road it is necessary to take the subway. Facing south from the mosque, the eye follows the bend of the dual carriageway until it reaches the large roundabout with its choice of right to 'Derham', left to the town centre, and straight on to Templebrough and the southern by-pass. Standing in front of the mosque facing east, one can see, on the opposite side of the narrow street on which the mosque is situated, the eyesore of a lorry repair yard, which is just one of the small-scale local businesses that make up the trading estate that now takes the place of the former 19th-century courts and back-to-backs. The site of the lorry repair yard has been offered for sale to the mosque committee, but after a big effort was made to raise the funds for purchase, the owners have reneged on their promise. The owners of the yard complain to the mosque about parking because it hinders their access. To the north, the mosque faces, to the left, a long line of parked cars belonging to employees from the various small businesses on the estate. To the right, a small rectangular piece of wasteland is used for parking also, and was also promised to the mosque, this time by the Town Council. A deposit was paid to the council in the 1980s, but the Council changed its mind and returned the deposit. The tyre suppliers on the opposite side of the parking area have now erected a steel fence to prevent cars accessing the parking area from their side of the road. The mosque suspects no permission has been granted for this fence from the council but are resigned to the feeling that nothing will be done about it and, therefore, do not complain. Every lunchtime the loudspeaker declaims the call to prayer. This is in Arabic and is uttered by the mosque's unofficial caretaker, who

Plate 10 'Church' Walk Mosque and its setting

arrives early every day to vacuum the carpets of the prayer hall and check the central heating. The call to prayer is loud enough for all within 100 metres to hear it, but the noise of the traffic and the small factories often reduces the sound to a muffle. It is unlikely that the nearest Muslim residents, on the opposite side of the dual carriageway, beyond the grass rectangle and behind the large furniture warehouse, can hear the call to prayer. It might be audible in the early morning for the dawn prayer, but council permission has not been forthcoming for the call to prayer at this time. It is unclear as to the feelings of the local workers and other employees when they hear this quintessentially Eastern sound in their little part of South Yorkshire.

Introduction

In accord with the paradigm of literacy study outlined by researchers within the New Literacy Studies (Gee, 1990; Street, 1993; New London Group, 1996), it is also appropriate to examine the physical characteristics of the environment within which liturgical literacy takes place. In this part of the book, I will describe and discuss the homes and the two mosques involved as well as the geographical area in which they are situated.

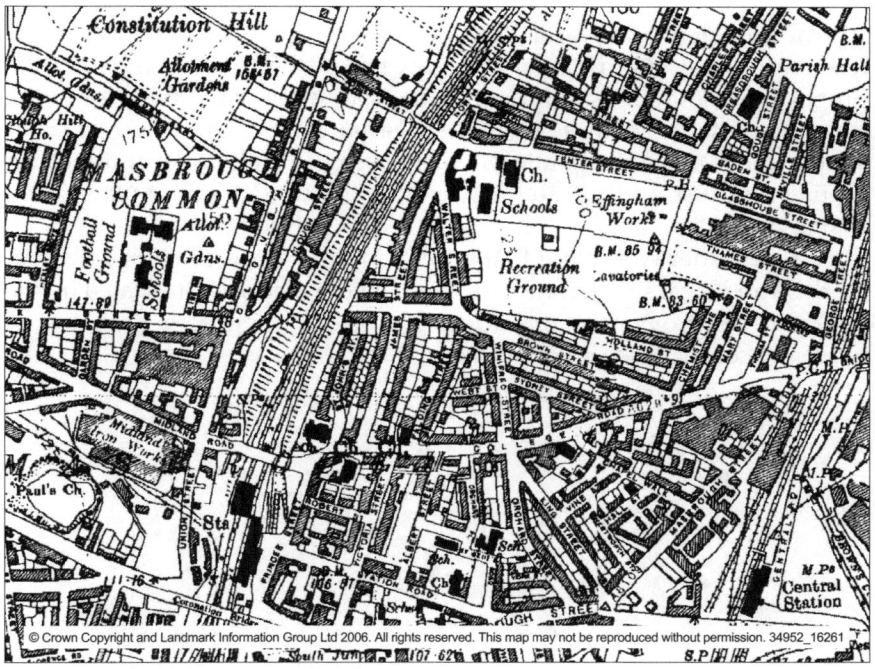

Plate 11 Rotherham and 'Midborough', 1938

Rotherham and 'Midbrough'

The square mile west of Rotherham town centre that contains the districts of 'Midbrough' and 'Derham' is historically very rich. One hundred years ago the heavily-built-up area of today still contained fields and open spaces, with the River Don still providing the principal communication route into the town from the west. An extension of the Sheffield and South Yorkshire Navigation Canal and the Midland Railway line had been constructed alongside its course. However, it was already clear where the future of the area lay, as some of the major iron and steel works (Midland Steel Works, Holmes Rolling Mills) were already well-established and providing increasing opportunities for employment. The Midland Iron works, later to become the bus depot, loomed large in the centre of 'Midbrough', and the railways hemmed the area in with its court houses and two-roomed back-to-backs reaching from the works to the centre of the town.

Rotherham today has six wards that feature in the 10% of the most socio-economically deprived wards in the UK. It has no wards featuring in the

10% of least-deprived wards. Although 10% of indigenous people in the town are unemployed, when it comes to those of Pakistani origin the proportion rises to 25%. 'Midbrough' and 'Derham' lie to the west of the town centre, with 'Midbrough' clustered around the main railway line and station and 'Derham' adjoining the large scrap metal-works and football ground and just north of the Sheffield and South Yorkshire Navigation Canal.

Until just after World War II, the area's industries were manned by local workers and local shops were run and owned by locals as indicated by the typical names from street directories and electoral registers. Residents of the many courts were seldom listed in these sources.

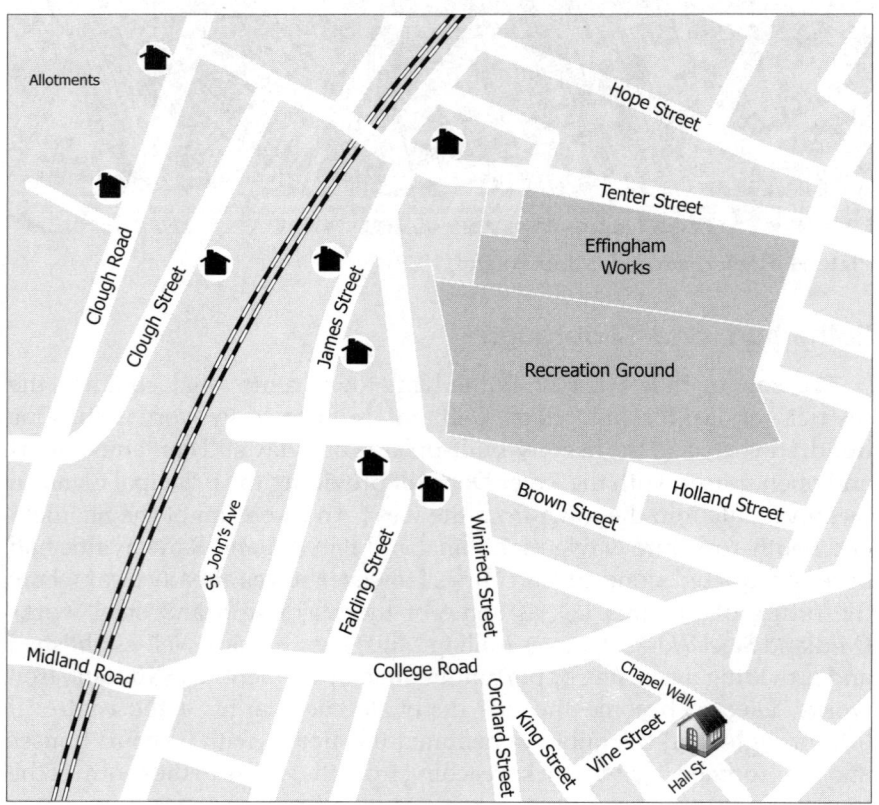

Figure 1 Street map of 'Midbrough' 1938, showing the houses that were later occupied by our interviewees (🏠), and the Wesleyan Reform Chapel (⛪) (later 'Church Walk' Mosque)

'Midbrough' Street, 'Midbrough'
79   Leech Herbert, pork butcher
81   Allen John, boot & shoe maker
83   Bray Henry & Co. grocers
85   Eaton John & Son, pawnbrokers
87   Adams Edwin Newton, grcr (from *Kelly's Directory*, 1888)

The labour shortage after the War led to an increasing demand for unskilled labour to fill vacancies in local industries. The traditionally-mobile Mirpuri community, who were well-represented in British merchant shipping at the time, supplying crew members for ships plying their trade around the world at the twilight of the British Empire, saw opportunities for employment onshore and soon the first Mirpuri settlers began to arrive at the iron and steel, and related, industries in Rotherham. Tenter Street, close to the railway, in 1950, could boast of two Italian residents, Antonio Maccio, at number 65, and Franco Annibaldi, at number 69; its other residents all had local names. By 1970, Mohammad Azam was at number 39, Ali Sher at 43 and Arif Mohammad at 45. We also notice here the custom of buying houses adjacent to one another which characterised the early purchase of houses by the Mirpuri community in the 1960s. In Josephine Road, in 'Derham', the first Mirpuri resident, Mohammad Sultan, appears in the street directory of 1970 which suggests a house purchase sometime in the 1960s. The electoral register for the same year has Mirpuri residents in 'John Street' from numbers 106 to 110, with the exception of 41. In Tenter Street, number 43, which is in the street directory under the name of Ali Sher, has five adult males living in the same house, whilst next door at 45 three adult males reside.

~~723~~	~~Guess, Joan~~	
724	Easthope, Sydney	104
725	Easthope, Iris Ida	104
726	Smith, Frank	106
727	Smith, May	106
728	Griffiths, Frank Anthony	108
729	Griffiths, Sheila Ruth	108
730	Couldwell, John	110
731	Couldwell, Pamela J.	110
732	Griffiths, Monica	112

830	Easthope, Iris Ida	104
831	Mohammed, Din	106
832	Zubeda, Begun Din	106
833	Abdul, Rashid	108
834	Altaf, Hussain—J	108
835	Altaf, Zubaida Begum	108
836	Afsar, Mohammed	108
837	Barasas, Khan	108
838	Mohammed, Riaz—J	110
839	Gulham, Akhter	110
840	Griffiths, Monica	112
841	Griffiths, Alfred	112

Plate 12 104–112 'John Street' 1960   **Plate 13** 104–112 'John Street' 1970

The Origins of 'Church Walk' Mosque

The 'Midbrough' district, therefore, changed dramatically during a period of less than 20 years. The history of the purchase of the local mosques has been described elsewhere (Chapter 6: Organisers). In this chapter I wish to briefly describe the relationship between the community and its institutions of liturgical literacy from a geographical point of view exploring the location of the buildings in relation to the homes of the community.

The mosque that was later to be named Jamia Mosque, or 'Church Walk' Mosque, began its existence as the chapel of the Wesleyan Reform Union. Unsurprisingly, this was located on 'Church Walk', though this street had got its name not from the place of worship in question, but from an earlier

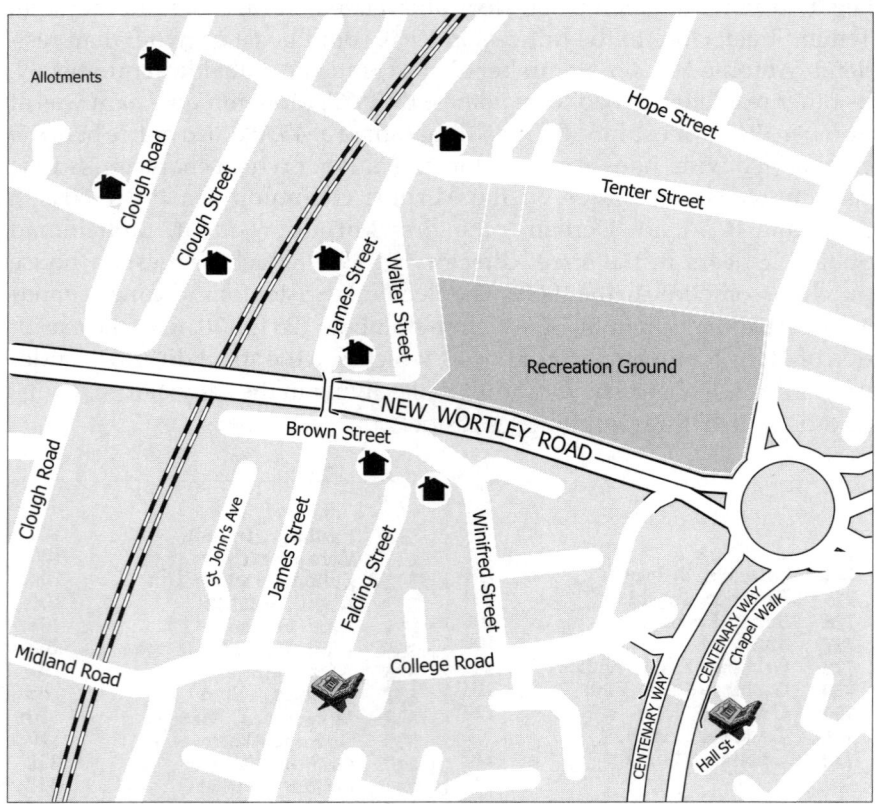

Figure 2 Street map of 'Midbrough' in 2005, new roads separate the homes of our interviewees (🏠) from the two mosques (🕌)

independent chapel built a little earlier situated at the other end of the street at its junction with 'University Road'.

The Rotherham and District Year Book mentions that the chapel was built in 1872, and a contemporary newspaper reported the event:

> New Wesleyan Reform Chapel at Masbro' – the members of the Masbro' Wesleyan Reform Church have determined upon the erection of a new chapel, and the cornerstone of the edifice will be laid on Monday afternoon. We understand that much success has attended the endeavours of the Church in this direction, but still there is great need of help from friends of the cause. The ceremony will be performed by S.H. Burrows, Esq., of Sheffield, to whom will be presnted a handsomely engraved silver trowel, from the establishment of Mr J. Mason, Jeweller, of High Street. It will bear the following inscription: 'Presented to H.H. Burrows, Esq., of Sheffield, on the occasion of laying the corner stone of the new Wesleyan Reform Chapel, Chapel Walk, Masbro', January 22nd, 1872'.

At the turn of the 19th century, services were held each Sunday at 2.30 and 6.00pm. Its 'pulpits are supplied with local preachers' (Plate 14).

The chapel was not exclusively a place of worship during its history, for a Sunday School took place regularly at the beginning of the 20th century. An early photograph (Plate 15) shows the Sunday School class presenting their work in the form of a display with their teachers. The children appear to have been working on the attributes of God or Christ and have chosen to present these both graphically through large card shapes as well as through text. The boy to the extreme left of the picture (one of the few boys in the photograph) has chosen to use the shape of a castle to illustrate his slogan 'New Heart Castle'. The rest of the boys and girls are presenting a message

---

WESLEYAN REFORM UNION.

This Methodist body has a Circuit called the Rotherham and Mexbro' Circuit which includes among its Churches, Societies at Masbro', Mexbro' Dalton, Parkgate, High Thorn, Swinton, and Bowbroom. The pulpits are supplied with local preachers. The local Chapel is situated in Chapel Walk, Masbro', and was built in 1872. The officers are—President : Mr C. Adams ; Secretary : Mr. A. Bailey, 28, Orchard Street ; Stewards : Messrs. L. Brierley and J. Hall. Services are held each Sunday at 2.30 and 6 p.m.

Plate 14 Extract from 'Rotherham and District' Yearbook

Plate 15 Wesleyan Reform Chapel (later 'Church Walk' Mosque) circa 1900
(By permission of Rotherham MBC, Archives and Local Studies Service, Photo 4409)

to the camera finishing with the uplifting ' ... Night and Day, In Mercy, At Death, Through Christ, How God Keeps, In Perfect Peace ... ' with each child having a shape, either a heart or a cross, featuring their words. The children are standing outside the chapel next to the north-facing wall in front of the exterior steps, which lead to the side entrance of the chapel. Their teachers, one male and one female, look appropriately pleased and proud of their students as they contribute to both their children's religious knowledge and their literacy. In the top-right corner it is just possible to see the rooftop of one of the terraced houses immediately behind the chapel.

The educating dimension of this photograph is clear and emphasises the reinforcing role that Sunday Schools played, and, to a much more limited extent, still play, in the acquisition of literacy, where much of the learning to read and write encountered in primary school was supported by activity in the church and chapel Sunday schools. No such obvious reinforcing role, as yet, exists for liturgical literacy in respect of learning how to read and write in English in contemporary primary and secondary schools. However, it has been reported elsewhere how the intensive experience of learning how to decode in Arabic in the mosque appears to have a beneficial effect on the ability to decode in general (Rosowsky, 2001).

Plate 16 Interior of Wesleyan Reform Chapel circa 1900
(*By permission of Rotherham MBC, Archives and Local Studies Service, Photo 4410*)

The large slogan in the chapel itself situated behind the pulpit is a reminder to the congregation of the time of the purpose behind their worshipping, and the hymns and tunes for the day are prominently displayed.

If we fast-forward to 1969, we see the same building in its latest guise. The chapel was purchased by the Rotherham Muslim community to be its first mosque. In Plate 17, we see the chapel soon after its conversion into a mosque. We can see clearly how the sign above the entrance announces the new role of the building. The houses which can be seen behind the mosque are in Vine Street. In front of the mosque is the beginning of wasteland created by the demolition of courts and back-to-backs in front of the building. The same fate awaited the houses behind the mosque 10 years later when the local council decided to drive a dual carriageway between the mosque and the community to its west. To the east of the mosque lie the railway, the river Don and the town centre. In the photograph, the mosque still has the tall windows on two sides of the building but these would soon be bricked up as the high ceiling of the interior was reduced later by the construction of a false floor in order to reduce heating costs for a building more regularly used than hitherto.

In the second photograph of the mosque (Plate 18), we can see how the demolition of houses has been extended to the west. The mosque now appears to stand in the midst of a wasteland. This isolation was strengthened soon after by the construction of the dual carriageway separating the

Plate 17 'Church Walk' Mosque soon after purchase
(*By permission of Rotherham MBC, Archives and Local Studies Service, Photo 4968*)

Plate 18 'Church Walk' Mosque in 1975e
(*By permission of Rotherham MBC, Archives and Local Studies Service, Photo 1341*)

mosque from its community. The decision to construct the dual carriageway was not informed by the needs of the community in respect of its mosque. No consultation of the community took place and parents, in particular, were now faced with the prospect of their children negotiating a busy road in order to attend their daily mosque class. This problem was alleviated to some extent by the subway joining 'Church Walk' to 'Midbrough'. However, later development of the area around the mosque into a light industrial estate hardly left the building in a congenial environment.

It is not unreasonable to trace much of the anti-council feelings of those interviewed in the Chapter 6: Organisers, to the decisions made about the area around the mosque in the 1970s. Nowadays, with feelings often running high about parking, matters are no better. Indeed, in 2003, the lengthy evening prayers of Ramadan (*tarawih*) clashed one evening with an important local football match at Millmoor, home of Rotherham United. Many northern football clubs (such as Bradford[1]) now have their grounds within or in close proximity to local Muslim, generally Mirpuri, communities. Cars of football spectators, who now came from parts of the town relatively distant from the ground, were boxed in by the cars of worshippers attending the evening prayers. Only sensible and prompt action by some of the mosque elders averted a nasty confrontation at the end of the match when football fans returned to their cars. The mosque is a busy place on a Friday and many worshippers come in cars. The local traffic wardens are always present at the time of Friday prayers in order to catch out anybody parked inappropriately. It is not therefore too difficult for the community to feel beleaguered and picked upon.

An Aside: Liturgical Literacy: A Matter of Life and Death?

The location of the mosque and its accessibility to the community has been a bone of contention since the establishment of the mosque in 1969. The construction of the bypass immediately to the west side of the building has already been described. In 1984 it was decided to construct an additional bypass to the north-west of the mosque. At that time, the district of 'Midbrough' was bordered on the north by 'Black Street', north of which was the district of 'Rosehill'. 'John Street', home to many Mirpuris, linked the two districts and at its northern end was one of the community's principal primary schools. The proposed new bypass would follow the route of 'Black Street' and link with 'Morley Road' to the west. This would, in theory, allow traffic to avoid the residential streets of 'Midbrough' and create a more effective conduit into the town centre. However, it would also split the community down the middle. The main teaching institution for

New £2m road eases congestion

ROTHERHAM'S new £2m dual carriageway has been opened to traffic for the first time.

And already the road, linking the inner by-pass with

Garden Street roundabout, is proving popular with motorists, who are finding it is cutting out a lot of congestion.

The road was officially opened by County Councillor

Wilf Cutts, chairman of South Yorkshire's Rotherham area highways committee.

A phase two development of the road, extending further into Wortley Road, is hoped to

be completed some time next year.

The crowds were out in force to try their new pelican crossing at Clough Road as part of the project, above.

Plate 19 Newspaper report of new road (*Rotherham Advertiser*)

the community's liturgical literacy found itself on one side of the new by-pass and many of its students on the other.

Despite concerns expressed by many, including a local councillor who drew attention to the lack of fencing separating the dual carriageway from a recreation ground where children played, the community's worst fears came to pass when a small child was killed as he attempted to cross the new road returning, not from playing in the recreation ground, but from his daily lesson in the mosque, now situated on the 'wrong' side of the dual carriageway. This happened six days after the official opening of the new road.

> Many people are now separated from the nearby school, playing fields, and shops. A large number of Muslim families are now cut off from their community centre where children attend for religious education. (*Rotherham Advertiser*, 20 March, 1984)

The event caused such an outcry in the community that the Council had to agree to the erection of a footbridge a year later, but before then one more young girl, again on her way back from the mosque, was run over by a car. Thankfully, she survived.

In Chapter 6, interviewees commented that the council was often unforthcoming in its support for community projects, and, in fact, sometimes appeared to obstruct rather than facilitate. These incidents with the dual carriageways are two very obvious situations where this has

POLICE last night lodged an inquiry on the scale of a murder hunt to find a hit-and-run driver who killed an eight-year-old boy on a new £2m dual carriageway.

Thousands of motorists are being questioned and their cars checked on the strength of what are believed to be a handful of vital clues provided by a taxi driver who chased the mystery driver along the newly-opened A629 by-pass in Rotherham after an accident in which schoolboy Askez Mohammed Ashraf died as he crossed a pelican crossing.

The taxi driver lost the other car, believed to be a gold or brown Mark III Ford Cortina.

Every car in South Yorkshire fitting that description — and there are believed to be about 3,000 of them — is to be checked and road blocks were set up last night to question drivers who could have been in the area at the time.

Chief Inspector Bob Lax said the measures reflected the seriousness with which police were treating the inquiry.

"If this had been a murder we would have had an incident room full of officers set up to deal with it, and it is almost like a murder," he said.

The boy died on his way home from a local mosque as he crossed the first phase of the new £4m A629 diversion road, which was officially opened last Friday.

Almost immediately, the road was at the centre of controversy when Rotherham councillor Bob Andrews criticised safety precautions in the area and forecast danger for children living close to it.

Yesterday Coun Andrews said he would be calling for better safety measures on the dual carriageway which effectively split in two the heavily Asian-populated areas of Masbrough and Thornhill.

"I still feel that a foot-bridge has got to go in there. If you look at the road, it is a fast dual carriageway, and drivers cannot be expected to see a pelican crossing suddenly coming up a them.

"There is a conflict between drivers and pedestrians because this road is splitting the community. Unless it is made safe, there might be a repeat.

"The people of the area are getting up a petition asking for a foot-bridge. It is too late for this little boy, but if we can prevent it happening again, then we must."

Relatives at Askez's home on James Street, Rotherham, yesterday joined Coun Andrews in criticising lack of safety precautions on the road.

Plate 20 Newspaper report on child's death (*Rotherham Advertiser*)

happened. The positioning of the Mirpuri community on the periphery of the town's life is a development which, though not strictly engineered, is an all-too-familiar example of that institutional racism that appears to pervade the structures and systems of British society at the present time. It also contrasts quite starkly with the mythical 'favourable treatment' that right-wing groups such as the British National Party accuse immigrant communities of receiving.

Educational Purpose of the 'Church Walk' Mosque

The history of the building now known as 'Church Walk' Mosque is an important aspect of this book and fulfils the important requirement when explaining uses of literacy to also explore the institutions and locales of literacy; without this understanding, the picture of literacies and their role within the community is incomplete. The references earlier to the Wesleyan Reform era of the building have solid relevance in that the activities of the chapel 100 years ago foreshadow its later use in the second half of the 20th century and beyond. They also bear witness to the continuity of those literacy practices that at that time were closely tied in to religion and the Christian Church. The literacies of the community in this book, although its children are well used to secular literacies in school and in the wider world, are still very much connected with religion and matters of faith.

Part of the motivation behind establishing the mosque in the first place was to provide a place of learning for the community's children. The older members of the community clearly recognised the importance to the community of the establishment of the mosque:

How long have they been teaching children in the mosque?

Mahmood: From the beginning, but mostly when we had the mosque at 'Church Walk'. At that time not mostly families, all single men. Families started coming to this country in 1965/1967. And when children arrived, need to be Muslim, realised that there needs to be teaching in the mosque. And they started teaching.

A mosque, in fact, is often seen as a place of learning as well as of worship; though this is a view expressed about mosques in this country rather than a general observation of all mosques. The imam, Maulana Shabbir, acknowledges the educational purpose of the mosque:

Maulana Shabbir: Well, first of all, it is necessary to understand that every *masjid* is an educational centre ... when we look at the *sirah* or the life of the Prophet, they used to do everything from the *masjid* ... everything was done from the *masjid* ... all the meetings, all the agendas ... all the teaching ... and everything was done from the *masjid* ... so the *masjid* is the educational centre ... So here in our place, like in every *masjid*, all the teaching is done in the *masjid* ...

This may be a fact of life in the UK Muslim communities as they seek to provide their children with an Islamic education that they cannot deliver at home. It is certainly not necessarily the case for mosques back home in rural Mirpur. This husband and wife had a different experience in Pakistan from that of their children in 'Midbrough':

Where did you learn to read the Qur'an?

Hanif [consulting his wife Ferzana]: In Pakistan. In the house ... like they are doing here

So it was separate from school?

Yes, separate. In somebody's house.

Same for you?

I learnt it a bit in Pakistan in somebody's house but when I came here, 'Church Walk'.

So if you went to somebody's house, does that mean you didn't go to the mosque, like they do here?

Not really, no. The girls couldn't go to the mosque anyway.

The boys?

Er, yes. In the towns maybe, but not in the villages. In the village you had to go to somebody's house I think. From what I can remember. I had to walk a few miles to go to somebody's house, to read.

In the UK the mosque has two jobs, a place of worship and a place to teach the children the Qur'an. That's not the case in Pakistan?

No, it's not the case. It's just for prayer. I think most mosques ... It was at 'Church Walk' mosque that I learnt it.

For these UK Muslim students, learning to read in the mosque is as significant a literacy experience as learning to read in school. The connection between reading and worship is so intimate for this community that it will talk about 'reading prayer' rather than 'saying prayers' as might be more common among Christians. This is, one needs to stress, a particularly Pakistani, or Urdu- or Mirpuri-Punjabi-speaking, custom, for Arabs will talk about 'doing prayers' or 'praying' rather than 'reading'. The Muslim call to prayer, the *Azan*, which is now recited once a day from the 'Church Walk' mosque through an external loudspeaker (a rare concession from the local council), is always referred to as 'reading the *Azan*' rather than any other expression. Children will, likewise, talk about 'going to the mosque to read'. It is often unclear whether they mean 'pray' or simply 'read the Qur'an', the distinction between the two is so blurred. This close tie between 'reading' and acts of worship underlines the primacy given to the act of reading in the mosque.

'Church Walk' Mosque in 2005

Nowadays, the building described above looks very different from how it appears in plates 17 and 18. It has now been whitewashed and extended to include a main entrance at the side of the building. The long wall-length windows have been bricked up at some stage and smaller windows inserted. All these modifications have been prompted by reasons of worship. The side extension contains the *wudhu* (ablution) facilities, the long windows were removed when the main auditorium of the building was divided into two by a new ceiling, creating two prayer halls. This allowed for smaller heating bills as the mosque had to be warm most of the day to accommodate the five daily prayers. The new side entrance allowed worshippers to enter and leave the building without having to pass through the ablution area and the large rectangular bulge in the south-east facing wall contains the prayer niche, the *mihrab*, which indicates the direction of prayer. Luckily, one side of the building stands facing south east and allows for the congregation to face Mecca as they pray. At the bottom of the steps leading up to the upper prayer hall there is a park bench, a collection of roses and a conifer.

Inside, a time-travelling visitor from the Wesleyan Reform congregation would find enormous changes. There are now two prayer halls devoid of any furniture except for the three-stepped pulpit, the *minbar*. The floors are covered in good quality carpet with the carpet of the upper prayer hall boasting a design based on myriad prayer mats arranged in rows facing the *mihrab*. In the lower prayer hall, there are three large bookcases. One has books on Islam in English. One has books in Urdu. The other also has books on Islam in English. These books are the legacy of the former imam, Maulana Shabbir, and the remnants of an efficient lending system (stamps, notebook) are evident in one of the bookcases. The books in the cases are, at the moment, rather untidily arranged and remain locked most of the time.

Plate 21 'Church Walk' Mosque 2005

Bookshelves around the hall all carry copies of the Qur'an, some in cloth covers, others not.

Our time-travelling non-conformist would find much that is strange, but also much that was familiar. The three-stepped *minbar*, although not as grandiose as the large pulpit from 100 years ago, serves the same purpose. It is from here that the imam delivers his weekly sermon sitting on the second step speaking in Urdu for approximately 30 minutes before the formal ritual of Friday prayer when he will stand on the bottom step and deliver a short ritualised sermon, or *khutbah*, in Arabic before the main prayer of the day.

The large wooden cupboard on the same wall as the mihrab is not a cupboard at all, but an elaborate and decorative wall-mounted prayer timetable. In every mosque in the world, one of the most important features is the display of prayer times for that particular day, week or month. This particular version is made of wood and allows for the days and times to be displayed by means of small wooden blocks, akin to a small child's bricks, inserted into appropriate holes (Plate 22). The language of this display is in Arabic, including the numerals, with the designer allowing the wood to inspire a design that is suitably cursive and florid. Our time traveller would also notice, however, an A3-sized poster by the wooden timetable, which carries the same information in English for every month of the year; useful

Plate 22 Wooden prayer time indicator

for those in the congregation who understand little Arabic, and especially Arabic numerals.

The sums of money that the community has expended on the purchase, modification and upkeep of the building are not inconsiderable. The principle of 'self help', retained from cultural and social practice back home, is naturally followed (see Chapter 6, and Ballard, 2001). These are comments from the Chairmen of the two mosques:

> *Ghulam* (translated by Hanif): We have spent nearly £40,000. Not asking anyone to give money – only money from collection. Ask this gentleman, he is writing it down in his book.
>
> *Mahmood:* So I was thinking myself and I told to committee if you are going to buy a place across the road, it's a lot of money, but they have collected it, the truck place, they are going to close it and the mosque wants to buy it, £120,000. And it's a lot of money. People have collected about £65,000.
>
> Because he is selling it [a yard across from the mosque], we decided that if we did not buy it we would lose the chance for progress. So we consulted our members and we decided that if we buy it, in the future, we might need some plans, we don't know, we can use it for many many things. We could extend the mosque. We could make the bottom part a car park and the top part for making *wudhu*. Or it could

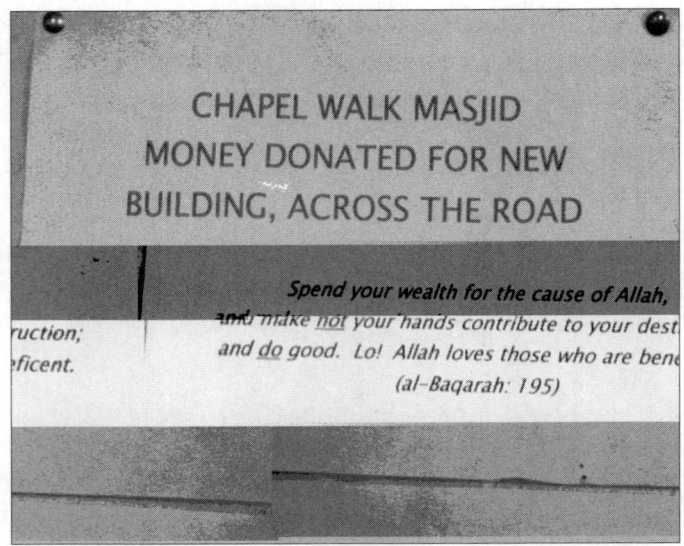

Plate 23 List of donors with Qur'anic verse in English

NAME (URDU)	NAME (ENGLISH)	ADDRESS	AMOUNT DONATED
	CH. MUHAMMED ABDUL MAJEED	QUEENSWAY	£1000 —
	CH. JANGHIR ALAM	BEAM GROVE	£1000 —
	HAJI MUHAMMED SAJAVAL	WARWICK ST	£1000 —
	HAJI ALI-SHAN	BROWN ST	£1000 —
	HAJI MUHAMMED RASHID	FEARNAM RD	£1000 –
	HAJI MUHAMMED AZAM	TOOKER RD	£1000 –
	HAJI ABDUL RASHID	LOZO ST	£1000–
	HAJI QURBAN HUSSAIN MALAK	BRINSWORTH	£1000–
	HAJI GHULAM YASEEN	GOODSTONE RD	£1000–
	MUHAMMED AMIN YASEEN	GOODSTONE RD	£1000–
	HAJI MUHAMMED NAZIR	BEACHWOOD RD	£1000–
	CH. MUHAMMED AMIN SABIR	TOOKER RD	£1000–
	HAJI GHULAM NABI	NORTH RD	£1000–
	ZAHID AZIZ QUERSHI	LINDUM TERRACE	£1000–
	HAJI MUHAMMED SIDDIQ	TOOKER RD	£1000–
	MASTER. M. AKRAM	HATHLEY RD	£1000–
	HAJI SHABAN HUSSAIN	FRASER RD	£1000–

Plate 24 List of donor names and amounts paid

be a facility for girls. Muslim girls don't like to be taught with the boys … And if we can do it, there is already a small building there …

In Islam, there are two acceptable manners of giving charitable donations. The first, and the most praiseworthy, is to give in secret, and thereby avoid any accusation of 'showing off' one's wealth or advertising one's generosity. The object in this case is to incur the pleasure of the Almighty which, by itself, should be its own reward. The second manner of giving charity, and the lesser valued, is to publicise one's donations, not to curry favour with one's peers, but to serve as an example to others. This latter custom is used extensively when collecting money for purposes connected with the mosque and its activities. In connection with the 'on-off' sale of the yard opposite 'Church Walk' mosque, a list of donors and the amount of their donations is prominently displayed, in English, on the back wall of the main prayer hall (Plates 23 and 24).

'University Road' Mosque

In 1980 a new imam was recruited from India. He began to speak about issues hitherto left undiscussed in the mosque. Back home in India and Pakistan, most mosques followed one of two prevailing schools of thought. These were based on the teachings of two renowned Indian Colleges of

Religious Sciences at their prime in the 19th century, The Deobandi College, or seminary, and the Berelvi College. The 'Church Walk' mosque until this time followed neither school of thought, and operated a 'welcome to all-comers' policy. The discussions prompted by the arrival of this imam led to fierce arguments and eventually to physical fighting. The community was split down the middle and it was decided that one faction would have to leave the mosque, and so another building was urgently sought. A stone's throw from 'Church Walk' is 'University Road'. In 1982 a trustee from the 'Church Walk' mosque organised a collection of money and, with considerable investment of his own, purchased an Irish working men's club on 'University Road' and the building next door, a bicycle repair shop. In the following conversation, Ghulam, the chairman, recalls the purchase of 'University Road' mosque. The bracketed comments are from Hanif, the treasurer of the mosque, who was acting as interpreter.

> **Ghulam** (translated by Hanif): This was three properties, you know. That was an Irish Club. This was for bikes selling and repairing. These two places and that is back garden. So I bought it and then after mosque.
>
> *When?*
>
> 1984 or 1985.
>
> *Have you any photographs of how it was before?*
>
> (**Hanif:** They were houses and a shop, one was a club, the other a cycle.)
>
> No, no. You know Foster's..? It belonged to his property. So I bought it separate. One and then the next one.
>
> *All at the same time?*
>
> Three times over two or three months. Because I not got enough money.
>
> *So **you** bought it? You personally?*
>
> Me. Bought myself. (**Hanif:** whole community together, so they choose a person who ...) I am a trustee, but not just myself who bought it ... everybody paid. Collection.

Over the last 20 years this building, the 'University Road' Jamia Mosque, (Plate 25) has become established as the second main mosque of the 'Midbrough' community. Unlike 'Church Walk', which was already a place of worship, developing the buildings has been a struggle for the chairman and, although heavily reliant on 'self help' for funding, he has been obliged to deal with the local council on many occasions because of issues around

Plate 25 'University Road' Mosque 2005

planning permission. From this experience has come a deep distrust of the council and its affairs.

Ghulam (translated by Hanif): Council gave me a headache. This extension. This extension has got a flat roof. It's leaking all the time. Three times the Council has rejected our claim. Planning permission to put pitched roof. We keep repairing, it keeps leaking, what can we do? Last time, when I applied again, John Holt, the architect, he keeps trying, to do half, pitched roof and half make extension. To change the toilet area.

So the Council have been difficult about it?

I don't know why. I am not saying. But the Council has never done us any favours. When I bought this mosque, they didn't give me planning permission. I got a solicitor and went to court. Glister. And when it went to court, Glister says, 'why are you not giving it to him planning for this place?' It is a residential area, they said. And that's why people need a place to pray! Not make a mosque in the jungle! That's what he said. Then the Council couldn't answer. Then he said, 'You give him part three of this paper ... because he pays rates, he pays taxes, for many years he is working, he is asking me in quite friendly way ... two people he ask the question, how long you been in this country, how long you been working here, do you pay tax, I told him, when I come in, working from the mill, seven days, six day week, then I pay tax, insurance, I pay rates, the solicitor said why you ... these people ... plan ...

From the outside, the red-brick 'University Road' mosque appears modern and tidy. It fronts 'University Road', once a busy thoroughfare into the town centre but now a minor road that ends in a cul-de-sac created by the building of the dual carriageway. There are double yellow lines in front of the building offering little in the way of ease of access for worshippers travelling by car. Interestingly, there are no yellow lines in front of the local church yards away on the same road. The building bears no traces of its former occupants. The extension built on to the front of the building contains the wudhu facilities and as you enter the main door you are faced with shoe racks to your left and to your right. Entering another door into the main prayer hall, you are surprised by the amount of space there is concealed behind the façade of the building. The prayer hall covers the space previously occupied by the working men's club, the cycle shop and their respective back yards.

In 1888 'University Road' provided a world of contrasts. To the south were terraced houses for skilled workers, engine drivers and miners, butchers and mechanics; while at Alfred Street were humble but lively courts and back-to-backs, for workers at the local factories.

By 1901 the large fields behind 'John Street' to the north of 'University Road' had been replaced by more terraced houses. The row of terraced houses on 'University Road' which now form the Jamia Masjid 'University Road' feature in the Street Directory as follows:

110   Post, Money Order & Telegraph Office;
        Benjamin Gregory, sub-postmaster
110   Gregory Benjamin, grocer
112   Wharin Joseph, butcher
112   Askin George, draper
114   Brown Henry, house furnisher (from *Kelly's Directory*, 1900)

By 1960, number 114 was St Bede's Working Men's Club, and number 112 was a bicycle suppliers and repairers. The former post office is now closed, and remains a derelict building at the end of the terrace.

The Materiality of Liturgical Literacy

The walls of the interior of the mosque are awash with pictures and texts.

Starting with the prayer niche, the *mihrab*, which is tiled, there is a rectangular LED display at the apex of the *mihrab*'s arch which alternates the two parts of the Islamic credo in Arabic, *'la illaha illa Allah; Muhammadu Rasul Allah'* ('There is no god except God; Muhammad is the Messenger of God'). This electronic display is complemented by a string of fairy lights draped around the edge of the arch. Both of these electrical devices have been installed by Bashir, a young man who is trained in microelectronics. A chandelier is suspended in the prayer niche to complete the light display, which underlines the centrality of the prayer niche to the rest of the prayer hall. On either side of the arch are two dish-shaped plaques bearing the Arabic, *'Ya Allah'* and *'Ya Muhammed'*. The significance of the word *'Ya'*, or *'O'*, is immense. In the case of *'O, Muhammed'* this saying has the implication in some schools of thought that the personage of the Prophet can still be addressed and be an object of a worshipper's supplications. A critic, as represented by the Deobandi school of thought, would consider such a saying as heretical and tantamount to *'shirk'*, or polytheism. A Deobandi mosque would allow plaques saying *'Allah'* and *'Muhammed'* but would consider the insertion of *'Ya'*, or *'O'*, to be an anathema.

Running anti-clockwise around the walls of the prayer hall, the following images are arranged: a large (100cm x 75cm) photograph of the Holy Mosque and Kaaba at Mecca in Saudi Arabia. Next to this is a smaller photograph (A4-size) of one of a series of relics of the Prophet Muhammed, the Holy Sandal, which is presently kept in the Topkapi Museum in Istanbul. Indeed, such a photograph would not be found in 'Church Walk' mosque, for it is typical of that branch of Islamic teaching derived from the Berelvi school of thought mentioned above. Furthermore, it is also true that more images and displays are found in Berelvi mosques than in the more 'puritanical' Deobandi mosques.

A large (150cm x 100cm) mass-produced printed cloth depicts in a stylised fashion the three principal mosques of the Islamic world: the Holy Mosque in Mecca, the Prophet's Mosque in Medina and the Al Aqsa Mosque in Jerusalem. Next to this are another two large photographs of the exterior and interior of the mosque at Medina, and another poster featuring relics of the Prophet comes next. This poster with captions in English includes the aforementioned sandal, an imprint of the Prophet's foot, his sword, his bow, his mantle and his flag.

After this is an interesting document in the form of a poster. As in many other religions, tradition is carefully preserved and called upon to support and verify matters of faith. In Islam, a common practice in religious teaching is to regularly establish lines of spiritual authority. This poster features the Kaaba at the top, with the names of those Prophets acknowledged in Islam arranged in chronological order below. The names, written in Arabic, have Muhammed nearest the top just below the Kaaba and include names such as Jesus, Moses and Abraham before ending (or starting, depending on one's perspective) with Adam, who, in Islamic tradition, is considered the first Prophet as well as the first man. Helpfully, there is a text-only version of this poster in English alongside.

Another large poster then features the Arabic words for the Prophet Muhammed and his closest Companions. As we reach the back wall of the prayer hall, a very large credo (200cm x 150cm) is displayed in white letters on a green background. This poster is framed and has the English translation in large capital letters underneath. The translation opts for the more archaic 'There is no deity save Allah' rather than the more straightforward 'There is no god except God'. This is an example of a problem that the English-speaking Muslim community often has to deal with. Many of the available translations of texts, be they translations of the Qur'an or other texts, belong to an era when mass readership in English was not an issue. One wonders what the children make of words such as 'lo', 'beneficent' and 'deity'. The quality of translated materials and their usefulness, especially to the children attending the mosque, will be referred to in Part 4: Languages.

The Emergency Exit sign above the rear door is sandwiched between two more large tapestries of the Holy Mosque at Mecca and the Prophet's Mosque at Medina. Next to this is an English version of the Prophet and his Companions with Muhammed in the centre and, in the four corners in anti-clockwise order, Abu Bakr, Umar, Uthman and Ali.

A wooden, handcrafted, prayer time board, similar to that in 'Church Walk' mosque, hangs on the wall next to the prayer niche. As the times are displayed in Urdu only, it is likely that this timepiece was brought from Pakistan. A '*salawat*' prayer, a supplication asking God to bless Muhammed, one of the most common prayers in the Islamic liturgy, is displayed in Arabic above a door leading out of the prayer hall. An Urdu Islamic calendar and prayer timetable is next followed by an English board with clockfaces depicting daily prayer time (Plate 26).

At the rear of the prayer hall are stacked the low benches used for teaching children every evening. The imam has arranged three of the benches at right angles to form a square enclosure so that he can sit with his back to the wall. A cushion is there for the imam's use. In the evenings the other benches are arranged in ever widening arcs from the inner square. Behind the imam is a wall-mounted whiteboard.

A large bookcase contains the copies of the Qur'an and *Qaidahs* (see Chapters 3 and 4) used by the young students.

On the back wall next to the entrance to the prayer hall is a small peg

Plate 26 Prayer times display

board with notices. Here there are advertisements in Urdu and in English from travel agents specialising in arranging pilgrimages to Mecca and Medina. There are also receipts pinned to the board displaying contributions to the mosque funds. There is also a poster in English explaining the ingredients of certain foods that contain forbidden substances.

The prayer hall is, therefore, very rich in texts, in a variety of languages

Plate 27 Wall sign in English

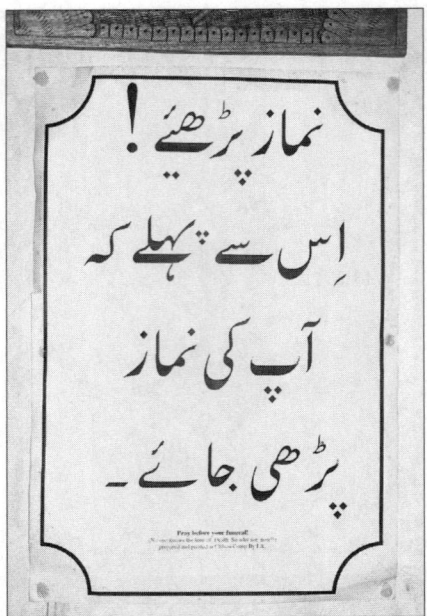

Plate 28 Wall sign in Urdu

and varieties of language. With the human form being proscribed in many Islamic contexts, it is the written word that, historically, has been developed into a fine art form. The words appearing in texts in 'University Road' and 'Church Walk' mosques do not generally aspire to fine art. With their varieties of languages, scripts, fonts, sizes and colours it is hard to imagine

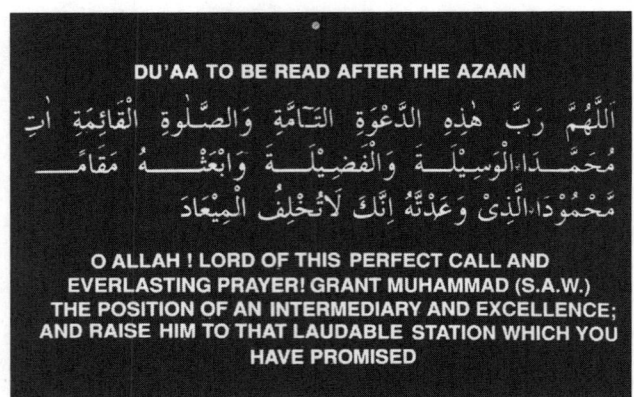

Plate 29 Wall sign in Arabic and English

Plate 30 Sign in ablution area

how such an impression could be made. On the one hand, there is the discrepancy between the scripts used for Arabic derived from the Arabic-speaking world and the scripts derived from the Indian subcontinent. The former tends to feature on bilingual texts featuring English and has a more angular form. The latter tends to be more cursive and features regularly in bilingual texts with Urdu, which itself is conveyed with a stylised Arabo-Persian script. The large posters featuring English seem to prefer capitalisation as a calligraphic technique, making them rather hard on the eye at times.

The prayer hall is not the only place in the mosque for displays of texts. In the *wudhu*, or ablution area, of each mosque there are toilets and washing

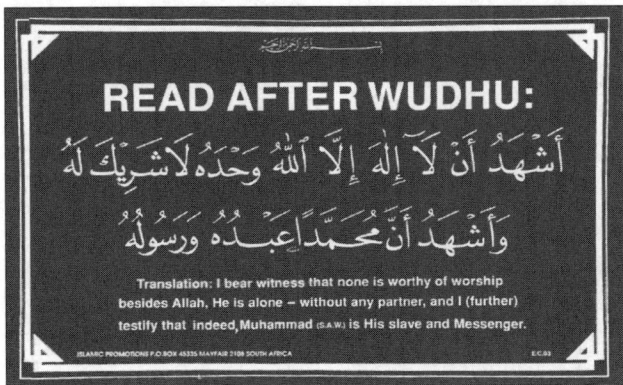

Plate 31 Sign in ablution area

faciltiies. There are many supplications to accompany preparation for prayer and these are often prominently displayed on the walls.

In every mosque that holds classes for children there is, inevitably, a high turnover of texts, copies of the Qur'an and the *Qaidahs* (primers). Despite the best of intentions, including the use of covers and careful handling, books become tatty and pages become detached. Islamic custom insists that material containing verses from the Qur'an, and that includes practically all materials used in the mosque, cannot be thrown away. It is customary, therefore, for a space to be identified in the mosque where such materials can be deposited safely. In the 'University Road' and 'Church Walk' mosques there is a cupboard in the large bookcase that acts as a depository for old Qur'ans and other texts. It is fascinating to reflect on the link that can be made across the centuries between this practice of

Plate 32 Fragments cupboard: a South Yorkshire *'genizah'*

preserving fragments of sacred texts in UK mosques with the identical practice carried out by the original readers of what have come to be called the Dead Sea Scrolls, a large proportion of which are considered to have been collected and preserved for very similar reasons 2000 years ago in the Jordanian desert! A synagogue has a similar depository called a *'genizah'*.

Summary

The children who attend their respective mosques every evening for two hours have little awareness of the history of the buildings in which they gather to learn how to read the Qur'an. Their elders tell a story that involves determination, struggle and frustration. Yet the story they tell is one that is mirrored in many of the towns and cities in the UK. The establishment of Muslim communities and their institutions, the mosques, has been a significant socio-cultural development over the past 50 years. In the most recent UK Muslim Guide (*Muslim Directory*, 2003), a 'yellow pages' for Muslim residents of the United Kingdom, there are listed over 800 mosques in nearly 200 towns and cities. The education that is on offer at the mosque for its young worshippers is, in many respects, a new phenomenon in UK society. In other respects, however, there is a great deal of continuity amidst this overriding impression of change. The children attending the Sunday School at the Wesleyan Reform Chapel in 1901, with their teachers, and their combination of learning faith and literacy, have their counterparts in the early 21st century with the young children of Mirpuri heritage and their imams and assistant imams now attending Jemia Mosque 'Church Walk' and Jamia Masjid 'University Road'.

We have seen in Part 2 how the community structures and organises this cultural and religious activity. The buildings in which the activity takes place, and their history, bear witness to the sacrifice the community is always making in order to preserve and maintain it. As we shall see in Part 4 when discussing the role of different languages within the community, no such similar sacrifice is made for Urdu or the mother tongue of Mirpuri-Punjabi.

The mosque, however, is not the only site for the practice and acquisition of liturgical literacy. The family home, too, reflects and helps shape the nature of liturgical literacy as it is practised within the community. This is the subject of the next chapter.

Note

1. In the 1985 Bradford fire, which took 52 lives, members of the local British Asian community living around the football stadium assisted with the rescue effort.

Chapter 8

Liturgical Literacy in the Home

Introduction

We have seen that the formal acquisition of liturgical literacy takes place mainly in the mosque. There are parents who assist their children with learning how to read the Arabic of the Qur'an, but most are content to support this acquisition by ensuring that their sons and daughters attend the mosque regularly. In a sense, this is very similar to their attitudes towards formal education in the state school. However, there is no doubt that the home provides one of the main contexts for the practice of liturgical literacy. Once liturgical literacy has been acquired, the main practical use for this literacy practice is in the performance of prayer, the recitation of Qur'an and, occasionally, other religious ceremonies. All of these take place in the home as well as in the mosque.

The Materiality of Liturgical Literacy in the Home

The interviews with parents took place exclusively in the homes of the participants. In general, the interviews were held in the 'front room' of the families in question. This room is, as in many communities in South Yorkshire, kept as the room for receiving guests. The material literacy in these rooms reflected the variety of literacies of the community with texts in English, Urdu and Arabic. With the exception of the Mufti's room, which, in fact, was more akin to an office or even a library, most of the rooms were similar in their contents. Texts were to be found on walls in the guise of pictures and posters, on tables in the form of books, newspapers and papers, or as books on shelves.

The ubiquitous large picture, often on cloth, of the Holy Mosque at Mecca was usually above the mantelpiece with occasionally a dish-like plaque on each side, one with the word 'Allah' in Arabic and the other with the word 'Mohammed'. Some homes had a framed picture of the 'Throne' verse from the Qur'an, a verse that is considered essential for protection from harm and evil (Plate 33).

This verse is also sometimes found on amulets and jewellery worn on the body. Another text usually found on the wall is the Islamic credo 'There

Plate 33 The 'Throne' verse in a family home

is no god except God; Mohammed is the Messenger of God' (Plate 34). This is more often than not in Arabic.

Not many books are in evidence. A copy of the Qur'an is kept in a cloth casing and placed either on the highest shelf in the room or on the top of a bookcase. This is to symbolise respect for the sacred text. It is interesting to

Plate 34 The Islamic credo

compare this practice with the practice of Muslims from the Arabic-speaking world. In these communities, the Qur'an is no less valued as a sacred text with all the same strictures regarding the handling and placing of the Qur'an. However, the text in Arabic-speaking homes is very much more a text in use. It will be on a shelf, but can appear tatty and well-thumbed. It may appear on a coffee table or on top of a sideboard. It may well have a bookmark inserted into its pages, or even a page corner turned over. Furthermore, it is very common in Arab countries to have a Qur'an on the dashboard of a car. Muslims may keep small copies of the Qur'an in their breast pockets of jackets or in handbags. It appears that the more meaningful the text is to the reader, the less likely it is that the book takes on a purely symbolic or reverential value. The Qur'an in a home of the community described in this book, which does not have direct access to its meaning, is very much an object of veneration rather than a text for regular consultation. The placing of the Qur'an in a high place, and its careful protection from damage and getting dirty – in a sense, a meritorious act of devotion – at the same time, acts against an active engagement with the words of the text and their meaning.

Other books, if in evidence, will be in Urdu and, as often acknowledged by the parents, are read only by the older members of the family.

Munir: *What was the last book you read?*
At this time it is mostly religious books. Mostly study in Qur'an. In Urdu as well. For explain. I read that mostly.

What was the last book you read?
Qurban: Islamic books.
In which language?
In Urdu.
Where do you get them from?
My brother left books, so his family are not reading them, so I brought them here.

Every home will have at least one, usually more, prayer mats. These are often imported from China and can be purchased in local Muslim grocers or milliners of which there are just one or two in Rotherham but many just a few miles away in Sheffield. They are usually made from brushed cotton or velveteen and depict stylised images of one or more of the three holy mosques of Islam (Plate 35). Occasionally, another image will appear. The Blue Mosque in Istanbul is sometimes seen. Daily prayers are conducted on these mats and they are kept clean and folded away.

Plate 35 Prayer mat featuring the Kaaba in Mecca

Another necessary accessory to prayer, and therefore liturgical literacy, is the rosary, or *tasbih* (or *subhah* in Arabic-speaking homes). These are kept in both mosque and home and often in pockets. The regular Muslim rosary (sometimes erroneously referred to as 'worry beads') consists of a string of 99 beads divided into three sections of 33 with a single large elongated bead called the 'imam' at the head of the string representing the beginning and end of the rosary (Plate 36). The divisions into 33 are designed to facilitate the counting of the phrases, *'subhan Allah'* ('glory to God'), *'alhamdulillah'* ('thanks be to God') and *'Allahu akbar'* ('God is great') which, according to tradition, are best repeated 33 times at the end of each prayer.

However, for some worshippers, the rosary has a more extended use than the above. Some Muslims will have a daily routine of *dhikr*, or remembrance, which they will carry out with the aid of a rosary in order to count the number of certain litanies and supplications. Again, this latter will take the form of Arabic words and phrases that have been learnt orally either by

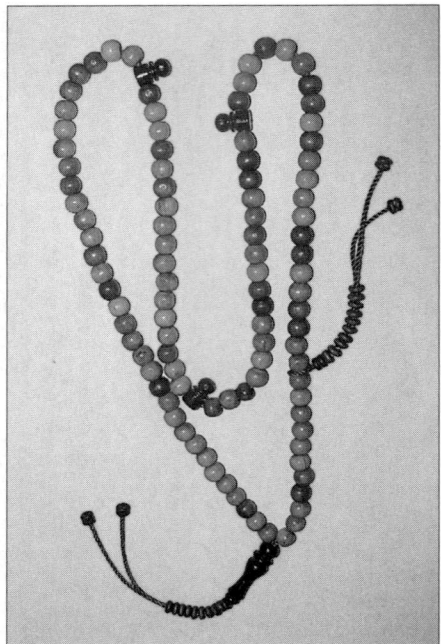

Plate 36 Muslim rosary, *tasbih* or *subhah*

heart, or from texts. Not all worshippers will carry out this practice, and children very rarely do so, and some will do it only in the mosque whilst waiting for the beginning of the congregational prayer. However, it would be unusual for a home not to have a rosary.

Liturgical Literacy Events at Home

Before leaving the subject of the home as a context for liturgical literacy, it is necessary to mention one particular liturgical literacy event that occurs in some homes on a reasonably regular basis. In Chapter 10: Urdu, a brief description is given of a *Mawlid*, a gathering of worshippers to celebrate the occasion of the birth of the Prophet. Many of the practices there described also, on occasion, take place in the home. It may be hoped that such a gathering is an auspicious event that may attract blessings for the house and those who live there or it may be to celebrate and give thanks for the birth of a new child. These are often family gatherings involving the extended family and close friends. An imam, or someone suitably qualified, will be invited to host the proceedings and a substantial meal will usually seal the event.

Plate 37 Example of amulet

As in the mosque, this is an occasion for poetry and song as well as the more formal recitation of the Qur'an and other recitations. Unlike the mosque gathering, there are not so many, maybe not any, formal speeches or addresses. It should also be mentioned here that not all the Mirpuri community will take part with equal gusto in such gatherings. The Berelvi–Deobandi split, described in Chapter 7, plays a role with the Deobandis often disapproving of such practices, particularly the *dhikr* and the singing.

Such events in the home are equally multilingual with recitations taking place in Arabic (Qur'an and supplications), Urdu (*naat*) and Mirpuri-Punjabi (*naat*). Indeed, many of the younger members of the family may be more confident to declaim the poetry they have learnt, either by heart or from texts. A more detailed description of this literacy practice will be found in Part 4, which deals with the languages of liturgical literacy.

Finally, many Muslim homes will contain texts and textual artefacts that are considered to have properties of protection for those living there. We have mentioned earlier (Chapter 2) how the liturgical texts of the Arabic language are sometimes used for esoteric purposes beyond that of their literal or figurative meaning. The Mende imams in Sierra Leone would also employ religious texts as a means of warding off evil and misfortune. The 'Throne' verse mentioned above is an example of this particular usage, and features not only on walls but on jewellery and on other personal objects such as credit-card sized insertions for wallets and purses. For more serious matters, among some members of the community, a religious teacher (not usually the local imam) will provide amulets designed to perform particular spiritual or worldly functions. These range from seeking protection from evil spirits to seeking success in school or university examinations. The Arabic words that feature on these amulets are not generally known by those who wear them, but usually consist of verses from the Qur'an and other Arabic prayers and formulations (Plate 37). The amulet is usually a smallish square piece of paper that is folded into a small triangle and inserted into a silver or leather pouch and worn around the neck or placed in a wallet. The amulet may also be placed somewhere in the home.

It should be noted that not all Muslims agree with this particular practice and believe it to be an example of superstition. Nevertheless, it is possible to witness usage of these amulets for various purposes in the community. Plate 38 shows an advertisement from a supplier of such amulets that was being distributed in 'University Road' mosque in 2005.

Plate 38 Offer of amulets (*taviz* in Urdu)

Chapter 9
Liturgical Literacy and School

Introduction

This chapter is sadly short. The relationship between schooled literacy and its principal institution, the school, and liturgical literacy and its principal institution, the mosque, is a simple one to describe, for there is very little relationship that is evident or recognised. There appears to be, at best, little or, at worst, no awareness or precise knowledge of the literacy practice experienced by, in this particular secondary school, one in five of its pupils.

The Local Secondary School

The secondary school in question is an 11–16 secondary mixed comprehensive school located to the west of 'Midbrough' in a different district of the town. Apart from its Muslim pupils, most pupils attending the school live on a large council estate, with a small minority living in some private housing near to the school. The majority of its Muslim pupils come from two main feeder primaries, one in the district of 'Midbrough' and the other in neighbouring 'Derham'. Until 2001, standards were satisfactory and progress made by pupils measured against similar schools was considered good. The council's decision to close the school and merge its pupil population with that of a neighbouring school half a mile away resulted in a number of key staff leaving the school and standards dropped, despite a slight recovery in 2003, the year before merger. Of the three secondary schools closed during the past 20 years, all three served the local Mirpuri communities in Rotherham and, despite local campaigns to save the schools, the pupil populations of each were merged with traditionally 'all white' schools. Although no parent expressed any indignation about this apparent trend to close those schools with larger minority ethnic populations, apart from some voices concerned about the most recent closure, it would be interesting to hear the response of the council planners if asked for an explanation of this apparent coincidence.

Teacher Perception of Liturgical Literacy

The fact that children from the school attended the mosque after school was generally known by teachers at the school but, beyond a non-specific awareness of pupils 'going to' mosque', little else was known. The majority of teachers in the school had no idea where the mosques were or how long the children spent there, and would have had a hard job identifying the streets and houses of 'Midbrough' where their pupils lived. At a school in-service training day in January 2003, where the theme of the day was cultural diversity, during a presentation to a group of teachers I projected an image of a map of 'Midbrough'. At least two teachers claimed they had no idea of what they were looking at. Their daily routine involved driving to school from an outer suburb that avoided Rotherham town centre and driving home at the end of the day. However, here I am conscious that I am not describing a unique situation and that many, if not most, teachers working in schools 'facing challenging circumstances' (to use the latest euphemism for schools in areas of severe social and economic deprivation) have little experience or knowledge of the areas surrounding the schools in which they work. A teacher in such a school who lives in its catchment area is a rare individual.

The main way in which liturgical literacy overtly interacts with the life in the school is perceived, sadly, as a nuisance factor. This manifests itself in two ways. Firstly, when Muslim children are placed in detention, they often use 'I've got to go to mosque' as an excuse for leaving early. This, then, is often the only reference to this literacy practice and, as a result, teachers can have conscious or subconscious negativity about its importance. It is seen as an intrusion into the systems of school life. Secondly, those few individual teachers who do have some awareness of the demands that attendance at the mosque places on their pupils may express their concerns that little time is, therefore, available for doing homework or coursework. If coupled with the erroneous and uninformed opinion that allows them to think that Muslim girls do nothing in the home except housework, their view of life in the community can be a very negative one.

The school environment reflects linguistic diversity in some classroom and corridor signs, though closer inspection of the signs will show that most of them are merely English words transliterated into Urdu script, rather than Urdu words.

The Effect of Liturgical Literacy on Reading in School

By and large there is little interaction between schooled literacy and liturgical literacy. However, covertly, there is evidence that the intensive experience of liturgical literacy has a significant influence over the literacy behaviour of Muslim children in school. It has been reported elsewhere (Rosowsky, 2001) that 11-year-old Muslim children who have experienced a mosque education for five or six years arrive in the secondary school with a very accomplished skill at decoding English. This skill is generally well in advance of the accompanying skills of knowledge of syntax and reading for meaning.

Most teachers are aware of this situation, but are often unaware of the possible reasons. The emphasis on decoding Arabic in the mosque is no doubt responsible for the parallel development of this skill in reading English. This is clear evidence of the Common Underlying Proficiency (CUP) (Cummins, 1984, 1989) in action. This theory of bilingual development suggests that certain language skills transfer readily from one language to another. Furthermore, there is evidence, apart from in this study, that suggests that this transfer takes place even where scripts are very different, such as in Vietnamese and Japanese (Cummins *et al.*, 1984).

Reading tests (NFER-Nelson, 1989) undertaken by 11-year-old Muslim pupils in the school that report both reading accuracy (decoding) and reading comprehension illustrate this discrepancy. Pupils on average had a two-year gap between their decoding and comprehension ages. Their proficiency in decoding in Arabic seems to be a significant contributing factor to their proficiency in decoding in English. Of concern, however, are the corresponding depressed scores in reading comprehension. Again the CUP principle would suggest that the lack of attention to meaning in the pupils' intense acquisition of liturgical literacy might contribute to a similar lack of attention to meaning when reading in English at school. Chapter 3 described how children, when asked, would say that they thought of various matters when reading the Qur'an but could not, obviously, reflect on the meaning of individual words and phrases. It was interesting to notice that a similar response was given when asked about reading in English. The CUP does not include accompanying physical behaviours within its remit, but were one to observe these Muslim boys and girls reading their English books in the school library rocking gently to and fro, one would observe how a very physical aspect of liturgical literacy has been transferred to a different literacy context.

Liturgical Literacy and Literacy Development in School

Discussion in previous chapters has touched on the issue of preferred language for instruction in the mosque and, although this issue is prompted by parental concern about their children's knowledge about their religion rather than a concern to complement literacy acquisition at school, if English were to become the main, or at least an equal, language of instruction in the mosque, one might predict a more mutually beneficial relationship between the two literacy practices. Indeed, it is possible to predict a relationship between school and mosque that is closer to that relationship shared, in another era, between school and Sunday school.

In the school, liturgical literacy is rarely acknowledged. All of the Muslim children attending the school have acquired an accomplished and secure knowledge of the decoding of Qur'anic Arabic. Many of them have also developed an interest and a skill in the declaiming of religious poetry. None of this is recognised by the school. Liturgical literacy remains a literacy practice that is developed apart from other more approved or more legitimised literacy practices. At present its 'capital' has little exchange value .

Yet the liturgical literacy of the children attending the secondary school is an identifying factor in their concept of self and self-worth. The acknowledgement of an important aspect of one's identity by validating institutions such as schools should enhance the general feelings of self-esteem expressed by these young people. Self-esteem is well documented as an essential element in the educational success of young people. To have a crucial dimension of one's identity denied or ignored by the institution which is responsible for formal learning, and, therefore, acts as the gatekeeper to future pathways and careers, can act as a debilitating factor in a child's educational progress.

Benefits of Liturgical Literacy

The practice of liturgical literacy can be criticised, and has been (see Chapter 1), if this literacy practice is pursued narrowly and without recourse to other more meaningful aspects of religious instruction. However, as educationalists, we should be aware of the enormous success the institutions of liturgical literacy have with teaching the initial acquisition of reading. The method of teaching initial reading in Arabic has already been described (Chapter 4: Teachers) in detail. The proficiency that is developed in decoding is no mean achievement against the rather less effective mastery of decoding experienced by many children in decoding English. Without going into the ins and outs of the never-ending debate about the teaching of reading, it seems obvious that the methods used in our mosque schools for the teaching of reading need examining to account for their spectacular success. The quasi-synthetic phonics system that is employed by the mosque teachers is a traditional form of teaching initial reading that has altered little since it was developed many generations ago. The current call for a greater emphasis on phonics in the teaching of reading within UK primary schools, and national programmes for tackling phonics even in the secondary school, suggests there is scope for a greater awareness of those teaching techniques that have proven their longevity and continuing success.

Summary

Liturgical literacy is acquired in the main in the mosque and is intimately linked with that institution. The home is a context for liturgical literacy and provides a literacy environment for its practice with its wall designs, photographs of the Holy Mosque in Mecca and copies of sacred texts and prayer mats. Daily prayers will occur in some of the homes on a regular basis, particularly for the female members of the household, and occasional religious gatherings will provide a vital context for the practice of liturgical literacy. Schools would benefit considerably from a greater awareness of this substantial and universal literacy practice.

As we will see in Part 4, it is liturgical literacy that is prioritised by the community. Without serious attention and significant structural change, the home and community languages of Mirpuri-Punjabi and Urdu (though it could be argued that Urdu has never been a secure language within this community) will soon be supplanted by English in nearly all contexts, including religious ones. Only liturgical literacy is actively supported and encouraged by and within the community. The formal institutions of schools need to recognise this linguistic fact of life.

Part 4

The Languages of Liturgical Literacy

Chapter 10

Urdu

Introduction

In this part we provide a brief description of the languages involved in the literacies of the community studied in this book and an account of their respective functions, roles and interrelationships with one another.

Urdu is the national language of the Islamic Republic of Pakistan. It enjoys this status alongside the 'official' languages of Sindhi and, still, English. The population of Pakistan is around 148 million, of whom nearly 11 million consider themselves to be mother-tongue speakers of Urdu. The worldwide figure for mother-tongue Urdu speakers is 60 million and includes substantial numbers of speakers in India, South Africa and Mauritius. If we include those who consider Urdu as their second spoken language, the number of Urdu speakers rises to 104 million.

Linguistically, Urdu belongs to that family of languages generally known as Indo-Aryan, which includes most of the languages spoken on the Indian subcontinent. Further back, Urdu is also part of a wider family of languages known as Indo-European. As such, in terms of its linguistic roots and grammatical principle, it has more in common with English, which also belongs to the Indo-European family, than it does with, say, Arabic, with whose history it has become enmeshed.

It shares mutual intelligibility with Hindi, the principal official language of India, but has a great deal of formal vocabulary borrowed from both Arabic and Persian. Traditionally associated with Islam, most Muslims from this part of the world, or whose families originate there, will have knowledge of Urdu, either as a spoken language or as a language encountered and employed in education and other formal contexts. Most Pakistanis would consider Urdu as at least their third language, if not their second.

Urdu is always written in Arabic script modified by the addition of several extra characters. According to the latest UN statistics Pakistan at present has a literacy rate of only 26% of the adult population. As the majority of the population is having to acquire literacy in a second or third language (the largest, spoken, language group in Pakistan is Punjabi), this is not totally surprising. In fact, the driving force for the present campaign

173

for a Punjabi-based literacy (see next chapter) is to increase the literacy rate of native Pakistanis as well as those based abroad.

Literacy Campaigns in Pakistan

In recent years (since the early 1980s) there have been numerous state and locally-run literacy campaigns designed to increase the numbers of Pakistan adults who can read and write. These campaigns have had varying degrees of success. One major concern has been the number of rural female adults who remain illiterate. Although the gap between male and female literacy rates is decreasing, there is still concern that female literacy rates remain alarmingly low.

One interesting example of these literacy campaigns has been the Qur'anic Literacy Project, which ran between 1991 and 1995. In this campaign, an attempt was made to employ the much greater mastery of Qur'anic literacy possessed by adult females in a number of districts, including Islamabad and Rawalpindi, to develop literacy in Urdu. It was hypothesised that the women's knowledge of the Arabic script would, with some additions, facilitate their learning of Urdu. Some 10,000 women were admitted to the scheme and nearly 7000 were deemed to have 'fully benefited' from the scheme (Prime Minister's Literacy Commission, 2002).

Urdu Use in the Community

Although it is not part of the remit of this book to assess the Urdu literacy levels of the adults in the sample, it nevertheless arose as an issue in many of the interviews conducted with parents and other adults. Remembering that the majority of the adult males who arrived in the 1950s and early 1960s came from a rural background and that literacy rates among both men and women in rural areas of Pakistan were low at that time, it would not be a surprise to find Urdu illiterates among the Mirpuri community in South Yorkshire. On the other hand, it may be argued that the resourcefulness of those migrating to find work abroad is predicated upon, at least, some elemental literacy in order to facilitate the arrangements of such a venture.

How old were you when you came to the UK?

Ghulam (translated by Hanif): About 17.

So all your education was in Pakistan?

I have never been to school! That time was war time you know.

In the case of this respondent, it would not be too outrageous to conclude that his knowledge of Urdu was insecure. However, it is also probable that this man's knowledge of spoken Urdu is much more secure. The relationship between spoken Urdu and the Mirpuri-Punjabi mother tongue of the community will be explored more fully in the next chapter. Suffice it to say that Urdu and Punjabi are located on a dialectal continuum, or diglossia (Ferguson, 1959), which allows for some mutual comprehension at both ends and greater mutual intelligibility as the speaker becomes more familiar with each variant.

Literacy in Urdu among adult males in the community is correlated with level of education reached back home in Pakistan. We have already seen that it was quite possible for someone to arrive in the 1950s with little or no Urdu literacy. This was because of the upheaval in India created by World War II and Partition. Later on, if a male arrived in the UK at the age of 15 or over, it is fairly likely that an adequate level of literacy in Urdu had been reached for future use. However, boys arriving at a younger age ran the risk of having a rather insecure level of Urdu literacy that often manifested itself as a reluctance to read and write in Urdu or even wilful neglect.

Here is a typical response from someone who arrived in Britain at around the age 11:

Akhtar: In Pakistan. Well, all I can remember is ... In fact there isn't a great deal I can remember ... Truthfully, I can't. I cannot remember. I can read. I can still read a little bit...if it has been written by a novice or if it has been written by ...

Read in Urdu?

Yeah, in Urdu. But as far as my experience in Pakistan concerning school work. ...

So you can't, for example, remember how you learnt to read?

No, absolutely not.

Would you have gone to school in the village?

Yes. I remember the school. Just can't remember what we did in the classes.

Other men who arrived at a similar age felt a need to continue working on their knowledge of Urdu, despite an initial acquisition of Urdu literacy, which they considered inadequate for adult purposes. The following responses are typical:

When you left Pakistan, when you were 11, was that the end of your formal Urdu education?

Wajib: Yes. That was the end of my formal education in Urdu.

And was that enough for you to be able to read and write in Urdu later, like reading the paper and books?

No, it wasn't enough, but I've been doing a lot of work in Urdu myself.

Was that your choice or your parents' choice?

I think it was my choice. I think ... I can read and write. Maybe write wasn't that good but I could read pretty good Urdu. I could read almost anything in Urdu and quite understand it. Most of it. Spoken Urdu is maybe lacking a bit. Written Urdu is maybe lacking, but I can read. Because most of the books I have read were in Urdu. I carried on Urdu.

So could you read and write in Urdu by the time you left and came to England?

Hanif: Yes, I could. I polished it up later in life. I left it for English a bit. I polished it up later in life by reading books and the newspaper and things like that. Mainly my education level is primary level.

Purposes for using Urdu in the home were mainly for reading and writing letters from and to relatives back home in Pakistan, though this was becoming, as elsewhere, less and less of a literacy practice as more electronic forms of communication have developed:

Do you write in Urdu?

Munir: Letters, well only my brother's daughter is in Pakistan. She was married there. Anything that happens here, she just reads about it.

Reading newspapers such as the *Jang* and other magazines:

Qurban: I read the *Daily Jang*. That is our newspaper.

Though this is not necessarily a literacy practice universally shared across the community:

Do you read the Daily Jang?

Jabbar: Sometimes I buy that. Mostly I look at the TV. All the news is there.

If you bought a newspaper every day, what would it be?

Wajib: I don't know. It depends how I feel. One day I might buy the Daily Star, another day it could be *The Times* or something like that. In Urdu, there's no choice, only the *Jang*.

Do you read it every day?

No, very rarely. If I wanted to buy a paper I would buy an English paper. I wouldn't buy the _Jang_ or any Urdu paper.

Do you read the Jang?
Akhtar: The English section only. Excellent paper. That is the standard of _The Times._ I've met the editor. Very clever man.

If books were read in Urdu, they were often religious books that provided commentary or explanation of Arabic texts. Indeed, Urdu has an extremely rich tradition and history of religious literature including some of the most beautiful religious poetry. After Arabic, Urdu is considered by many, alongside Persian and Ottoman Turkish, to be one of the principal languages of the Islamic faith.

What was the last book you read?
Hameed: Islamic books.
In which language?
In Urdu.
Where do you get them from?
My brother left books, so his family are not reading them, so I brought them here.

What was the last book you read?
Munir: At this time it is mostly religious books. Mostly study in Qur'an. In Urdu as well. For explain. I read that mostly.

Finally, the main role for Urdu within the wider community lies in its importance as a lingua franca, together with its close sister, Hindi, in the Bollywood film and music industry, which just may be the saviour for the language among young people in the UK:

Which other languages do you know?
Akhtar: None.
What about Urdu, the actual language of books?
Yes. I would say I can understand that. I can't speak it as well as someone who is educated.
For _example, if you went to Pakistan and watched the TV?_
Yeah, oh yes. And the films ...

A regular cultural and social activity for both boys and girls is to listen to songs in films, on the radio or on CD and transcribe the words to aid memorisation. The transcription, interestingly, is done mainly in Roman script.

Urdu in the Mosque

In this community, Urdu is used most often in the formal setting of the mosque. On a Friday, the imam gives a sermon to the congregation just before the formal Friday prayer. This tends to last approximately 30 to 40 minutes and is delivered in Urdu with Arabic verses and sayings quoted liberally within it. The sermon can often be a literary tour de force with Qur'anic verses quoted in the original Arabic followed by their Urdu translation, sayings of the Prophet, or *hadeeth*, quoted in Arabic and explained in Urdu. As the sermon proceeds, the subject matter moves from general principles introduced by scriptural references, to teaching stories involving historical personages from the history of Islam. These may be named contemporary companions of the Prophet, or historically later figures who have achieved renown in the Islamic world for their piety. In the 'University Road' mosque it is rare for the imam not to also include some religious poetry. Such verses may be in Urdu, Punjabi or even Persian. Even to someone with no knowledge of the individual languages spoken during the sermon, it is difficult not to be impressed with the imam's erudition as he effortlessly recites and declaims without the aid of any notes, and with no apparent speaking by rote.

Sadly, much of what the imam says is increasingly lost on the younger members of the congregation as they grow up without access to the wealth and history of this rich language.

You know on a Friday, when the imam speaks before, what language is that in?
Akhtar: Urdu.
Pure Urdu, he doesn't use dialect?
No. Not as far as I know. I'm not the expert on this ...
I do notice that some of the boys might sit towards the back. They can't follow it really ...
Yeah, it is. Tanveer doesn't understand him.
Some do and some don't? Why is that?
Yeah, that's right. That's true.

What about all the boys who come to Friday prayer and sit at the back?
Munir: I told them, and in the month of Ramadan, the imam from Eastfield Mosque, they used to come to *tarawih*, and try to explain in English, but I think it is very very important, that our young boys, of 20 or 26 years old coming to the mosque, but our imam is only speaking Urdu. And it should be in English. Then they can understand what Islam says. They are coming there and just sitting there.

These young people are not only losing access to the meaning of much that is taught in the mosque, but are also losing access to a deeply-rooted and intensely-poetic branch of literature that has inspired Urdu speakers for generations.

Four or five times a year, the mosque will host a religious gathering to celebrate an important event on the Islamic calendar. This could be *Mawlid* (the anniversary of the birth of the Prophet), the *Laylat-ul-Miraaj* (the Night of the Ascension), *Laylat-ul-Shaaban* (the middle night of the month of Shabaan) or *Laylat-ul-Qadr* (the Night of Power, 27th of Ramadan). These are all auspicious events in the Islamic calendar that are celebrated by a programme of Qur'anic and poetic recitations as well as speeches that may contain storytelling or prophetic accounts as well as exhortations, supplications and singing. The amount of the latter will vary from mosque to mosque as the more puritanical Deobandi variety of Islam will generally disapprove of singing and raised voices in the mosque, believing them to be inappropriate. Nevertheless, both mosques will host gatherings.

Vignette: Laylat-ul-Miraaj at 'University Road' – a Literacy Event

This event is a very popular one throughout the Islamic world and is celebrated in all countries and in most mosques. The event commemorates the moment when the Prophet was taken by miraculous means from Mecca to Jerusalem and then onwards through the seven heavens to the presence of the Lord Almighty. There are many accounts of this journey and it has been remembered also in poetry and depicted in paintings. There are, obviously, verses and a chapter of the Qur'an devoted to this incident.

The event is organised by the imam, who, with the permission of the committee, or in this case, the chairman of the trust, makes use of the local and regional network of imams to construct a viable programme for the event. He invites an imam from a mosque in a nearby town who is a Qari ['he who recites the Qur'an'] and, therefore, excels in the recitation of the Qur'an. The imam, himself, could do this, but he knows that the event will last a long time, and he needs to have a variety of speakers and reciters in order to retain the congregation's attention. He invites an imam from Derby, who is particularly good at relating religious teaching stories, to relate the principal story of the celebration, the account of the Night Ascension. Although most of the congregation would be familiar with this narrative, there are a number of different versions of the story in existence in Urdu, and the iman's narrative will be embellished with other sayings and poetic verses.

The imam also asks two of his students to take part in the proceedings. Rashid is 14 and is already an accomplished reciter of naat [religious devotional verses]. The imam wants him to recite before the congregation an ode, in Urdu, on the life of the Prophet. Rashid understands the gist of what he is going to recite. Imran is 15 and is well on his way to becoming a hafiz, or memoriser, of the Qur'an. He is asked to prepare a very accurate recitation of the first 18 verses of the Qur'anic chapter, Najm, the Star, as they refer to the Ascension of the Prophet. Imran understands none of the words of what he is asked to recite.

> *By the Star when it sets,*
> *Your companion is neither astray nor misled*
> *Nor does he speak from himself*
> *It is but an inspiration to him,*
> *He was taught by One mighty in power,*
> *And in wisdom; for he appeared*
> *While he was at the height of the horizon,*
> *And he approached and came closer,*
> *And was at a distance of but two lengths or nearer,*
> *So did God convey the inspiration to His Servant*
> *What He meant to convey;*
> *His mind in no way falsified that which he saw*
> *Will you dispute with him concerning what he saw?*
> *For indeed he saw Him at a second descent,*
> *Near the lote tree beyond which none can pass,*
> *Near it is the Garden of the Abode,*
> *Behold, the lote tree was shrouded,*
> *His sight never swerved, nor faltered,*
> *For truly did he see,*
> *Of the Signs of his Lord,*
> *The Greatest!*

(Najm, *or* The Star, *Chapter 53, translated by Abdullah Yusuf Ali, 1934*)

The event is publicised in all the local mosques that share the same school of thought. The 'Church Walk' event will be publicised in one other Rotherham mosque as well as the mosque in Doncaster and also in the three mosques in Sheffield. The 'University Road' mosque publicises its event in two other Rotherham mosques as well as in four mosques in Sheffield. A poster is designed at a local Muslim-run printers and is distributed to the mosques with the request that the event be mentioned during the announcements which take place after the sermon on Friday.

On the day of the event, the mosque is given a spring clean by helpers. Bashir, who designed the LED displays around the mihrab in the prayer hall, lends a hand with the Hoover and others tidy up, removing the teaching benches from the hall to create more room, and rearranging the books on the shelves. Bashir also makes sure the public address system is working. The prayer hall is smaller than a school hall, but the mosque committee feels a need to demonstrate that it is in tune with modern technology. A place by the loudspeaker is not to be recommended.

Finally, no such event could take place without refreshments. A member of the congregation has offered to provide a meal at the end of the afternoon for all who attend. As sometimes the gathering could be attended by over 100 people it is no mean feat to arrange for the catering which usually consists of savoury and sweet rice, a curry and chapattis all washed down with pop or water. Each mosque usually has in a cupboard somewhere a large roll of catering paper that is unrolled along the floor at the end of the proceedings to enable people to eat on the floor.

The event begins at two in the afternoon with the afternoon prayer. At the end of the prayer, which lasts 20 minutes, the congregation remains sitting as the guest speakers sit at or near the front. The imam begins by speaking in Urdu. He introduces the guests and outlines the programme for the afternoon. Most of the congregation can follow this; even the younger members sitting near the back of the prayer hall can follow this simple information. Imran is then asked to recite his learned verses which he has spent a week preparing. He had to learn these verses from scratch because as yet he has not reached them in his gradual learning of the complete Qur'an. He has concentrated, with the help of the imam, on achieving as perfect a recitation as possible. This includes perfect pronunciation as well as the appropriate tone and rhythm. He is nervous as he has never recited in front of so many people before. Moreover, when he finishes at the mosque he has to go home and complete two outstanding pieces of English coursework.

The congregation listens attentively to Imran, and some of the elders, occasionally interject Arabic expressions such as 'subhan Allah ['glory to God!'] in between verses, a customary practice during Qur'anic recitations in mosques all over the world. His father observes Imran proudly, whilst his brothers try to avoid looking him in the eye, as it might break his concentration, and they might start giggling. No one, neither reciter nor listeners, understands what is being recited.

The Qari from the local mosque is then introduced by the imam and invited to begin his recitation. Again this is in Urdu and some of the elders in the congregation nod approvingly as the Qari's credentials are listed during the imam's introduction. We learn that he is Qari Hafiz ['he who has memorised the entire Qur'an'] Maulana ['our master'] Seyed [honorific title for someone claiming lineage to the Prophet] Muhammed Iqbal, Al-Hanifi [announces the owner's allegiance to the Hanifi school of Islamic law] Al-Qadiri [this latter title announces the owner's allegiance to a prominent Sufi order]. The Qari breathes deeply and begins to recite the first verse of the chapter in the Qur'an entitled, Bani Isra'il, the Children of Israel, which is translated by Abdullah Yusuf Ali in the following manner:

In the name of God, most Gracious, Most Merciful
Glory to God Who did take His servant
For a journey by night
From the Sacred Mosque
To the Farthest Mosque,

Whose precincts We did
Bless – in order that We
Might show him some
Of Our Signs: for He
Is the One Who hears and sees all things
(Bani Isra'il, The Children of Israel, *translated by Abdullah Yusuf Ali, 1934*

The reciter uses his breath to structure his recitation, with his breaths becoming ever longer as he seeks to recite an ever-longer string of words. As the convention whilst reciting is to complete a phrase only at a set point, when the reciter's breath obliges him to pause inappropriately, he returns to the beginning of the phrase, takes a longer breath, and 'tries' again to reach the point in the verse convention has decided is an appropriate stopping point. However, this is not quite what it sounds, because this is not an exercise in trying and trying until eventual success, for this process has now become a very stylised and deliberate method of recitation and is expected at the beginning of every recitation. The Qari spends 20 minutes on this short verse and his extended recitation is punctuated with the interjections of the congregation and the occasional feedback from the PA system. Again few in the mosque understand what is being recited.

After the recitation, the imam thanks the Qari and begins a short talk cum introduction to the next speaker, the imam from Derby. The imam's Urdu address includes Qur'anic verses and Prophetic sayings and lasts for about 15 minutes before the introduction is made. Again, most of the imam's address is understood by the members of the congregation but, as he begins to include Arabic verses and sayings and their more formal translations and explanations, the Urdu used begins to be rather hard for some of the younger boys to follow. The imam who takes over has an equally long name and proceeds to relate the story of how the Prophet travelled to Jerusalem upon a magical flying beast and then ascended to the heavens accompanied by the Angel Gabriel. The imam is wise and canny. He knows that the majority of the congregation are Mirpuri-Punjabi speakers, and intersperses Mirpuri-Punjabi words and phrases into his formal Urdu account. This makes for much more audience attention, especially among the younger members who are more familiar with the Mirpuri-Punjabi language than they are with Urdu. The speaker uses humour and pathos to engage his audience and accompanies his words with extravagant arm gestures and facial gesturing. He is able to deliver a very serious and important religious message with vivacity and empathy. At many points in his talk, the audience will laugh or express surprise or wonder. The Ascension account contains many descriptions of marvellous and horrific sights as the reader or listener is taken on a journey of the Heavens and Hell too.

Those who do understand Urdu well are very appreciative of the speaker's use of poetry during his talk. Whenever he arrives at a point in the narrative that lends itself to a particular poetic verse, the imam declaims the verse with gusto and enthusiasm.

Those who recognise a verse will occasionally recite with the imam, and for some very well-known verses up to half of the congregation will join in, chorus fashion.

The younger members of the congregation can participate in this part of the after-noon, for there is enough meaningful discourse to engage their attention. They are also helped by the speaker's talents in performance. However, it should be noted that not all speakers will be as sensitive to their audiences as the imam from Derby. In 'Church Walk', the imam, through no fault of his own, for he originates from a non-Punjabi speaking part of Pakistan and speaks only in Urdu, is unable to communicate to the young boys who attend on Fridays and on other occasions such as the event described here.

By now it is 4 in the afternoon and it is time for the late afternoon prayer. Some take this opportunity to leave the mosque, but most stay and some newcomers arrive. After the prayer, the congregation stands and a naat session takes place. Naat are declaimed or sung on auspicious occasions such as those mentioned above, though some mosques will have naat sessions at the end of every Friday prayer.

The imam is an accomplished naat reciter and he begins with a well-known Urdu naat that nearly everyone in the congregation knows. This means that the verses are mainly declaimed by the imam, and the entire congregation responds with the chorus. In some traditions, but not represented in this mosque, this form of recitation is accompanied by the beating of a drum. After the imam, with the congregation still on its feet, Rashid has his opportunity to recite the naat that he has learnt. His voice is still unbroken and his tenor notes ring out across the prayer hall. Through careful control of his breathing Rashid is able to deal with the tricky rhythm and cadence of his verses. At the end of his performance, many of the elders mutter the congratulatory 'ma sha'Allah' ['What God has willed' (is good)].

This is an opportunity for more humble members of the congregation to contribute to the proceedings. Many of the worshippers, young and old, have learnt various naat and are asked to recite. The collecting of naat is an activity that is being given a recent boost by the Internet. In the next chapter we will describe the cultural phenomenon that of electronic naat-swapping that is currently engaging many younger members of the UK Mirpuri communities.

The naat at this recital are all in Urdu, although such is the relationship between Urdu and Arabic that some of the refrains sound almost totally in Arabic. Again, in the next chapter we will discover the use of Punjabi naat within similar settings. It is also worth recording that occasionally Persian naat are recited at events such as this.

The Urdu naat session is followed by the end-of-event 'dua', or supplication, session. It is customary to ask the most prestigious guest to undertake this supplica-tion on behalf of the congregation. The imam asks the Derby imam to make the suppli-cation on behalf of everyone. He begins by supplicating in Arabic using well-known Arabic verses from the Qur'an and sayings of the Prophet. The congregation, despite not understanding most of these pleas and requests, respond with the universal 'ameen!' The language of the supplication changes into Urdu and the congregation, understandably, become more responsive as they react to meaningful phrases and expressions. Sometimes the supplication session can last for as long as twenty minutes.

Finally, the congregation is asked to recite the 'Fatihah', the first short chapter of the Qur'an, which serves as a seal on all that has preceded it. Some members of the congregation stand up and start sorting out the eating arrangements and everyone else lines up on either side of the spread-out catering roll and sits down opposite someone else. There are so many people in attendance that there are three lengths of catering roll running lengthways towards the back wall of the prayer hall and one more running at right angles to them across the back wall. With a minimum of fuss and an efficiency born of many previous similar events, the food is distributed and the congregation eats.

I decided to include a detailed description of this particular literacy event in order to portray the richness and creativity of the Mirpuri community as it engages in a religious celebration common to the Islamic world. The literacies that are encountered in such an event are complex, rich and diverse. No participant has full access to all the potential of any particular literacy here represented. The Arabic, much in evidence, is understood by few, and even then, in a limited way. The Urdu is understood fully by some, partially by others and not at all by many. Mirpuri-Punjabi, a language that the community speaks, makes its first full appearance at the meal at the end of the afternoon. English, the language of the wider society outside the mosque, remains an interloper, spoken in snatches by some of the younger members of the congregation.

It should also be obvious that the participants in this particular event are exclusively male. However, equivalent events for females are often arranged and held either in the home or in the mosque at another time.

Future Status of Urdu in the Community

The key language, here, is Urdu. Without knowledge of Urdu, much of what is described above is incomprehensible. There is obviously no danger of the disappearance of Urdu back home in Pakistan where its role as the national language and its role in education and the media secure its position and ensure its development. In the UK, within Mirpuri communities, struggling to maintain their liturgical literacy in the mosque, and adamant about ensuring their children succeed at school, in English, the decision to support the development of Urdu is a difficult one. I end this chapter with the words of one parent that encapsulate the dilemma all these parents and their children are facing in respect of language maintenance:

Munir: One way, actually, if I try to learn here, it is very difficult for the children. Because sometimes parents do not give pressure on children to carry on with our language, Arabic, Urdu, and they go to an English school as well. I myself think that if they link with the school, there is this Urdu language, then children will try to learn, that because it comes into his mind, that is one subject actually. And when I have tried at home, they think we give to them pressure. And they are confused like. They say too much work in school, then going to mosque, then Dad asking about our language ...

Do you think they could do it in the mosque?

Well, actually, before they tried to teach it on a Sunday. Children come Sunday and try to teach them Urdu. But sometimes children want to play ... And to go for seven days is very hard for the children. But we are British, so why don't the British accept our language into education? I think myself, that Urdu is very important in school, you know. When they finish school, they are here only one hour and then they are going to the mosque. It's too much. He says if he goes to mosque then he has no time for homework. That's why he is going to leave maybe next year.

Summary

At the end of the literacy event described above the congregation sat down to eat. At this juncture it was possible to discern the encroachment of other languages upon the proceedings. The formality of Urdu is reserved at present for those occasions that demand it and will be maintained for as long as there is a critical mass of Urdu users within the community. The vital and necessary languages for everyday communication fill the space Urdu that leaves behind when these occasions of formality end. At present there are two such lingua francas in use within the community, Mirpuri-Punjabi and English. The next two chapters examine the role that these languages play in the life and literacies of the community.

Chapter 11

Mirpuri-Punjabi

Introduction

Despite being the largest language group in Pakistan, Punjabi, or more correctly, Western Punjabi, is not considered an official language. With up to 45 million speakers according to the 1981 census, the language is spoken in the Punjab area of Pakistan. It is obviously linguistically-related to Eastern Punjabi which is spoken in India. In fact, there is a continuum of varieties between Eastern and Western Punjabi and with Western Hindi and Urdu. There is also a variety of dialects within Western Punjabi, of which Mirpuri-Punjabi is one. *Ethnologue* (Gordon, 2005) includes Mirpuri-Punjabi as a separate language distinct from the occasionally-heard Potwari or Pahari, although Mirpuri is listed as a dialect of the latter.

Figure 3 Mirpur, where the Mirpuri dialect is spoken

Mirpur, Punjabi and Mirpuri-Punjabi

The Mirpur area of Pakistan lies next to the border with India, and forms part of the Pakistani side of the disputed territory of Kashmir, in an area known as Azad Kashmir. This accounts for many UK-based Mirpuris claiming to be Kashmiri as well as Pakistani or Mirpuri. Mirpur itself is a relatively small area and officially has a population of only 30,000 or so. There are actually more Mirpuri speakers residing outside of Pakistan, particularly in the UK, than there are in Pakistan. However, other sources indicate that there up to 7 or 8 million speakers of Mirpuri in Pakistan and up to a million in the UK. This discrepancy is explained by the uncertain status of dialects (in particular, the names given to dialects) in censuses and other linguistic surveys. Another contributing factor to the language's uncertain status is its lack of a recognised written form. A written form, with its associated literature and educational support, ensures a recognisable status for a language, providing it with legitimacy, a history and a material form capable of being preserved, analysed and developed. A spoken language is dependent on its speakers alone for its integrity and, if not supported officially or educationally, remains a low status language.

Linguistically, Western Punjabi and its varieties of Mirpuri and Potwari belong to the same language family as Urdu, Indo-Aryan and, further back, Indo-European. Their intelligibility with other varieties of Punjabi and Urdu itself varies according to the geographical extremes of the continuum. At their most extreme, Western Hindi and Potwari dialects are the most removed from one another and speakers from each group would be the least intelligible to one another. The fact that Mirpuri, Potwari and northern Western Punjabi dialects are so close to one another geographically explains their mutual intelligibility as well as the confusion around what to call them.

Unlike Eastern Punjabi which has a written form, and a rich literary tradition, Western Punjabi is rarely written. When it is, it uses the same Perso-Arabic script that is used for Urdu. The extant literature is limited at the present moment to poetry. Speakers of Western Punjabi are predominantly Muslims. Eastern Punjabi enjoys a much more enhanced status both in India and around the world because of its association with Sikhism. The Gurmukhi script, used for all Sikh sacred scriptures, and for all Eastern Punjabi literature, serves as a reinforcing and preserving factor in the status and development of the language.

Self-perception of Language Use

Confusion regarding the name of particular languages or dialects is common within the Mirpuri community, particularly among the young.

Most adults refer to their spoken language as Punjabi. Their responses also reveal a certain awareness of the lack of prestige their own language possesses.

Munir: My language is not Urdu. It's like a Yorkshire, you know.

Jabbar: My mother tongue is called Punjabi. This speech is like slang like.

Most are aware that their spoken language is a variant of the more standard Punjabi, and many draw a parallel between the differences between Mirpuri and standard Punjabi and the dialects of South Yorkshire and standard English.

Wajib: That [Punjabi] is not my language. It's like a Punjabi, you know.
Mirpur?
Mirpur language, yes. My mother language, you know, it's not a Punjabi, like a Yorkshire, you know.

Sometimes, someone might suggest that his or her mother tongue is Urdu. However, it is quite possible that the speaker may be intending to signal some form of cultural and educational status by doing so. There is no doubt that the community considers Urdu to be a much more prestigious language.

Jabbar: Urdu. [His wife, Rukshana, interrupts.] No, Punjabi. [Rukshana interrupts again.] We speak Punjabi at home.
Rukshana: Some people speak Urdu.
Jabbar: Here we all speak Punjabi. Urdu. I think it's a dialect, isn't it? Really. It's Punjabi I think.
[Consults Rukshana here.] Punjabi dialect. I speak more from the Mirpuri side and my wife from Deena is more from the Punjabi side. Different dialects but more or less the same. No big difference.

Gender Difference in Language Awareness

In a significant number of interviews where both husband and wife were present, it was soon apparent that the wife possessed a greater sensitivity to and awareness of language difference than her husband. Indeed, what was obvious in a number of families was that the wife was generally more educated, and definitely more familiar with Urdu than her husband was. It was also apparent that the wives tended to come from urban environments such as Lahore. Socially, what seemed to have happened is that Mirpuri males, despite originating from rural area with relatively low levels of education, because of their residence in the UK, in terms of arranged marriages were now esteemed to be suitable matches for more sophisticated and educated females from families in urban areas. This would definitely explain situations such as the comments from the family below when asked about their respective knowledge of Urdu and Punjabi. At first, Rukshana, the wife, characterises the difference between the language practices of herself and her husband to be that between Mirpuri, or Potwari, and standard Punjabi:

> *Nafisah* (their daughter): My mum is just saying that she's from a city, my dad is from a village and they speak the Potwari language, and my mum speaks the Punjabi language proper. Village people don't know that much, they don't go to school [Rukshana interrupts]. It's different – *jaana* – *jaassa*.
>
> *Is that an example of two words?*
>
> Yes, like 'we're going' in the two languages.

As the conversation proceeds, this distinction is made even clearer by references to Urdu and to education.

> *Nafisah*: She is just saying that people coming from Mirpur originally or somewhere like that, they speak Punjabi, the people coming from the cities, with a good education and that, they speak Urdu.

The links between knowledge of and speaking Urdu to social manners and privileged language use are also very apparent within this family:

> *Nafisah:* My mum speaks Urdu, doesn't speak Punjabi, she speaks in a more mannered way. More than my dad. My mum speaks good Urdu so we all speak Urdu with her. So they (the children) come up with better language and that.

It is also obvious that Urdu maintenance is in the hands of the mother, as she has the skill and knowledge to enable her to do this. Socially, girls in the Mirpuri community spend more time with their mothers than they do with their fathers and this, by itself, is often sufficient reason to explain the more confident use of Urdu and spoken Mirpuri-Punjabi, among young females:

> *Nafisah:* I learnt it [Urdu] from my mum. Because she knows a lot.
>
> *When and who taught you?*
>
> At a small age.
>
> *Did she teach you to speak Urdu as well?*

Reading and writing. She used to help us with that. She learnt us to speak a bit of Urdu, it's more in a mannered way. We speak a bit different from other girls and they always say you speak a bit ... It's because my mum is a bit different you see. It's mixed Urdu and Punjabi, it's not full. Punjabi is like a slack language you see, and Urdu is more mannered. So we speak both.

Are there other families that speak Urdu?

Only one or two families. But not a lot. Most of them just don't care.

Is that because of your mum?

Yeah. Because she's from Lahore. If she was from Mirpur it would be different.

Perhaps the most perceptive comment about the confusing linguistic profile of the Mirpuri community came from this man, Wajib, when asked for the name of his mother tongue. It was unusual for someone to have such explicit awareness of language and dialect:

Wajib: Punjabi. Or Mirpuri, a dialect of Punjabi. Yes. The language that we speak is very very similar to Potwari. It would be the closest one linked. Potwari is spoken in Pakistan, a few areas of Pakistan. Potwari is spoken in Kashmir. And where we live, most people from that area.

And is that the same for most of the community?

Yes. Most of the community would speak that language. Some people might call it Potwari. But Potwari is basically spoken mainly in some area of Pakistan. The official language though of the whole area of Pakistan is Urdu.

Potwari or Mirpuri-Punjabi Literacy

Potwari is the name given to the variant of Western Punjabi spoken by people of Mirpuri origin resident in the UK by the language activist Tariq Mehmood, based in Manchester, UK. He uses the term to cover all the different dialects that might be spoken by UK-based Mirpuris. That his term is disputed by members of the Mirpuri community is indicative of the uncertainty that surrounds the language. However, it is a useful umbrella term for referring to the Mirpuri speakers in the UK and elsewhere. Mehmood characterises it as:

... an ancient language of the hill tracts of what is today Pakistan and Kashmir. Its general linguistic 'border' would start at the North bank of the river Jhelum going up to the south bank of the river Atack in Punjab,

Pakistan and eastwards towards the western face of the Pirpanjaal mountain range, crossing into Jammu Kashmir. (*Our Suppressed Language*, n.d.)

Mehmood claims that the number of active speakers of Potwari or Mirpuri in the UK to number up to 700,000, which, after Welsh, would make it the most commonly-spoken second language in the UK. He lists Bradford, Leeds, Manchester, Sheffield, Oldham and Birmingham as among the main British cities where the language is spoken.

> Our language has primarily been kept alive by workers and toilers, with the middle classes, following a policy left behind by the British, teaching their children Urdu, maintaining that the people's language is crude, rustic and worthless. (*Our Suppressed Language*, n.d.)

Mehmood is trying to address illiteracy within the Mirpuri community both in the UK and in Pakistan by developing a Potwari literature. It is hoped that by using the Perso-Arabic script used for Urdu, many more people will be able to develop literacy in their mother tongue. It should be remembered that the script, or at least the Arabic script from which it is derived, is known through the liturgical literacy acquired in the mosque. This is obviously akin to the Qur'anic literacy campaign carried out in Pakistan in the 1990s. So far, some short stories and some children's books as well as a magazine, *Chitka*, have been published using this script.

There is little doubt that the development of reading and writing is heavily influenced by a person's command of the language in question. To read initially in one's mother tongue is the ideal situation. A child's experience of the world is enmeshed with his or her language development. To begin reading in a second or even a third language is to put that child at a considerable disadvantage. The Common Underlying Proficiency (see Chapter 9: School), which might facilitate subsequent reading in different languages, is less satisfactorily acquired when one is reading for the first time in a language that is not the mother tongue. Even in those specific situations where individuals learn to read in a language that they do not know (for example, an English-speaking scientist learning to read academic Russian), they would be hard pressed to do this had they not learnt to read in their own language in the first instance. The strength in Mehmood's campaign is that, unlike the Pakistani government sponsored Qur'anic Literacy, which aimed to develop Urdu literacy, he is attempting to develop literacy in the mother tongue. Set against him is a generations-old, and state-supported, prejudice against literacies other than Urdu and liturgical literacy in Arabic, originating in Pakistan and transferred to the UK. Linked to this are the community's own feelings of self-worth in respect of its mother tongue. Nearly all those questioned spoke in rather disparaging terms of their own language, likening it to 'village' or 'slang' language. Only occasionally, would a respondent speak positively about his own language:

Jabbar: I only speak Punjabi, you see, I like my language. I like it.

There was also the strong feeling that, were a language to be retained and preserved for the future generation's use, that language should be Urdu rather than Punjabi.

How important do you consider your first language is for you? Your children?

Fameeda: Punjabi language I am not really, I think is important, but Urdu language is very important actually. Punjabi language is basically a village language. But if children get to know Urdu, Urdu is a proper language.

So you don't think it is important for the children to know Punjabi?

The children catch Punjabi from us, how we speak, they speak in that way. But Urdu is a subject concerned with education. Punjabi is not just language. It is not mostly concerning writing and reading. Where we live in Kashmir, they speak Punjabi but all paper they write in Urdu, educational system in Urdu. I myself think in my opinion, if a child learns Urdu, it is better for them.

Mirpuri-Punjabi Usage

We have already described how the formal language of the mosque, Urdu, is employed and privileged. It is in the home that Mirpuri-Punjabi remains strongest. Among the first two generations of settlers, those who came as single males in the 1950s and 1960s and those who came as children in the 70s, Mirpuri-Punjabi is still the dominant language of business and relationships. As children have been born here, English has begun to make serious inroads into this linguistic monopoly and this will be explored more fully in the next chapter.

It is in the home that Mirpuri-Punjabi has its widest scope. When asked to whom, when and where they spoke Mirpuri-Punjabi it was family and friends contexts which occurred the most regularly.

Munir: Actually, mostly when we meet each other in the community, we speak to each other our language. Punjabi like.

Hameed: With old people who have come from Pakistan. And a lot of the people living round here. From my family, you know. We speak our language. I mean a lot of my relatives don't know English fully. They can't understand. So also you know, language, if you speak English some other one does not understand, it's no good speaking English. I mean this is our mother language. When we speak to each other they can understand very well. And they can answer right. A lot of English words are very difficult to understand. And if I say people living in Rotherham they are qualified and educated, no. They are not educated.

With whom do you speak your first language?
Nafisah: At home.
Is it spoken in the mosque or do they use Urdu there?
Urdu.
[**Rukshana** interrupts: No, Punjabi.]
Some they speak Punjabi, some they speak.
If you are sitting in the mosque after the namaz, and you are talking with your friends ...
Punjabi.

However, even among those parents who speak exclusively with one another in Mirpuri-Punjabi, there is not a straightforward choice of speaking Mirpuri-Punjabi to their children.

Do you speak to your children in Punjabi? All the time?
Munir: I myself sometimes speak to them in Punjabi language.
At home?
Well, these all children they speak mostly English. To brother and sister, you know. When I speak to them, if they don't understand in my own language, in mother language, I speak to them English. I try to explain to them. So they understand.

As this parent recognised, it was quite common for siblings to converse in English at home. Sometimes this was denied by parents who prided themselves on running a purely Mirpuri-Punjabi speaking household, but this was often in the face of direct evidence to the contrary. In this extract a mother is responding to questions on the use of Mirpuri-Punjabi whilst her teenage son (Munir) is interjecting his own observations:

So, for example, if you were arguing with your brother, you'd be doing it in Punjabi.

Munir: No, I'd be doing it in English! [laughter]

So when is English used in the house? When do you use English in the house?

Fameeda: I don't use English in the house. I only speak English when my English friends come or people who do not understand Punjabi. Or Urdu. Then I speak with them English. With the girls I strictly at home speak Urdu. Because English I know, my kids know. Everybody knows.

So who speaks English at home?

Munir: Actually, we speak among ourselves in English.

Fameeda: Sometimes they do. [*Munir:* A lot of the time.] Oh, yes. But when we speak with the children we speak Urdu. I mean, my daughters, they speak very good Urdu. And now I am teaching my grandchildren to speak Urdu. And I taught all of them to speak in Urdu.

Among some of the younger parents, those who were born or, at least, educated here, there is a greater tendency to rely on English. One young man whose wife was educated in Pakistan was very aware of what was happening to his peers. Indeed, his wife being from Pakistan rather from the UK was a significant factor in his children growing up bilingual:

Bashir: The great majority of the time they are English speakers ... I have a large family in Birmingham ... and they go the local mosque ... they acquaint themselves with Asian children ... but the majority of everything they speak is in English ... they don't have a mother tongue like we do ... if my wife spoke in English I don't think my children would know as much ... of Urdu ... this is what I am seeing with my family members in Birmingham ... where their children have been brought up with this atmosphere and background where both parents speak English ... the only time their parents speak Urdu, is possibly when they meet up with their parents ... because our forefathers have started to disappear ... the new generation ... it's not a case they have no connection with their grandparents ... the thing is they don't have to speak Urdu ... they can speak English ... and if both people know English ... to read and write ... say, for instance on the television remote control it says 'on', where you turn it on, so even if I were to speak in Urdu, I would say 'can you turn the television on', even to my wife, who doesn't speak a great deal of English ...

Another parent, from an older generation, with grown-up children, was keenly aware of the precarious status of their mother tongue:

Akhtar: For example, take my son, and his wife, they're both English, she's a Muslim and Pakistani, but she's English, the same as my son is ... And there's nothing to support it ... they're kids who will speak even less Urdu than we do ...

Mirpuri-Punjabi, Urdu and Popular Culture

Finally, in this chapter it is worth describing the growth of a recent cultural and religious activity that may contribute to a delay or even postpone the total loss of the Punjabi language from the Mirpuri community as the generations ensue. In the previous chapter a literacy event known as the *Laylat-ul-Miraaj* was described in detail as an example of the use of Urdu within the community. In the final session of the event, a number of members of the congregation recited *naat*, or religious verses, in Urdu. It would have been equally possible for the *naat* to be in Punjabi. Many young people, both male and female, are now discovering, composing, transcribing, recording, learning and reciting privately and publicly religious *naat* in both Urdu and Punjabi. What is of most interest is that the transcription that takes place is in fact transliteration, and that these young people are making use of the more familiar, to them, Roman script.

A typical literacy event for one of these young people can look like this. Sitting at home listening to a *naat* on either a CD or downloaded MP3 file from the Internet, the young person listens carefully to the Punjabi words and, with no recourse to Perso-Arabic script, he or she chooses to transcribe them using Roman letters. One *naat* follows another and soon a whole pocket-sized notebook is full of transcribed verses, some in Urdu, some in Punjabi, and some even in Arabic. When asked to recite a *naat* at a gathering, the notebook is carefully removed from a pocket and the *naat* is recited word for word. However, when asked to share one's transcribed *naat* with a friend, excuses are offered because the system used for transcription is a very personal and idiosyncratic one. No two people, as yet, have developed a common method of transliterating the Urdu or Punjabi poetry. The only available official method of transliteration has been consulted by some of the young people, and discarded as too complicated and unhelpful. This is a truly living and elemental literacy that is arising from a practical need to record sound on paper, quickly and for a specific purpose.

Many gatherings of the kind described in the previous chapter take place in cities and towns up and down the UK. It is encouraging to witness so many young people involved and contributing to what are significant events of liturgical literacy. Muslim gatherings are usually gender-specific and the gatherings observed and described here have been all-male events.

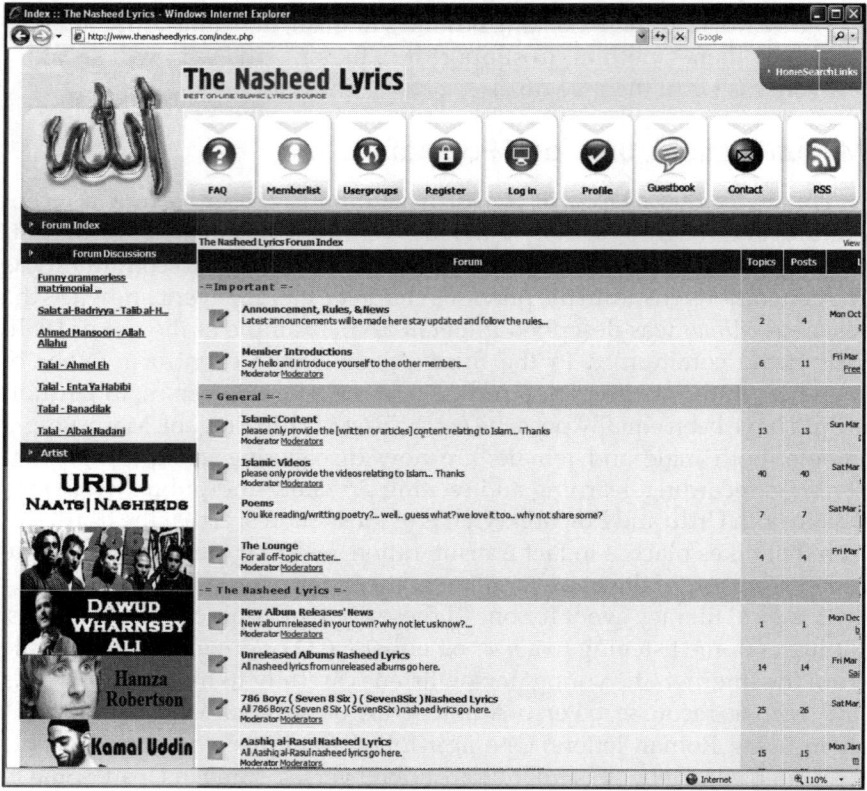

Plate 39 Web page offering *naat* downloads (*Nasheed Lyrics*, n.d.)

However, all-female events of a similar nature take place in homes within the community. Moreover, there are now a number of UK and worldwide websites that assist people in collecting and downloading *naat* in a variety of languages (Plate 39). These sites, usually in English, also allow users to discuss through forums the relative merits of different *naat* and information about their provenance and country of origin.

Summary

Although the principal theme of this study is the acquisition and maintenance of liturgical literacy, it is impossible to examine this literacy practice in isolation from the other literacy practices with which it interacts. The future of the mother tongue of this community, Mirpuri-Punjabi, hangs in the balance. Its lack of an officially-recognised script hinders its survival, though even that development is no guarantee of a future. The position within the community of Urdu, which does have a rich and strong literate and literary legacy, as I indicated in the last chapter, is uncertain. The growing use of Roman script to capture the sounds and words of popular religious songs and poems is helping the two languages to survive, albeit in a transformed way. The younger generation is, in a true sense, using the linguistic resources it has at its disposal to harness and engage with an art form, and a literacy, that risked being beyond its linguistic reach. The community's relationship with its mother tongue is, therefore, an ambivalent one. This ambivalence is even more evident in its relationship with English, the subject of the next chapter.

Chapter 12
English

Introduction

Of all the languages in use within the Mirpuri community at present, less concern is expressed by parents about English than about any other. The parents have acquired enough English to enable them to work and function within and interact with the wider society. The children are growing up speaking English both at school and at home. They even tend to speak English among themselves more and more. It is probable that, in time, English will become the principal language of the Muslim community in Rotherham.

In this chapter we will examine further the role that English plays within the educational provision of the mosque. There is no doubt, and I hope previous chapters have demonstrated, that the liturgical literacy taught and practised in the mosque is focused fully on the acquisition and use of accurate decoding of Qur'anic Arabic. Where instruction in connection with this teaching takes place, it is principally done through the medium of Urdu. This is because, on the one hand, this is the tradition of the mosques in question and, on the other, because the teachers themselves can only teach using Urdu, though sometimes recourse may be made to Mirpuri-Punjabi. Urdu remains the language most readily associated with learning and scholarship. Many imams are still recruited on the basis of their Islamic scholarship mediated through the Urdu language. The use of English in the mosque is now a controversial issue with Home Secretaries (Blunkett, 2003) and other European politicians (*DR Nyheder*, 2004) entering into the debate. What was a local and often parochial matter is starting to become a national and even international affair.

Parental Feelings

In discussions with parents, it is apparent that many of them are dissatisfied with certain aspects of instruction in the mosques to which they send their children. In general, these parents are content with the manner in which children are taught how to read the Arabic of the Qur'an. It has been mentioned on a number of occasions already what an efficient and effective job the mosques do in terms of young people acquiring accurate and fluent decoding skills. However, most parents are united in their belief that this is not adequate to equip children with at least a basic understanding of their faith. They put this failing down to language. As more and more of the young people attending the mosque classes rely on English as their principal language for meaning-making both in and outside of school, there is more and more of a communication gap between teacher and student in the mosque.

Literacy Learning and Meaning-making

In Chapter 5; Teachers, I described briefly the methods of instruction in the mosque and the opportunities that exist for learning activities outside of the intensive decoding acquisition and practice. In the previous two chapters I have outlined the possible risks involved in the community losing its access to the rich heritage of the Urdu language and the potential contribution that mother-tongue Mirpuri-Punjabi could make to religious practice. However, the common element in all activities described in the previous two chapters – the sermons, the gatherings, the recitations – is the apparent lack of meaningful engagement with the texts employed. Beyond an intangible sense that one is reciting something holy and pure, which should not be underestimated as an authentic and genuine purpose, there is little or no sense of the words themselves. The *naat* provide a taste of meaning for those with enough Urdu and Punjabi to access them. Many in the audience, unfortunately, do not have such access.

Parents have expressed quite clearly their desire to include the English language within the mosque system of education and instruction. In the following extract, Munir refers to a book called *Taalim ul-Haq*. This is a book available in English that outlines the basic tenets of the Islamic faith for children. Munir is complaining that too much attention is paid to mere decoding.

> *Munir:* I have seen the system in the mosque is not very good. So I have discussed with the committee about the children. They should read *Taalim ul-Haq*. Because lots of things in the *Taalim ul-Haq* they can understand. And if they do not read *Taalim ul-Haq* they don't know what Islam says. So *Taalim ul-Haq* is very important for our children who are born here. If they read the Qur'an they do not know what the Qur'an says. Because Arabic only they can read. But they don't know what is meaning of Qur'an. Because they don't understand. To read with English translation. If the teacher tries to explain the meaning then they can understand. Otherwise these children do not know anything about Islam.

What does the committee say when you tell them this?

They make an excuse. They say we are only paying £150 to £200 pounds a week to the imam. And they say this is too much for an imam. They have two teachers, one an imam, the other is a teacher. They pay him £50. And he knows English. He can understand Islam very well. He knows about Islam. But they don't give education of *Taalim ul-Haq*. They are also saying we need another teacher because there are so many children. So they want to make a separate group. Try to teach them *Taalim ul-Haq*! If you are saying to them, you are sending your children to the mosque for teaching Islam. But they are only learning and reading the Qur'an. They don't know what the Qur'an says. So we want a teacher who can teach them, learn them good ways. They should understand, but our imam can't speak English, he knows only Arabic. He's a Qari, you know. He knows about the Qur'an very well. This is very important for our young generation. If we don't do that, they won't know. It's wasting time. Only that Dars, Dar-ul Uloom, of Shabbir, he's very good and is giving a good education. A lot of children are going there, 40 children are there and a waiting list of about 70. I'm not sure but he has eight teachers, and they are teaching. Because they know very well English. And about Islam. The children come from all over. All children are going one day, if they have a big hall for children, then all children will go there but he has no room, that's why there is a waiting list. He's going to extend the place for those children who are on the waiting list. And when he has got plenty room all children will go there. Because the people know he is giving a good education. He is trying to make a proper human, when he grows up he is not making bad things.

In the extract above, Munir mentions the success that a former imam of the mosque is having through using English extensively to teach the children. Others are aware that Urdu is no longer an appropriate medium for teaching Islam to their children:

Wajib: Yes, because of the language as well. Because most of the kids, they are very fluent in English and were born here and most of the kids speak English and some of them have difficulty understanding Mirpuri or Urdu. Especially Urdu. Mainly Urdu they have difficulty understanding it. I mean if they don't understand it how are they going to learn? So what I have been suggesting is that the teachers can communicate well with kids and they get the message across. This is why we're falling behind.

There is often poignancy in comments made about the community's loss of Urdu

Akhtar: The biggest gripe I have with them is that they won't preach in English ... There's a guy, Mr Shabbir, who's got a private school. He's doing excellent work. Because it's in English! This is what you've got to do...They're preaching in Urdu ... Urdu is not our language ... Urdu is not the language of my children ... although it is a beautiful language ... beautiful language ... and I regret not keeping it up ...

There is also an awareness that the imam not only needs to know English, but also needs to be knowledgeable about the society and environment his students inhabit:

Akhtar: For the future of the kids yes, something like that, where the imam can speak English, translation, and taking both cultures into one and explain to them this is how it should be and this is Islam and all that. So the youngsters can understand. On a Friday they can't understand what the imam is saying.

Is that because he is speaking in Urdu?

Yes. Very like Shakespeare Urdu. If you know what I mean. Really deep Urdu that I have to listen to it carefully and it takes me a long time to understand some of the words.

So who is he speaking to? Who understands it?

Mainly the older generation.

Parental Acquisition of English

The generation of parents who arrived in the 1950s and early 60s in order to work often came with little or no knowledge of English, and there was little in the way of English classes to help them acquire the language. Most acquired their knowledge of English on the job and more widely in their interactions with the community.

When you first came, was there any opportunity to learn English?

Jabbar: At that time, there was no option. I could write down my name and address.

Did you learn English at school?

Just from working with people.

The nature of the employment undertaken meant that language learning was not a priority at that time. The unsocial hours of shift work also militated against attending evening classes though some managed to do so:

Hameed: I came to England. I was only young at that time. 16 or 17 years old. That time when we came to this country we had no facilities like now, at that time people were thinking about jobs. I started in 1963. I went only a few days to that school in Park Street. Used to be a lot of people who couldn't read and write. Now in this country there are all facilities for people who don't speak English to learn.

Was the school in Park Street for everybody?

It was classes for our people at night. Evening lessons.

Those who arrived in the late 60s and early 70s fared a little better. They came when they were still at school age, often just as they were finishing primary or beginning secondary schools, usually accompanying their mothers. There is clear evidence that this generation of men encountered considerable frustration in their educational experience. Their parents, particularly their fathers, who, of course, were based here, perhaps under-estimated the difficulty their children would have learning English quickly enough in order to benefit from a UK education. By bringing their children to the UK later, rather than earlier, a considerable language hurdle was placed before these young people who had to make up in four or five years what they had missed in the first six years or so of compulsory schooling.

What about here then, did you just have to pick it up? Thrown into 'Kings-wood' School and just had to survive ... ?

Wajib: That's why I was quite backward ... because I wasn't thick or anything, but I was quite backward because it took me so long to pick up the language. To learn the language. When it came to maths, I was always top of the class. Because that's the same. And when we were taught maths times tables up to 20 times tables off by heart, we had to learn them, before we were 5 or 6 years old. We learnt before we were 10 or 11. We had to learn them off by heart. Whenever it came to maths I was top. But it took me so long to pick up the English. I was lacking in other subjects. So, when I did CSEs I mean some of the questions I couldn't understand so if you don't understand the question, just one word even, you don't understand the question do you? So obviously, I didn't do very well. That put me a lot back ...

Is that typical? Of men of your generation?

Yes, it was typical.

Hanif: Here, I went to 'South Ash' School, not comprehensive, I got some CSEs, that's about it, I didn't go to college. Started work in a garage. I left at 15, no 16, that was the year it changed. 1974–75. I wasn't urged to go into the academic side in them days for some reason. I still remember the careers adviser, he goes ... into the academic side, more told to work, don't know, some reason, I could just remember right if I get another chance I might have gone into college, or university, but them days, no.

So how far did you go with school here?
Akhtar: CSEs. In those days, you either did CSEs or O-levels. Depending on how bright you were. And I did CSEs.
So you left at 16?
Yeah. Because in them four years, I had to learn English, I had to learn the language, and then, I think without trying to sound pretentious, I did quite well. To get the CSEs in them four years. Thinking back I should have gone on to further college, further education, life is such. My dad was getting on a bit. So we decided to start working.

It is impossible to hear or read these words without identifying the very obvious feelings of regret and frustration of these men. There is a strong sense of wasted ability behind these comments. The first man spent most of his working life as a taxi driver, the second is a car mechanic and only the third has managed to achieve some sense of fulfilment by becoming a councillor.

Parental Opinion about Children's Progress in English

However, despite their own unfulfilled experiences of UK schooling, they have not developed a negative attitude towards UK schools in general and consider their own children to have had all the opportunities they themselves were denied.

What is your opinion about schools in UK?
Wajib: I think they're doing a good job. Most of my children did well. For themselves. So obviously I can't blame schools as regard that obviously. Pupils have to try themselves and parents have to force it ... I think we're lacking in that respect as well. Parenting.

Akhtar: That's an interesting one. I think by all accounts from my own experiences I think they do a very good job. As far as the educational standards are concerned, I can't really comment that much because my children have done very well at school. They have all done exceedingly well. They have not gone on to build on that, the two of them, the third one, God willing is going to be a barrister. She is doing very well in her A-levels.

There is also a very strong sense of a generation of parents desiring for their children something better than they had or experienced.

Akhtar: The thing is all the work that my father did. He worked 16 hours a day, six days a week. If I don't make my life more comfortable than his, he has failed. I'm the second generation. And, *alhamdulillah,* Allah has been very good to me. More than I deserve. A lot more than I deserve! Now for us to ... as a family, and as a race as well, for us to make my dad's sacrifice worth it, my children must go to the next level ...

Do better than you?

Absolutely, that's when I will think of my life as a success ... Now unless I get someone professional from my family, I don't think I will have failed but, the next day I want him an MP, and maybe the next generation a minister. That was my hope and my dreams for my kids and for my people

To a certain extent, one can understand the positive slant these parents place upon the education their children have received. Their children, in general, have succeeded at school with a number of them going on to higher education. Yet, there is also the sense that their opinion of UK education and schools is a rather benign one. When problems do arise, it is not unusual for the source of the problem to be from within the community rather than one that the school might be able to do something about.

Wajib: Most of the young people in this area are going haywire because most of the Asian people from Kashmir just I think they ... I think that's bad upbringing personally.

The national picture regarding the educational achievement within this minority ethnic group is not one about which there seems to be a great deal of awareness. The majority of parents spoken to had only good things to say about their local schools.

In respect of learning English, it would appear that most parents are content with a natural acquisition of the language that takes place through attending school and interacting with others. They claim that there is no real problem with learning English because their children will pick it up willy-nilly. There is an obvious link to be made here with Cummins' theories (1984, 2000) on bilingual development where he makes a distinction between conversational language proficiency and academic language proficiency. The former is that variety of a spoken language one acquires relatively quickly when living among speakers of that language. It is a 'survival' and social form of the language that enables users to interact with and 'fit in' with that language community as quickly as possible. For children, the desire to 'fit in' is often paramount, particularly in a school context. As a result, it often takes a short amount of time for learners to develop conversational language proficiency. Academic language proficiency, on the other hand, is that variety of a language most closely associated with formal and literate contexts. The language of school, and particularly, the language of success at school, is very much an example of the latter. This academic variety of a language takes considerably longer to acquire. Parents witness their children speaking and interacting in English with their friends, their siblings and sometimes even insisting on speaking English with them. They conclude, quite naturally, that their children cannot be experiencing any problems with English at school because of the apparent ease in English they demonstrate.

> *Nageena:* Actually I am not worried about language, English. Mother tongue. These are good for our children.
>
> *Munir:* Not really, no. Personally I consider this country to be home, our country, so I don't think language makes any difference to them.
>
> *Hameed:* Yeah, because, I know they can pick up English quite well, I mean obviously their English is quite good.
>
> *Wajib:* No, no, no. I don't have worries about my children or any children. They learn enough English. I am more worried about them losing out on their own mother tongue.

Indeed, there is a great deal of concern that children are relying too much on English and are, therefore, neglecting their mother tongue of Mirpuri-Punjabi.

> *Wajib:* My own idea was that children are quite capable in English, and should be encouraged to speak Mirpuri, or Potwari, at home, amongst themselves as well as their parents, you know, and that way they don't use it. Because they have already picked up English, so they don't need to improve English as much. They do need it academically, but at home, if they carried on.... That's why I encouraged my children not to speak English ...

This would all seem rather strange to a recent UK Home Secretary who, in early 2003, claimed that British Asian families spoke too little English at home and that this was partly responsible for the community's isolation from mainstream society (Blunkett, 2003). On the one hand, we have a generation of frustrated parents whose children are leaving their language and culture behind them and, on the other, what appears to be an ill-informed minister complaining that the same community is reducing its employment and educational opportunities by jealously hanging on to its language and culture.

Summary

We have mentioned in previous chapters the various uses of English within the educational provision provided by the mosques. There is no doubt that the mosques, their teachers and their students are entering a period of significant transition. With the gradual replacement of mother tongue Mirpuri-Punjabi by spoken English, and with the weakening of Urdu as the community's literary language, the language of communication and instruction is likely to be English. We have already seen evidence of this in the breakaway school of Maulana Shabbir where English is the principal language of instruction for teaching the tenets of the faith, and also in the gradual encroachment of Roman script into some methods of teaching Arabic. The political interference into the language issue relating to liturgical literacy that has arisen since September 11th 2001 is one example of the scrutiny the Muslim community of the UK and elsewhere has come under. There are strong arguments for an increased use of English in UK mosque schools. It is to be hoped that such arguments can be conducted on a purely educational and sociolinguistic basis without outside political influence. However, whatever the future role of English may look like within the mosque school, there is little possibility of the central role and position of Arabic being affected in a similar way to that of Urdu and Mirpuri-Punjabi. The place of Arabic is the subject of the next chapter.

Chapter 13
Arabic

Introduction

Standard Arabic is the official language of the Arab world. It is the national language of all Arab countries and is used for education, all official purposes, written materials and formal speeches. Classical Arabic is used for religious and ceremonial purposes and has, in comparison with Standard Arabic, an archaic vocabulary. Standard Arabic is a modernised variety of Classical Arabic. Standard Arabic is not a mother tongue. In each Arab country there is a spoken variety of Arabic that is spoken by most people. Some varieties of spoken Arabic are more intelligible across the Arab world than others. This is due to a particular country's role and status within the Arab region. For example, Egyptian spoken Arabic is known practically everywhere in the Arab world because of the widespread popularity of the Egyptian film and music industries. Standard Arabic acts as the lingua franca for the Arab world, but only among the well-educated.

Arabic speakers, therefore, grow up with a mother-tongue variety of Arabic and an educated variety, Standard Arabic. The language itself, unlike the other languages that feature in this book, traces its origins to the Semitic family of languages which, in turn, is part of the much broader Afro-Asiatic language group.

There are approximately 260 million Arabic speakers around the world. It is estimated that only about half of these have adequate proficiency in Standard Arabic as well. Classical Arabic, which is the Arabic of the Qur'an, as a written language is known throughout the Islamic world of approximately one billion people. It is known by most Muslims in the same form and to the same proficiency as the liturgical literacy described in this book. Only Arabic-speaking Muslims have a linguistic advantage over the rest of the Muslim world. There is enough similarity between the different varieties of Arabic, both Standard and spoken, to allow for some comprehension when someone reads the Qur'an. However, this should not be overestimated, for Classical Arabic still differs significantly from most varieties of modern written and spoken Arabic.

Qur'anic Arabic

The Qur'anic Arabic that has been perhaps the central preoccupation of this book is acquired by Muslims throughout the world in a manner very similar to that described here. A competent reciter of the Qur'an in the UK would sound very similar to a competent reciter from Malaysia. Both would be understood by Qur'anic scholars from the Arabic world. Its importance and role as a liturgical language means that as a written language it rivals Mandarin, with 1 billion speakers, as the most widely known language in the world.

The Value Placed upon the Qur'an

The position of Qur'anic Arabic within the community of this book is valued and supported. There is little doubt that, of the four languages that interplay within the community, it is the Classical Arabic of the Qur'an that is the most closely preserved and nurtured. If one measures the importance of a cultural practice of a community by the amount of time, effort and resources given to it by members of that community, it is overwhelmingly evident that liturgical literacy is this community's most important cultural practice. Fishman (1989: 229) reminds us that in any minority-language context where spoken vernaculars and religious classicals (the term Fishman uses for liturgical literacies from different religious traditions) are under threat from majority language usages, it is the religious classicals that tend to survive best, to the disadvantage of the community's spoken vernaculars. This book has demonstrated the complex and extensive arrangements that have been and are in place for the continuance of this 'religious classical':

How long have they been teaching children in the mosque?

Mahmood: From the beginning, but mostly when we had the mosque at 'Church Walk'. At that time not mostly families, all single men, families started coming to this country in 1965/1967, after that start to come in this country. And when children arrived, need to be Muslim, realised that there needs to be teaching in the mosque. And they started teaching.

In the 'Midbrough' area what percentage of children attend the mosque classes, do you think?

At the early age of 5 or 6, I think all children.

Are there any families who do not send their children to the mosque school?

As far as I know, I think it is all families. No one refuses to send their children. They contribute money as well for reading. One pound a week for each child.

Your brother mentioned about how hard it is to pay the imam a decent wage ...

All the people who go to the mosque they pay everything.

Does the mosque have to pay for the imam's house?

Actually, they do. They pay wages which includes rent and everything.

We can see from this brief exchange the commitment that is given to liturgical literacy within the community. Of course, the principal advantage liturgical literacy has over its secular rivals in the language maintenance race is that liturgical literacy is an essential part of the community's deeply-held religious faith. We have already seen that knowledge of liturgical literacy is necessary in order for a Muslim to pray. Reading, in the decoding sense outlined in this book, is a cultural activity, not about seeking knowledge from books in order to inform faith, but the very stuff of religious worship. A Muslim believes that he or she is participating in a sacred act whilst reciting the Qur'an. With religion being the principal identifying factor within the community, it is no surprise that the community's resources are directed towards liturgical literacy.

How important is it for your children to learn the Qur'an?

Munir: Very very important, this is our religion you see. Qur'an is part of our life. And there is a big *thawab* [reward], you know. For reading the Qur'an. When I was young, I didn't know anything about this Qur'an. Now I understand, I am a Muslim, I should know.

Hameed: We are Muslims, I myself think so it is very important for Muslim children actually. Because we are here and we live, children need to learn the Qur'an, no matter where they are, this country, or somewhere else. This is very important.

Hanif: Very, very important. To the children. Especially on the religious side. More important than Urdu or Punjabi. The Qur'an. I tend to believe it is very important. It doesn't matter where you live, to keep one's religion is very important.

Furthermore, there is evidence in the comments made by interviewees that this particular religious and literacy practice is, unlike spoken Mirpuri-Punjabi and written Urdu, gaining strength within the community. Many of the fathers mentioned how their experience of liturgical literacy children was less intensive and more casual than that experienced by their own children.

Where did you learn to read the Qur'an?

Munir: I learnt in 'Church Walk' mosque.

So you didn't learn when you were a child?

No, no. At that time actually, I was only young and nobody guided me, this is very important ...

You grew up in a village, and you had a school, did they do the Qur'an in the school?

Yes, they used to give a lesson in middle school. Not in primary school. When I went to middle school at about 12 years old, I finished after about 3 or 4 years, and they used to give a lesson, and I can't understand at that time, I was young.

So the young ones didn't go to the mosque after school to learn Qur'an like they do here?

At that time, the children used to go the mosque, but our father used to work at sea, on a ship, and nobody in our family told us to go the mosque it is very important. It's like now, the children go the mosque and they go to school as well. And at that time, we weren't bothered about it. And now I am grown up and I understand this is very important, you know, reading the Qur'an. Very, very important.

In addition, they, too, had taken advantage of the arrangements made for their children to learn or re-learn liturgical literacy. With the presence in the community of scholars and qualified imams, they could, for the first time, benefit from informed and experienced teaching. This was not necessarily the case back home when they were children themselves where facilities and personnel were not always available:

When you came to England when you were 16, was that it, you could read the Qur'an, or have you learned more while you have been here?

Hameed: I have learned in the last two years in here. I have tried to learn it for about two months. With the imam in 'Church Walk' mosque. And they teach very very different there than how we read in our village. He teaches us very different there ...

Does he teach you more accurate pronunciation?

Yeah, more accurate ... because the reading of the Qur'an is where the words come out from the throat, the nose. And he tries to explain that. It is not easy for us ...

Did he just teach you or was there a group?

We were a group of 5 or 6. Same as my age. 50–55.

Once a week?

No, every day we did that.

Therefore, not only are the children of the community benefiting from the expertise of experienced scholars and teachers, but so are their parents. Mufti Siddiq, whom we met in Chapter 5: Teachers, finds time every week to provide lessons in Islam to those attending afternoon prayers. The imam at 'University Road' mosque teaches not only the children but also adults in the afternoons.

Knowledge of the Qur'an

The limitations of their knowledge of Qur'anic Arabic are admitted by those who practise liturgical literacy:

So your knowledge of just reading the Qur'an, you wouldn't consider that knowing Arabic?

Wajib: No, no. Not at all. Nowhere near. Not even basics. Though I'd like to learn Arabic. Because I went to Hajj and ... I was lost. Because last year I went to Hajj I was lost, I couldn't ... I didn't know ... .what I was talking to ... what I was saying ... you know, picked up a few words here and there while I was there ...

Knowledge in liturgical literacy is bound up, not with understanding, but with accurate and precise pronunciation and melodious and correct recitation. Thus, expertise in Classical Arabic is to do with, within the community, the beauty of the sound of the Qur'an. The recitations that took place at the *Laylat-ul-Miraaj* celebration are listened to for their sound and the association they have with the word of God, not for the profundity of their words.

Mahmood: Do you see, so the child, I want for Qur'an better Arabic teacher. With better pronunciation.

What are the qualifications for an imam?

Ghulam: He reads the Qur'an well.

Maulana Shabbir: The main duty of an imam is ... his recitation of the Qur'an has to be perfect ...

For those who take an active interest in their faith, and who read more widely, in English or in Urdu, a restricted comprehension of Arabic words and phrases develops that can give satisfaction to the reader.

How much do you understand? You have already touched on this when you said that you recognise names ... anything else?

Bashir: I recognise the names ... there are some landmarks I recognise ... like, *Bayt ul Quds* [The Holy Mosque in Jerusalem], *Masjid al Haram* [The Holy Mosque in Mecca], even other people, not only including *rasools* [Messengers of God] of Allah, I'm talking about *Nabis* [Prophets of God], I'm talking about the people of the Book as well, whether they be good-doers or evildoers ... the places ... like as I said, *Bayt ul Muqadus, Bani Israil* [The Children of Israel], the children of Israel, basically the connections between what I have just read, until I read it in English, it doesn't come into any focus ... there are some sayings like, '*ghafoor ar-raheem*' ['The Forgiving, the Compassionate'], '*rabbi alameen*' ['Lord of all worlds'], where you do have this basic understanding that 'the most gracious, the most merciful'. There are so many different ...

The Qur'an in English Translation

There is growing evidence that Mirpuri-Punjabi-speaking Muslims, both adults and children, are beginning to make much more use of translations of the Qur'an available in English. Born of a desire to reach the meaning of the texts they are reading, and a growing availability of Islamic texts in English and inability to read Urdu translations and commentaries, many families now have access to English translations of the Qur'an generally on bookshelves at home or sometimes on the Internet.

Could you read it in the Urdu translation like your mum or dad?

Shazad: We can read the English off the Internet but we haven't got it at home.

Can you understand, for example, the Fatihah?

Akhtar: Only now though, because I have been reading that in translation recently ...

Bashir: Then I've got my Qur'an, which is translated into English ... I have another one which is in Urdu ... that's for my wife ...

Do you prefer to read the Qur'an in an English rather than Urdu translation?

I can't read the Urdu translation, but the thing is because I understand everything that is thrown at me, I accept it in English, I accept it in Urdu, it means the same to me as in English as it would do to me in Urdu ... as in Punjabi ...

As more and more recourse is made to these translations, a word needs to be said about their quality and overall usefulness. For much of the 20th century, anyone wishing to gain access to the meaning of the Qur'an through the English language would have had a very limited choice in translations available. Moreover, within this limited choice there were even more restrictions imposed by publishers. The best-known translation and the one that is seen in most Muslim homes in the UK, is the 1934 translation by the Indian Muslim, Abdullah Yusuf Ali (Ali, 1934). Because of its ubiquity, and there are copies of it in all Rotherham mosques, there are a number of observations that should be made about this translation and its usefulness to modern readers, and particularly to children, wanting to seek the meaning of the original Arabic. Notwithstanding that the original Arabic of the Qur'an originates from the 7th century and is a highly poetic and elaborate text, which itself poses plenty of comprehension issues for Arabic scholars, the intention of Ali, and his contemporaries, was to render the Arabic into an English text that caught the original meaning but which also attempted to emulate one of the greatest ever English texts in style and tone, namely the King James's Bible. Consequently, we are left with a text that serves the first aim reasonably well, but in striving for the second aim, seeking validity and credibility, the text ends up obscuring any clarity of translation that might have been achieved. The text abounds in 'lo's, 'behold's, 'verily's, forsooth's and has no end of 'thereof's and 'herein's. The Elizabethan second and third person pronouns and verb inflections are used throughout.

God doeth What He willeth. (Ch. 14, v. 27)

Seest thou not how God sets forth a parable (Ch. 14, v. 24)

It is God Who hath created the heavens and the earth and sendeth down rain from the skies, and with it bringeth out fruits wherewith to feed you (Ch. 14, v. 32) (Ali, 1934)

Unfortunately, the Ali translation, though of interest and useful to enthusiasts and to those whose faith allows them to be forgiving about the quality of the translation, has become somewhat of a classic, and, therefore, now serves as a yardstick against which other translations are measured. As a result many more modern translations still cannot avoid 'doffing their caps' to Ali's work and vestiges of his archaic and anachronistic style pop up everywhere. A very recent translation of the Qur'an, and one that has found its way into many mosques as a free gift from the publishers, is a committee-translated version from Saudi Arabia which, despite its recent date, cannot avoid looking over its shoulder at Ali.

O my Lord! They have indeed led astray many among mankind. But whoso follows me, he verily is of me. And whoso disobeys me, still You are indeed Oft-Forgiving, Most Merciful. (Ch. 14, v. 36)(Al-Hilali & Khan, 1419/1998)

As we can see, the text includes the superfluous 'indeed' (twice) which is non-existent in the original Arabic. The archaic 'whoso' (twice) and the Biblical 'verily' are present, when modern English would suggest 'whoever' and 'truly'.

The trouble with these well-intentioned translations is that they assume a particular kind of educated reader. This reader is familiar with Shakespearean English and has a decent store of archaic metaphysical and Biblical expressions and phrases. Such a reader is also not put off by a plethora of brackets that are there to allow the translators to paraphrase wherever they see fit.

There are some decent, readable translations available but, unfortunately not published widely. As I have shown previously, the Muslim communities have begun to employ English more and more both in the home and in the mosque, and so they will need the most accessible and readable translations in order to bring meaning-making into the process of acquiring liturgical literacy. Compare these two translations, the first by Ali (1934) and the second by Aisha Bewley (2005).

Such as fear not
The meeting with Us
(for Judgment) say:
'Why are not the angels
Sent down to us, or
(Why) do we not see
Our Lord?' Indeed they
Have an arrogant conceit
Of themselves, and mighty
Is the insolence of their impiety! (Ch. 25, v. 21) (Ali, 1934)

Those who do not expect to meet Us say,
'Why have angels not been sent down to us?
Why do we not see our Lord?'
They have become arrogant about themselves
And are excessively insolent. (Ch. 25, v. 21) (Bewley & Bewley, 1999)

One wonders what the eleven-year old boy or girl curious as to the sense of what he or she is reciting might make of the excruciating syntax of 'Such as fear not the meeting with Us say' or the preponderance of nouns in 'mighty is the insolence of their impiety!'

Summary

The primacy of Arabic in Islamic liturgical literacy is self-evident. The tradition of insisting on the use of Arabic in prayer and other ritualised practices ensures that all Muslims are initiated into the written code of Qur'anic Arabic. Even if a Muslim never reads the Qur'an, he or she will only ever be able to perform prayer in Arabic. These restrictions ensure that the ability to decode and recite Arabic is at the heart of the process of acquiring liturgical literacy. The educational process involved in its acquisition is a time-honoured and universal literacy practice and, as Wagner reminds us (1982), is one of the largest forms of alternative schooling in the world today.

Part 5

Concluding Remarks and Implications

Chapter 14
Concluding Remarks

Introduction

What I have hoped to demonstrate throughout this book has been the prestigious and valued position that liturgical literacy maintains within this particular Muslim community, which, as I have argued elsewhere, is far from being untypical and unrepresentative among the mosaic of Muslim communities, at least in the UK . Children, parents, their teachers and those charged with the responsibility of the two mosques depicted all see this literacy practice as central to their lives. For the children, attending the mosque and acquiring Islamic liturgical literacy is an important formative stage in their forging of a social, cultural and religious identity. For the parents, ensuring their sons and daughters acquire liturgical literacy is a central element in their role as Muslim parents and, in contrast with their desire to maintain either the mother tongue of the community, Mirpuri-Punjabi, or the literary language of Urdu, the process of acquisition of liturgical literacy, on the evidence of this book, is well-supported and administered. Indeed, throughout my discussions with all members of the community, the forging of a religious identity was far more essential to them than developing feelings of a common ethnicity or nationality, which suggests that the place of liturgical literacy within the community, as a factor in identity, is more secure than that of Urdu or Mirpuri-Punjabi.

But, within this strong sense of importance and value, there is, equally clearly, a significant tension emerging between advocates of traditional approaches to the teaching of liturgical literacy and those calling for more accommodating, more contemporary approaches involving pedagogy, curriculum and language. To a certain extent, such tension can be explained by generational differences. An older generation, keen to preserve tradition and valuing continuity and fearing innovation and change that might damage its religious and cultural heritage, is pitted against a younger generation, much more at ease with life outside the community, and with a broader outlook in regard to language and learning.

When the research for this book began, the tensions just referred to were a product of local origin, derived in the main from the playing out of generational attitudes within the community. True, a similar situation applied to a lesser or greater degree in many other UK Muslim communities and one might, therefore, safely generalise across many towns and cities.

Since the terrorist events of September 11th 2001 and July 7th 2005, the issues raised in this book have been brought sharply into focus not only locally, but also throughout the country and, indeed, the world. The Muslim community, both locally and globally, has had much of its religious and cultural practice exposed to the glare of media spotlight and made the subject of the soundbites of political opinion. It has been rather disconcerting for me as a researcher, and definitely uncomfortable for me as a Muslim, to have both my research and my faith so 'in the news'.

Quite recently, Lord Carey, the former Archbishop of Canterbury, was reported to have said:

> It is sad to relate that no great invention has come for many hundreds of years from Muslim countries ... (*Daily Telegraph*, 2004)

A recent Home Secretary, David Blunkett, made a number of interventions regarding the language of Muslim communities, as well as directly referring to the languages spoken by imams in UK mosques:

> At the moment in France, 60% of Muslim preachers do not speak French. We should be working together with the Muslim community in Britain to ensure we are not going down the same road ... (Blunkett, 2003)

The ministerial advice that British imams should speak English in the mosque is echoed across Europe. In Denmark, Integration Minister, Bertel Haarder, completed a bill that clamped down on Muslim imams who were said to propagate fundamentalist views and so slow down the integration of Muslim immigrants. Under the new regulations, imams who have the right to marry Muslim couples must be fluent in Danish, or take classes in Danish language and culture (*Nyheder*, 2004). His counterpart in Holland, Hilbrand Nawijn, had earlier set this precedent:

> 'Imams have a duty to convince their fellow Muslims that [they] have to be loyal to the values and norms of Dutch civil society,' the immigration minister, Hilbrand Nawijn, said at the opening of a controversial new college to instruct imams in Dutch attitudes towards homosexuality and women's rights ... The college ... will give imams intensive Dutch language lessons ... (*The Guardian*, 2002)

In an earlier speech organised with subheadings such as '11 September', 'Defending Democracy' and 'Security and social order', the same British Home Secretary chose to criticise the British Asian community for not speaking English at home. It is no wonder that the UK Muslim community at the present moment feels beleaguered when even its language use is linked indirectly with international terrorism in such a way.

[S]peaking English enables parents to converse with their children in English as well as their historic mother tongue, at home and to participate in wider modern culture. It helps overcomes the schizophrenia which bedevils generational relationships. In as many as 30% of British Asian households English is not spoken at home. (Blunkett, 2002)

As this book has demonstrated, the issue within the communities to which Blunkett is referring is not, ironically, the lack of English in the home, but rather its dominance that is resulting in the loss of heritage languages among the younger generations.

Disparaging remarks about forms of liturgical literacy similar to those quoted at the beginning of this book, in the light of the political atmosphere created by September 11th and July 7th, and to a lesser extent, by the earlier riots involving Muslim youths in Oldham, Bury and Bradford in the summer of 2001, are beginning to be heard more and more once again. On an international level, schools in Pakistan that promote 'rote memorisation of Arabic texts' turn out students who are said to be 'ignorant of basic events in human history such as the moon landing' and are, of course, actually 'terrorist training schools' (Singer, 2001).

The *Christian Science Monitor* juxtaposes the following comments and the reader cannot but draw negative conclusions:

As in most Madrassahs, or Islamic religious schools, rote memorisation is the key method of learning the Koran and virtually no other subjects are tackled.

This is Islamic scholarship as it should be, argues Zarif, who supports the Taliban. (*Christian Science Monitor*, 2002)

What should be a matter for Muslims and Muslim educationalists has suddenly attracted the attention of the entire world.

The irony is that the Muslim community itself, and the data in this book supports this, has for some time been acutely aware of a need for change in the content and language profile of the mosque and the mosque school. The late Zaki Badawi, a former principal of the Muslim College, had long advocated improving the quality of leadership of British mosques.

Among the younger generation there is also concern that liturgical literacy, on its own, will not fulfil the needs of the new generations of Muslim youth.

Inevitably, their experiences of rote learning without any understanding left them bored and alienated not only from the *madrassah* but from religion itself. (*Q-News*, 2000, quoted in Lewis, 2001)

The above comment, from a young journalist writing for British young Muslims echoes the fears and concerns of many of the parents in Chapter 4: Parents, who whilst acknowledging the importance of liturgical literacy, realised that their children need more in order to hold onto their faith.

There is an urgency to discuss openly the problems of criminality and drug dealing ... to appoint English-speaking Imams as a matter of priority, and to conduct as many programmes as possible in English which deal directly with issues facing young Muslims today. Imams should be properly paid, and they should also be expected to take up pastoral youth work outside the mosque. It is a crime that many of the young scholars who have graduated from British seminaries have not been able to find employment as imams. (*Q-News*, 2000)

Again, the comments about English-speaking imams reflect the concerns of the parents in Chapter 4 and I have described the success that Maulana Shabbir had in Rotherham by incorporating English into the life of the mosque. He was one of the lucky graduates of a British seminary who found employment, although he did have to set up his own school and mosque to do so.

This book has presented a detailed description of the literacy practice I have termed liturgical literacy as practised within a typical UK Muslim community in the north of England. Hitherto, this literacy practice has been analysed and referred to only in respect of other literacy practices, usually schooled and mainstream practices. The liturgical literacy of Mumtaz, in Barton and Hamilton's *Local Literacies* (1998: 182–187), is touched on briefly as one of a number of literacy practices with which she is associated. The Qur'anic classes described by Gregory (1996, 1997) are contrasted immediately with reading practices at mainstream school. This book has deemed it timely and necessary to dwell a little on the practice of liturgical literacy, with its participants and its institutions, in order to provide future researchers with a fuller picture of its nature, its acquisition and its role within communities. Of course, liturgical literacy in this community is not identical to that in all Muslim communities. However, it is safe to assume that many Muslim communities seeking to establish themselves within a mainly non-Muslim wider community, and originating from outside the UK, face similar issues regarding the maintenance of liturgical literacy, as well as the maintenance of other languages and literacies. Nevertheless, it would be a valuable development of this book to carry out similar studies of other communities where liturgical literacy is central.

I hope this book has shown what a rich and complex practice liturgical literacy is. There is little doubt that this form of literacy has its opponents. The quote from MacDonald (1916) at the beginning of this book is separated from the *Q-News* quote above by nearly a century and reflects a view that is still very much apparent in the words of politicians and in the media. The literacy practice of acquiring a thorough command of a script and learning to decode accurately a foreign language based on the central scripture of one's religion is, I have argued, a laudable skill and, for its practitioners, a highly rewarding cultural and religious activity. That it is a literacy practice that is generally absent from mainstream schooled literacy practices should not suggest any unfavourable comparisons. In fact, as I have shown elsewhere (Rosowsky, 2001), this form of accurate decoding can also be a very significant cultural practice outside of religion:

> There are many instances of using decoding bereft of understanding in many cultural practices around the world. In the Western cultural tradition, professional opera singers spend considerable time being coached in the ability to decode accurately libretti in a range of languages ... Gone are the days when a singer would limit him- or herself to their language of birth or known languages. A modern professional now has to sing in a whole host of European languages. A few of them become proficient in the language, but many of them, and all of them for certain languages, are merely learning the skill of decoding. When Domingo sings the role of Hermann in the original language at La Scala or Covent Garden, he is decoding the text as he sings. Does he communicate meaning, and is meaning communicated to the non-Russian members of the audience? The answer must be yes. Yet through the art form of opera a meaning is communicated which transcends the literal meaning of the words sung. The same is true, only more so, for the member of the professional choir, who may be asked to sing, and initially read, texts in a number of languages, both living and dead, including the High Latin of masses and the vulgar Latin of *Carmina Burana*. Whilst agreeing with Smith's statement, 'What is the point of any activity if there is no understanding?' [Smith, 1994: 7], one has to admit to the possibility that our definition of understanding must be sufficiently broad to accommodate those reading activities which appear, on the surface, to be divorced from meaning. (Rosowsky, 2001: 60)

Likewise, the complexity of this literacy practice and its cognitive demands must also not be understated. The attention paid to accuracy and the fine distinctions that are made in the teaching of decoding and recitation by teacher and student alike require concentration and application. This has been remarked upon by Robertson:

> Somewhere at the back of my mind – though I was only aware of it later on – I had simplified this kind of reading. I had simplified the nature of the task, the range of words, sounds and nuances of sound, to a meaningless mumble. And the fact that the girls were keen to test each other, that they took a firm view when they disagreed, surprised me, but revealed the depth of their engagement in their reading. (Robertson, 1997: 172)

I hope I have also shown the tension that exists between safeguarding the maintenance of liturgical literacy and other community-based literacies. Parts 2 and 3 of this book have illustrated the considerable resources invested by the community in the maintenance of liturgical literacy. This, it would appear, has been at the expense of the maintenance of Urdu literacy and Mirpuri-Punjabi oracy, particularly among the younger generations. However, causes of language loss are complex and beyond the remit of this book and it would be unfair to post such a development solely at the door of liturgical literacy. Fishman (1989) informs us that American Jews are much more protective of Prayer book/Biblical Hebrew than they are of their Yiddish vernacular and that Palestinian Arab-Americans continue to maintain their children in Qur'anic Arabic even after they are fully and exclusively English-speaking third generation.

> Because religion is concerned with eternals rather than externals, it is more conservative, less compromising and more compelling insofar as boundary maintenance is concerned. (Fishman, 1989: 229)

And although the future maintenance of other literacy and language practices is not the central question of this book, it was impossible to focus solely on the community's liturgical literacy without discussing its relationship with Urdu and Mirpuri-Punjabi. Indeed, Urdu literacy, when present, plays a significant role in the community's religious practices, though as I showed in Chapter 10, is becoming less and less accessible to the younger generation. The use of Mirpuri-Punjabi in the transcribing and memorisation of religious poetry (*naat*) is also a form of what is best termed religious literacy, in contrast to liturgical literacy. The support the community can provide for the maintenance of Urdu literacy is affected by limited resources, personnel and time. The community values highly the effectiveness and efficiency with which liturgical literacy is acquired. They are reluctant to introduce anything that might disturb this equilibrium – increased teaching of Urdu or more expansive teaching curriculum (see

Chapter 4). It is still too early to judge the impact that recently-published initiatives and policy statements (DCLG, 2006) on the part of the UK Department of Communities and Local Government, all under the umbrella title, 'Preventing Violent Extremism – Winning Hearts and Minds', will have on the nature and quality of education on the mosque school. Suffice it to say that such moves, presented intelligently and sensitively – not an easy matter – should resonate with many of the views outlined in this book.

Implications for the Community

I have shown how there is at present a tension within the community regarding the use of the English language in the mosque context. This is linked to a need, expressed by many parents, to provide a fuller Islamic education than that which is available. This tension can be understood not only in terms of different opinions regarding the aims of children attending the mosque on a regular basis, but also as an inevitable consequence of generational differences within the community. In the light of the heightened political interest in Islam and Muslim cultural and religious practices, it is perhaps more urgent that the community resolves this tension sooner rather than later. However, at the same time, the community needs to feel secure and confident about the value of its liturgical literacy practice. It must withstand the accusation of it being 'mechanical' and 'monotonous' (Zerdoumi, 1970), and be able to articulate its strength as a cultural and literacy practice that engages and enriches the religious life of the community.

Implications for the Wider Society and its Schools

As the community and its mosques set about resolving the tensions they perceive in the maintenance of liturgical literacy, mainstream society and, in particular, its schools should adopt a more positive and inclusive attitude to this literacy practice which children bring with them to the school gates. It is not helpful for schools and teachers to recognise this important religious and cultural practice only as a nuisance or distracting element in the lives of their young students. The community has demonstrated its fidelity to liturgical literacy by assigning resources and time to its maintenance. Schools should be aware of the importance attached to this literacy practice within the community and seek to accommodate its demands in a more conciliatory fashion than at present. For example, Maulana Shabbir has had a room at his centre equipped with computers and is offering his students a place to complete their homework. Although he has undertaken this independently of the local schools, there is here obvious potential for cooperation and collaboration.

There is a rich and longstanding tradition of supplementary, or complementary (Martin *et al.*, 2003), schooling within ethnic minority communities in the United Kingdom. Those that feature in studies (Martin *et al.*, 2003) or government reports (Strand, 2002) are generally focused on mother-tongue maintenance and provide education on cultural history and identity. Few studies or agencies include Qur'anic schools as supplementary schools. It is interesting to note that a recent study (Martin *et al.*, 2003: 9) found that only a minority of these supplementary schools had contact with state schools. There is much less reported about the education provided by places of worship, but the lack of contact remains the same. Yet the same educational benefits that can be identified for mother tongue supplementary schools are there in the mosque schools too:

> The skills learnt in these contexts are transferable to other learning contexts. The multilingual experiences students have in the schools, then, provide important learning experiences and an improvement in cognitive and academic achievement. (Martin *et al.*, 2003: 9)

Although it is not appropriate here to advocate a particular method for the teaching of initial reading in the mainstream school context, it is right to acknowledge that the methods used in the mosque for the acquisition of liturgical literacy could have something important to contribute to the ongoing debate about preferred methods of teaching reading. The recent recommendation (DfES, 2007) in the UK that systematic phonics teaching be an entitlement for all children learning to read in primary schools and the accompanying resource material and training (DCSF, 2007) present an opportunity for a rapprochement, or at least, a sharing of ideas, on similar approaches to reading acquisition albeit taking place in different settings. I have shown that the age-old methods employed in the acquisition of liturgical literacy are without any doubt both efficient and effective.

The emphasis on memorisation so often disparaged and devalued in modern pedagogy is another area that could have important and fruitful benefits for schools. I never cease to be staggered by the prodigious amounts of text the young people featuring in this book have learnt by heart. Although the true hafiz of the Qur'an is a rare individual, many Muslims have learnt by heart pages and pages of Qur'anic verses. For example, many children claim to have learnt a siparah by heart. This amounts to approximately 40 pages of closely-printed text, which corresponds to one third of the Alexander edition of Shakespeare's *Romeo and Juliet*. Being able to memorise large amounts of detail is not an insignificant skill, and is one that could be employed in school to a much greater extent than at present.

There is the possibility, sad but true, that the place of Urdu literacy within the community is seriously under threat. Without a sufficient support network for the maintenance of Urdu within the community, it is difficult for the language and its literacy to survive. The support network is there for liturgical literacy because, mainly, it has the institutional base of the mosque to provide and support it. The secondary school that features in this book provides Urdu GCSE courses, but finds it hard to find suitably qualified staff and struggles to deal with the extremely varied range of prior knowledge of Urdu that students demonstrate. The obvious confusion that exists among many schoolteachers about the differences between Urdu and Mirpuri-Punjabi also reflects a lack of awareness of the community and its cultural and linguistic make-up. A serious and determined effort by schools to support Urdu would have to begin much earlier than GCSE, and probably begin in the primary school. More importantly, the school would need to feel confident that the community supported such an enterprise. In Chapter 4: Parents, Chapter 10: Urdu and Chapter 11: Mirpuri-Punjabi, I hope I have conveyed some of the ambivalence that exists within the community regarding Urdu where many parents have less concern about the maintenance of Urdu than they do about the maintenance of liturgical literacy.

Culturally, it is significant that members of the community, in particular the younger members, are making use of the literacy resources they have in order to engage with the literacy practice of *naat* recitation. Just as the Mende of Sierra Leone utilise and re-interpret aspects of literacy and mould them into their own cultural systems, these young Muslims are applying their literate skills to suit their own purposes and needs.

It would also behove schools to have a greater knowledge of the cultural and intellectual resources within the community. As indicated in Chapter 5, Teachers, the Muslim community can boast of personnel with qualifications, expertise and status sufficient to place them among the most prestigious scholars nationally, and occasionally, internationally. Mufti Siddiq's prestigious position nationally is ignored in the schools attended by his children. The poetry and oratory of Hafiz Shakeel could be an invaluable resource locally outside of the Muslim community. Schools' work on poetry could be dramatically enhanced by careful links with a local imam who excelled in religious verse in Urdu, Punjabi and, even, Persian.

Final Comments

What initiated this book was my concern over the discrepancy that existed between reading accuracy and meaning among young Muslim students. I have sought in this book to reveal the concerns there are within the community about the lack of meaning that characterises much teaching of liturgical literacy. The call for greater use of English in the mosque in order to improve the basic understanding of Islam was made by each parent interviewed. Events in the world, to an extent difficult to imagine even until quite recently, have overtaken this previously private and modest demand, yet the reality remains the same for all those involved in liturgical literacy. That some are attaching questions of national security to what is, in the final analysis, a sociolinguistic and curricular matter should not deflect attention from the very real concerns of Muslim children, young people, their parents and their teachers. It is obvious that any increase in the role of English will not only placate parental concerns about religious knowledge, but will also complement the students' acquisition and use of English more widely. The fear that an increased role for English might erode the primacy of Arabic or affect adversely the hitherto very successful acquisition of liturgical literacy contributes to the tension that presently exists.

Finally, I hope to have shown in this book that it is impossible to analyse the practice of liturgical literacy without taking into account also the competing, or contrasting, literacy practices evident within this community. The complex picture these languages and literacies create require a multi-dimensional and multi-disciplinary approach, which brings out the tension that exists between them and the fluidity of those who practise them. I end with a brief comment from a respondent that captures this tension and fluidity:

> *Hameed:* Very, very important. To the children. Especially on the religious side. The Qur'an is more important than Urdu or Punjabi. The Qur'an. I tend to believe it is very important. It doesn't matter where you live, to keep one's religion is very important. I think myself, if children go to the mosque, they should read in Arabic and also in English as well. They should understand what is the meaning of this word. I mean, if they are reading that, and they don't understand, don't know what is the meaning of this, they are just wasting time. We want proper teachers, qualified teachers, who can teach these children born in this country.

Glossary

Arabic/Urdu/Punjabi Words and Phrases Used in the Text

Please note that the transliteration of these words and phrases has not followed any particular system, other than the author's attempt to consistently represent the sounds of the original. All words listed are Arabic unless indicated.

Abu Bakr Companion of Prophet Muhammad and his successor.

alif, bah, tah First three letters of Arabic alphabet (cf. ABC).

alhamdulillah 'thanks be to God'.

alhamdulilllah rabbi-alameen 'thanks be to God, Lord of the worlds' – first verse of *Fatihah* (see below).

Allahu akbar 'God is greater'.

ameen 'amen'.

ash-hadu a-laa ilaaha ill-Allah, ash-hadu ana Muhammada-r-asool Allah 'I testify there is no god except Allah, and that Muhammed is the Messenger of Allah' – the first *kalimah* (see below).

Astaghfirullah 'May God forgive'.

Bani Israil the Children of Israel.

Bayt ul Quds Jerusalem/Dome of the Rock.

biraderi (Urdu/Mirpuri-Punjabi) system of kinship favours.

Bismala Abbreviated form of *bismillahi rahmani rahim.*

bismillahi rahmani rahim 'in the name of God, Most Merciful, Most Compassionate'.

dars lesson.

Dar-ul-Uloom College of Religious Sciences.

dhikr the practice of repeating liturgical verses or formulations on a regular basis.

dua' prayer.

durood sharif (Urdu) see *salawat* below.

eid Islamic festival.

fajr dawn prayer.

fatihah or Al-fatihah opening chapter of the Qur'an, 'the Opening'.

fiqh Islamic jurisprudence.

ghafoor ar-raheem 'forgiving and merciful'.

hadeeth sayings of the Prophet.

hafiz someone who has memorised the Qur'an.

hajj pilgrimage to Mecca.

harakat letters.

hifz memorisation.

hizb one sixtieth of the Qur'an.

hufaaz plural of *hafiz*.

imam the man who leads the prayer in a mosque.

imamat imam-hood – learning to be an imam.

iman faith.

iqra' 'read' – the first word of the Qur'an revealed.

insh'Allah 'if God wills it so'.

jamaat congregational prayer.

juma Friday congregational prayer.

juz' one thirtieth of the Qur'an.

kalimah a formulation learnt as part of Islamic credo.

Khalifah caliph.

khutbah sermon.

kitaab book.

kutaab school for learning the Qur'an (Arabic-speaking world).

la illaha illa Allah; Muhammadu Rasul Allah 'there is no god but Allah; Muhammed is the Messenger of God'.

Laylat-ul-Miraaj/ Laylat-ul-Shaaban/ Laylat-ul-Qadr various celebrations that take place annually.

madrassah school.

ma sha'allah 'what Allah wills'.

masjid mosque.

Masjid al Haram The Holy Mosque at Mecca.

Mawlid birthday of the Prophet.

mihrab prayer niche.

minbar pulpit.

moulvi (Urdu) imam.

mufti religious title designating authority to make legal judgements.

Musa Moses.

naat (Urdu) religious poetry.

nabi a prophet.

Najm 'The Star' – a chapter of the Qur'an.

namaz (Urdu) prayer.

pir religious guide.

Potwari sometimes used for Mirpuri-Punjabi.

photi (Urdu, Mirpuri-Punjabi) shortened version of Qaidah.

Pushto language spoken by Pathans.

Qaidah primer for learning how to read the Qur'an.

Qari qualified reciter of the Qur'an.

qunut a specific supplication relating to one of the daily prayers.

Qur'an The Holy Book of Islam; literally 'the Reading'.

rasool a messenger.

rasool Allah 'Messenger of God'.

salaam alaykum 'peace be upon you'.

salah or *salat* prayers.

salawat prayers asking God to bless Muhammad.

siparah (Urdu) one thirtieth of the Qur'an.

sirah the biography of the Prophet.

siraat ul mustaqeem 'the straight path'.

subhah rosary.

subhan Allah 'glory to God'.

sunnah the practice of the Prophet and his Companions.

surah chapter.

tafseer exegesis of the Qur'an.

Taalim ul-Haq a children's book that teaches the basics of Islam.

taharah ritual purification.

tarawih the special night prayers that take place in the month of Ramadan.

tasbih rosary.

tashahud a recitation made during prayer.

tashkeel the diacritic marks around letters that aid pronunciation of the Qur'an.

taviz (Urdu) amulet.

thawab reward.

topi skull cap.

ustaad teacher.

wudhu ritual ablution.

Yasin chapter of the Qur'an known as the 'heart' of the book.

zakat the giving of alms.

References

Ali, A.Y. (1934) *The Holy Qur'an: Translation and Commentary.* Various publishers.

Anwar, M. (1985) *Pakistanis in Britain: A Sociological Study.* London: New Century.

Asad, T. (2003) *Formations of the Secular: Christianity, Islam, Modernity.* Stanford: Stanford University Press.

Baker, J.N. (1993) The presence of the name: Reading scripture in an Indonesian village. In J. Boyarin (ed.) *The Ethnography of Reading.* California: University of California.

Ballard, R. (2001) *The Impact of Kinship on the Economic Dynamics of Transnational Networks: Reflections on Some South Asian Developments.* Workshop on Transnational Migration. Princeton University.

Barton, D. (1994) *Literacy: An Introduction to the Ecology of Written Language.* Oxford: Blackwell.

Barton, D. and Hamilton, M. (1998) *Local Literacies.* London: Routledge.

Basit, T.N. (1997) *Eastern Values, Western Milieu: Identities and Aspirations of Adolescent British Muslim Girls.* Aldershot: Ashgate.

Baynham, M. (1993) Code-switching and mode-switching: Community interpreters and mediators of literacy. In B. Street (ed.) *Cross-cultural Approaches to Literacy.* Cambridge: Cambridge University Press.

Bewley, A. and Bewley, A. (1999) *The Noble Quran: A New Rendering of its Meaning in English.* Norwich: Bookwork.

Birt, J. (2006) Good imam, bad imam: Civic religion and national integration in Britain post-9/11. *The Muslim World:* 96.

Bledsoe, C.H. and Robey, K.M. (1993) Arabic literacy and secrecy among the Mende of Sierra Leone. In B. Street (ed.) *Cross-cultural Approaches to Literacy.* Cambridge: Cambridge University Press.

Blunkett, D. (2002) Integration with diversity: Globalisation and the renewal of democracy and civil society. In *Rethinking Britishness.* London: Foreign Policy Centre.

Blunkett, D. (2003) *One Nation, Many Faiths: Unity and Diversity in Multi-faith Britain.* London: The Home Office.

Bruyn, S.T. (1966) *The Human Perspective in Sociology: The Methodology of Participant Observation.* New Jersey: Prentice-Hall.

Catholic World News (2003) 13 May. Online at http://www.cwnews.com/news/viewstory.cfm?recnum=22353. Accessed 04.08.

Cazal, Y. (1998) *Les Voix du Peuple, Verbum Dei: Le Bilinguisme Latin-langue Vernaculaire au Moyen Age.* Geneva: Droz.

Choudhury, T. (2007) *The Role of Muslim Identity Politics in Radicalisation.* DCLG. London: HMSO.

Christian Science Monitor (2002) 30 January. Online at http://www.csmonitor.com/2002/0130/p07s01-wosc.html. Accessed 04.08.

Cummins, J. (1984) *Bilingualism and Special Education.* Clevedon: Multilingual Matters.

Cummins, J. (1989) Language and literacy acquisition. *Journal of Multilingual and Multicultural Development* 10 (1), 17–31.

Cummins, J. (2000) *Language, Power and Pedagogy: Bilingual Children in the Crossfire.* Clevedon: Multilingual Matters.

Cummins, J., Swain, M., Nakajima, K., Handscombe, J., Green D. and Tran, C. (1984) Linguistic interdependence among Japanese and Vietnamese immigrant students. In C. Rivera (ed.) *Communicative Competence Approaches to Language Proficiency Assessment: Research and Application.* Clevedon: Multilingual Matters.

The Daily Telegraph (2004) 23 March. Online at http://www.telegraph.co.uk/news/main.jhtml?xml=/news/2004/03/26/ucarey.xml. Accessed 04.08.

DCLG (Department for Communities and Local Government) (2005) *Preventing Extremism Together: Working Group.* London, Home Office. On WWW at http://communities.homeoffice.gov.uk/raceandfaith/reports_pubs/publicationsrace_faith/PET-working-groups-aug-Oct05?view=Binary. Accessed 15.3.06.

DCLG (Department for Communities and Local Government) (2006) *Preventing Violent Extremism: Winning Hearts and Minds.* London: HMSO. On WWW at http://www.communities.gov.uk/communities/preventingextremism. Accessed 21.12.07.

DCSF (Department for Children, Schools and Families) (2007) *Communication, Language and Literacy Development Programme.* London: DCSF.

Desai, S.A. (1998) *Taalim ul-Haq.* Mumbai: Idara Islamiyat

DfES (Department for Education and Skills) (2007) *Independent Review of the Teaching of Early Reading: Final Report.* London: DfES.

DR Nyheder Online (2004) 11 February. Online at http://www.dr.dk/nyheder/fremmedsprog/English/article.jhtml?articleID=14924=. Accessed 12.05.

Ferguson, C.A. (1959) Diglossia. *Word* 15, 325–340.

Fishman, A.R. (1988) *Amish Literacy: What and How it Means.* New Hampshire: Heinemann.

Fishman, J. (1967) Bilingualism with and without diglossia: Diglossia with and without bilingualism. *Journal of Social Issues* 23, 29–38.

Fishman, J.A. (1989) *Language and Ethnicity in Minority Sociolinguistic Perspective.* Clevedon: Multilingual Matters.

Fishman, J.A. (1991) *Reversing Language Shift.* Clevedon: Multilingual Matters.

Fishman, J.A. (ed.) (2001) *Can Threatened Languages be Saved?* Clevedon: Multilingual Matters.

Gee, J. (1990) *Social Linguistics and Literacies: Ideology in Discourses.* London: Falmer Press.

Geertz, C. (1973) Thick description: Toward an interpretative theory of culture. In C. Geertz (ed.) *The Interpretation of Cultures.* New York: Basic Books.

Goody, J. (1968) *Literacy in Traditional Societies.* Cambridge: CUP.

Goody, J. (1977) *The Domestication of the Savage Mind.* Cambridge: CUP.

Goody, J. and Watt, I. (1963) The consequences of literacy. In J. Goody (ed.) *Literacy in Traditional Societies.* Cambridge: CUP.

Gordon, R.G. Jr (ed.) (2005) *Ethnologue: Languages of the World* (15th edn). Dallas, TX: SIL International. On WWW at http://www.ethnologue.com/. Accessed 15.04.08.

Graff, H.J. (1979) *The Literacy Myth: Literacy and Social Structure in the 19th Century City.* New York: Academic Press.

Gregory, E. (1996) *Making Sense of a New World: Learning to Read in a Second Language.* London: Paul Chapman.

Gregory, E. (ed.) (1997) *One Child, Many Worlds.* London: David Fulton.

Gregory, E. (1998) Siblings as mediators of literacy in linguistic minority communities. *Language and Education* 12, 1.

Gregory, E. and Williams, A. (2000) *City Literacies.* London: Routledge.

Grimes, B. (ed.) (1992) *Ethnologue: Languages of the World.* Dallas: SIL.

The Guardian (2002) 1 October.

Hardy, G. and Brunot, L. (1925) *L'enfant marocain.* Rabat-Paris: Edition du Bulletin de l'enseignement du Maroc, no. 63.

Havelock, E.A. (1976) *Origins of Western Literacy.* Toronto: Ontario Institute for Studies in Education.

Hawkins, E. (1981) *Modern Languages in the Curriculum.* Cambridge: CUP.

Haykal, M.H. (1976) *The Life of Muhammad.* Philadelphia: North American Trust.

Heath, S.B. (1983) *Ways With Words.* New York: Cambridge.

Al-Hilali, T. and Khan, M.M. (1419/1998) *Translation of the Meanings of the Noble Qur'an.* Madinah: King Fahd Complex for the Printing of the Holy Qur'an.

The History of Rotherham (n.d.) Online at http://www.rotherhamunofficial.co.uk/history/20th.html. Accessed 04.08.

Hussein, A. (2000) *Emigré Journeys.* Serpent's Tail: London.

Impact of Kinship (n.d.) Online at http://www.transcomm.ox.ac.uk/working%20papers/Ballard.pdf. Accessed 04.08.

Institute of Islamic Scholars (2002) *First Bi-annual Report.* Batley: Institute of Islamic Scholars.

Jameel, Hafiz M. (n.d) *Namaz Book.* Lahore: Self-published.

Johansson, E. (1977) *The History of Literacy in Sweden.* Umeaa: University of Umeaa Press.

Kapitzke, C. (1995) *Literacy and Religion: The Textual Politics and Practice of Seventh-day Adventism.* Amsterdam: John Benjamins.

Kelly's Directory (1888).

Kelly's Directory (1900).

Lankshear, C. (1997) *Changing Literacies.* Buckingham: Open University.

Lankshear, C. and McLaren, P. (eds) (1993) *Critical Literacy: Politics, Praxis and the Postmodern.* New York: State University of New York.

Lewis, P. (2001) *Between Lord Ahmed and Ali G: Which Future for British Muslims?* Supplementary report for Bradford Race Review. Bradford: City of Bradford MDC.

Liberman, I.Y. and Liberman, A.M. (1992) Whole language versus code emphasis: Underlying assumptions and their implications for reading instruction. In P.B. Gough, L.C. Ehri and R. Treiman (eds) *Reading Acquisition.* Hillsdale: Lawrence Erlbaum.

Linguistics Minorities Project (1983) *Linguistic Minorities in England.* London: University of London Institute of Education.

Luke, A. (1996) Genres of power? Literacy education and the production of capital. In R. Hasan and G. Williams (eds) *Literacy in Society.* New York: Longman.

MacDonald, D.B. (1911) *Aspects of Islam.* New York: Macmillan.

Manguel, A. (1996) *A History of Reading.* Harper Collins. London.

Martin, P., Creese, A. and Bhatt, A. (2003) *Complementary Schools and their Communities in Leicester.* Final report for the ESRC for Project no. R000223949.

Millard, E. (1997) *Differently Literate: The Schooling of Boys and Girls*. London: Falmer Press.

Millard, E. (2003) Toward a literacy of fusion: New times, new teaching and learning? *Literacy* 37 (1), 3–8.

Miller, G.D. (1977) A study of behavior in a classroom of a Moroccan primary school. In L.C. Brown and N. Itzkowitz (eds) *Psychological Dimensions of Near Eastern Studies*. Princeton: Darwin Press.

Ministers of religion (n.d.) Ministers of religion, missionaries and members of religious orders. On line at UKBA website: http://www.ukba.homeoffice. gov.uk/workingintheuk/ministersofreligion/eligibility/. Accessed 04.08.

Muslim Directory (2003) MDUK Media Ltd. On WWW at http://www.muslim directory.co.uk/. Accessed 04.08.

The Muslim Parliament (2006) *Child Protection in Faith-based Environments: A Guideline Report*. Online at http://www.muslimparliament.org.uk/NatReg Madrasas.html. Accessed 04.08.

The Nasheed Lyrics (n.d.) Online at http://www.thenasheedlyrics.com/index.php. Accessed 04.08.

NFER-Nelson (1989) *Neale Reading Analysis* (revd British edn). Windsor: NFER-Nelson.

New London Group (1996) A pedagogy of multiliteracies: Designing social futures. *Harvard Educational Review* 66 (1).

Olson, D., Torrance, N. and Hildyard, A. (eds) (1985) *Literacy, Language and Learning*. Cambridge: CUP.

Ong, W. (1982) *Literacy and Oracy: The Technologising of the Word*. New York: Methuen.

ONS (Office for National Statistics) (2003) *Region in Figures: Yorkshire and the Humber*. London: HMSO.

Our Suppressed Language (n.d.) Online at http://www.sangionline.com/eng/ index.php?option=com_content&task=view&id=349&Itemid=69. Accessed 04.08.

Prime Minister's Literacy Commission (2002) *Adult Literacy in Pakistan: Quranic Literacy Project*. Paper from the 2nd Asian Regional Literacy Forum. Online at http://www.literacy.org/products/ili/webdocs/islama.html. Accessed 04.08.

Pennycook, A. (2000) Language, ideology and hindsight: Lessons from colonial language policies. In T. Ricento (ed.) *Ideology, Politics and Language Policies*. Amsterdam: John Benjamins.

Q-News (2000a) February.

Q-News (2000b) October–November.

Qaidah (n.d.) Book Centre Publications: Bradford.

Rashid, N. and Gregory, E. (1997) Learning to read, reading to learn: The importance of siblings in the language development of young bilingual children. In E. Gregory (ed.) *One Child, Many Worlds*. London: David Fulton.

Reder, S. and Wikelund, K.R. (1993) Literacy development and ethnicity: An Alaskan example. In B. Street *Cross-cultural Approaches to Literacy*. Cambridge: Cambridge University Press.

Robertson, L. (1997) From Karelia to Kashmir: A journey into bilingual children's story-reading experiences within school and community literacy practice. In E. Gregory (ed.) *One Child, Many Worlds*. London: David Fulton.

Rosowsky, A. (2001) Decoding as a cultural practice and its effects on the reading process of bilingual pupils. *Language and Education* 15, 1.

Said, E. (1985) *Orientalism*. Harmondsworth: Penguin Books.

Said, E. (1997) *Covering Islam: How the Media and the Experts Determine How We See the Rest of the World*. New York: Vintage.

Shakespeare, W. (1597/1972) *Romeo and Juliet*. Alexander Edition. Collins Educational: London.

Singer, P.W. (2001) *Pakistan's Madrassahs: Ensuring a System of Education not Jihad* Analysis Paper. Washington: The Brookings Institute.

Smith, F. (1994) *Understanding Reading*. Hillsdale: Lawrence Erlbaum.

Strand, S. (2002) *Surveying the Views of Pupils Attending Supplementary Schools in England in 2001*. Report for CFBT and the African Schools Association relating to the Supplementary Schools Support Service.

Strand, S. (2007) Surveying the views of pupils attending supplementary schools in England. *Educational Research* 49 (1), 1–19.

Street, B. (1984) *Literacy in Theory and Practice*. Cambridge: Cambridge University Press.

Street, B. (1993) *Cross-cultural Approaches to Literacy*. Cambridge: Cambridge. University Press.

Street, B. (1999) *Multiple Literacies and Multi-lingual Societies*. Watford: NALDIC Literacy Papers.

Travers, M. (2001) *Qualitative Research through Case Studies*. London: Sage.

Trudgill, P. (ed.) (1984) *Language in the British Isles*. Cambridge: Cambridge University Press.

Wagner, D.A. (1982) Quranic pedagogy in modern Morocco. In L.L. Adler (ed.) *Cross-cultural Research at Issue*. New York: Academic Press.

Wagner, D.A. (1993) *Literacy, Culture and Development*. New York: Cambridge University Press.

Wagner, D.A., Messick, B M. and Spratt, J.E. (1986) Studying literacy in Morocco. In B. Schieffelin and P. Gitmore (eds) *The Acquisition of Literacy: Ethnographic Perspectives* (Advance in Discourse Processes, XXI). New York: Academic Press.

Weinstein-Shr, G. (1993) Literacy and social process: A community in transition. In B. Street *Cross-cultural Approaches to Literacy*. Cambridge: Cambridge University Press.

Zerdoumi, N. (1970) *Enfants d'hier: L'education de l'enfant en milieu traditional Algerian*. Paris: Maspero.

Zinsser, C. (1986) For the Bible tells me so: Teaching Children in a Fundamentalist Church. In B. Schieffelin and P. Gilmore (eds) *The Acquisition of Literacy: Ethnographic Perspectives* (Advance in Discourse Processes XXI). New York: Academic Press.

Index

administration 19, 80-1, 90
adults 17, 29, 33, 45, 48, 54, 174, 211-2
Ali, Abdullah Yusuf 180-2, 213
alphabet 20, 57, 59, 70, 96, 100
amulets 2, 22, 33, 158, 163-4, 232
Arabic 8, 9, 20-1, 25-6, 43-4, 52-5, 100-3,
    151-2, 158-9, 183-5, 206-7, 213-5
– alphabet 1, 24, 57-8, 72, 99, 100, 111, 229
– script 17, 29, 44, 51, 66, 97, 101, 173-4, 191
    and Arabic language 43
Arabic-speaking world 8, 21, 154, 160, 231
Arabic teachers 6, 22, 124, 211
Arabic-Urdu script 36
attitudes, children's 68, 71
authority 12, 14-5, 21-3, 35, 80, 90, 95, 114-5,
    231

Baker, J.N. 13, 25-6, 233
Barton, D. 11-4, 16, 222, 233
Beatson Clark 73, 122
Bible 23-4, 237
– school 24
Bledsoe & Robey 6, 19-22
Blunkett 90, 198, 205, 220-1, 233

children 29, 30, 43-9, 51-7, 61-9, 73-81, 85-9,
    99-102, 104-5, 192-4, 198-205, 208-13
'Church Walk' mosque 46, 80, 83, 94-5, 99,
    114, 143, 147-8, 151-2, 154, 210
classes 23, 54-6, 71, 84-5, 94, 155, 175, 202, 220
Classical Arabic 9, 19, 37, 44, 52, 62, 66, 109,
    207-8, 211
Common Underlying Proficiency, see CUP
community
– languages 18, 48, 169
– literacy practice 236
comprehension 25-6, 32, 53, 207
council 119-21, 129, 140, 148-9
cultures 6, 13-5, 18, 20, 46, 66, 73, 96, 121,
    206, 234
Cummins, J. 167, 204, 234
CUP (Common Underlying Proficiency)
    167, 191, 234-6
curriculum 24, 62-4, 68, 76, 106, 124, 219, 235

Dar-ul-Uloom 89, 92-3, 110, 117
decoding 9, 15, 21, 25-6, 54, 66, 76, 109,
    167-8, 198-9, 223-4
dialects 29, 178, 186-8, 190
diglossia 175, 234

Eastern Punjabi 186-7
education, religious 77, 87, 109, 140
elders xi, 78, 89, 90, 104, 126, 157, 181
English
– language 34, 36, 65, 123, 126, 199, 213,
    225
– transliteration 102
ethnography 28-9, 31, 33, 35, 37, 233

faith 22, 30-1, 33, 66, 71, 79, 106, 109, 111,
    142, 151
families 10, 30, 48, 55-6, 73-6, 142, 160,
    188-90, 192-3, 204, 208
Fatihah 27, 66-7, 72, 109, 184, 212, 229
Fishman, J. A. 5, 11, 13, 208, 224, 234

Gee, J.P. 11-2, 130, 234
grandparents xi, 49, 50, 194
Gregory, E. 10, 13-4, 16, 31, 50, 63, 65, 222,
    234-6

hafiz 61, 92, 97, 111, 180, 226, 230, 235
Hamilton, M. 12-4, 16, 222, 233
harakat 100-1
hifz 61, 97
history 19, 31, 90, 95, 134-5, 141, 157, 173,
    177-8, 187, 235
Hmong 22-3
home language 35, 47

identity 17, 32, 35, 43, 68, 168, 219, 226, 233
– religious 16-7, 35, 82, 219
imam 35-6, 78, 82-3, 89-97, 115-8, 123-5,
    178-9, 181-3, 200-1, 209-11, 220
– home-trained 79
institutions of liturgical literacy 134, 168
Islam 62-4, 69-71, 77-8, 81, 83-4, 103-4, 106,
    116, 122-5, 178-9, 199-201

238